Pauline Eschatology

Pauline Eschatology

The Apocalyptic Rupture of Eternal Imperialism

PAUL AND THE
UPRISING OF THE DEAD,
VOLUME 2

Daniel Oudshoorn

Foreword by Larry L. Welborn

CASCADE *Books* · Eugene, Oregon

PAULINE ESCHATOLOGY
The Apocalyptic Rupture of Eternal Imperialism

Paul and the Uprising of the Dead, Volume 2

Cascade Books
An Imprint of Wipf and Stock Publishers
199 W. 8th Ave., Suite 3
Eugene, OR 97401

www.wipfandstock.com

PAPERBACK ISBN: 978-1-5326-7524-9
HARDCOVER ISBN: 978-1-5326-7525-6
EBOOK ISBN: 978-1-5326-7526-3

Cataloguing-in-Publication data:

Names: Oudshoorn, Daniel.

Title: Pauline eschatology : the apocalyptic rupture of eternal imperialism. / Daniel Oudshoorn.

Description: Eugene, OR: Cascade Books, 2020. | Series: Paul and the Uprising of the Dead, Volume 2. | Includes bibliographical references.

Identifiers: ISBN 978-1-5326-7524-9 (paperback) | ISBN 978-1-5326-7525-6 (hardcover) | ISBN 978-1-5326-7526-3 (ebook)

Subjects: LCSH: Paul, the Apostle, Saint—Political and social views. | Bible. Epistles of Paul—Criticism, interpretation, etc. | Christianity and politics—Rome—History—Empire, 30 B.C.–284 A.D. | Eschatology—Biblical teaching

Classification: BS2655.E7 O93 2020 (print) | BS2655.E7 (ebook)

Manufactured in the U.S.A.   FEBRUARY 10, 2020

TABLE OF CONTENTS

FOREWORD

THE SECOND VOLUME OF Daniel Oudshoorn's sweeping *Paul and the Uprising of the Dead* carries us to the conceptual center of his project: the drama of how the false eternity projected by the empire of Rome was shattered by the apocalyptic hope and longing of the first followers of Jesus. Oudshoorn grounds his account of the temporal rupture in a comprehensive, penetrating analysis of the ideological mechanisms by which Roman rulers and their intellectual servants—poets, historians, moralists—sought to persuade the public that the time of empire was divinely ordained and without end. Further, Oudshoorn describes how the ideological apparatuses of the Roman state—the family, patronage, constructions of honor and shame, the imperial cult—served to reify the conception of time as an unbroken continuum of power.

As in the first volume, Oudshoorn assembles the crucial primary sources and critically engages the most relevant secondary literature, both classical scholarship and Pauline studies. Especially striking is Oudshoorn's juxtaposition of the Golden Age fantasies of client-intellectuals such as Virgil, Horace, and Lucan with the intense revelations of an open, alternative future in the most poetic passages in the Pauline corpus (thereby bringing to fruition the prescient insights of Dieter Georgi). Oudshoorn's exposition of the apocalyptic resistance of the Pauline faction is deepened and enriched by his interaction with philosophers and theologians like Alain Badiou and Jürgen Moltmann, and critics of political economy such as Achille Mbembe and Sayak Valencia.

In one final respect Oudshoorn's account of a two-thousand-year-old uprising of the spirit of life goes beyond the works of conventional Pauline scholars: Oudshoorn never forgets those who are being deprived of life and left for dead in our perilous moment in late capitalism. May the reading of Daniel Oudshoorn's brilliant and impassioned trilogy inspire in contemporary Paulinists a solidarity with the stillborn in our society and a longing for the redemption of the groaning creation so that, like the original members of the Pauline faction, we begin to hope that, as Oudshoorn insists, "the future is not closed and that resistance is not futile."

Larry L. Welborn
Fordham University
Bronx, New York
September 2019

PREFACE

IN PAUL AND THE *Uprising of the Dead,* I attempt a comprehensive study of the Pauline epistles, paying especial attention to socioeconomic and theopolitical matters. I survey a broad range of positions and note how presuppositions related to the socioeconomic status of the early Jesus loyalists as well as presuppositions about Pauline eschatology heavily influence the conclusions that diverse parties draw in relation to these themes. I begin by surveying four prominent positions taken in relation to "Paul and politics," and then explore the socioeconomic and general eschatological arguments that are made to support these positions (volume 1: Pauline Politics). I then turn to examining Pauline apocalyptic eschatology in more detail and relate it to the realized eschatology of Rome, while studying the ideo-theology of Roman imperialism more generally (volume 2: Pauline Eschatology). This leads to a presentation of Paulinism that focuses especially upon the themes of living as members of the transnational family of God, embracing shame in solidarity with the crucified, engaging in sibling-based practices of economic mutuality, and loyally and lovingly gospeling the justice of God in treasonous, law-breaking, and law-fulfilling ways, within the newly assembled body of the Anointed (volume 3: Pauline Solidarity). This presentation is distinct, in many ways, from the most prominent conservative, liberal, and radical readings of the Pauline epistles. Ultimately, what is presented is an understanding of Paulinism as a faction within a movement that is actively working to organize the oppressed, abandoned, vanquished, and left-for-dead into a body that experiences Life in all of its abundance and goodness. This body necessarily exists in conflict with dominant (imperial) death-dealing ways of organizing life in the service of Death. The Pauline faction, then, are those who help to organize this resistance to Death—and all the ways in which Death is structured into social, economic, political, and religious organizations—within assemblies where justice is understood to be that which is life-giving and life-affirming, especially for those who have been deprived of life and left for dead.

ACKNOWLEDGMENTS

I BEGIN BY ACKNOWLEDGING the various sovereign Indigenous peoples who have allowed me to live and work and play and complete this project on the lands to which they belong—from the Wendat, Petun, and Mississaugas, to the Musqueam, Squamish, and Tsleil-Waututh, to the Attawandaron, Wendat, Lenape, Haudenosaune, and Anishinaabe—I lift my hands to them and thank them for the care that they have shown the land and for allowing me and my children and other loved ones to live, work, and struggle alongside of them. In many ways, my ability to complete this project is related to my own status as a white, cishet, male settler of Christian European descent. It is precisely people like me who have benefited most from the ongoing and genocidal process of Canadian colonialism. Thus, when I acknowledge various sovereign Indigenous peoples, as I am doing now, I do so with a sense of my own interconnectedness, liability, accountability, and responsibility. I hope that this work contributes to the ongoing process of decolonization and the uprising of those whom my people have left for dead in these territories. Were I to begin this project again, I would be more interested in writing about Paulinism as it relates to militant Indigenous movements pursuing solidarity, resistance, and liberation within the overarching context of colonialism. The parallels, to me, are striking and I believe that kind of study could be very enriching and, perhaps, help bring together two groups of people who are often at odds with each other.

I acknowledge my children, Charlie and Ruby, and my partner, Jessica Marlatt. You each played central roles in my own *anastasis* from the dead. Thank you for giving me the gifts of wonder, gratitude, gentleness, love, joy, kindness, fatherhood, companionship, and life—new creation life, abundant life, resurrection life. You are all marvels and wonders and I love you with all of my everything.

I acknowledge those scholars who showed me that we have to figure these things out in the streets, on the barricades, in our homes, in squats, in physical altercations with riot police, and in the midst of the struggle. Thank you, Charles and Rita Ringma and Dave and Teresa Diewert. Nobody else whom I have known who bothers talking about Paul has ever come close to embodying Paulinism in the ways that you all have and do. Bob Eklad and Don Cowie also helped me a great deal in this regard. Thank you also to all those involved in the fight who may or may not have cared one bit about Paul but who helped teach me (personally or from a distance) what it means to serve Life and fight against Death—thank you, Jody Nichols, Nicky Dunlop, Andrea Earl, Jan Rothenburger, Anthony Schofield, Ivan Mulder, Stanislav Kupferschmidt, Alex Hundert, Ann Livingston, Harsha Walia, John Clarke, Mechele te Brake, Haley Broadbent, Richard Phillips, as well as all the people at Boy'R'Us (Vancouver) and SafeSpace London, and everyone involved in creating overdose prevention sites across Canadian-occupied territories, and the old warrior from AIM who gave me his bandana late one night at a bar in Vancouver's downtown eastside. Indeed, it is Indigenous peoples who have spent generations organizing against colonialism, capitalism, patriarchy, and the devastation of Turtle Island—from the Wet'suwet'en camp, to Elsipogtog, to Amjiwnaang, to Kanehsatake, to Ts'peten, to Aazhoodena, to Esgenoopititj, to the Tiny House Warriors—who, to my mind, show us the closest example of what something akin to Paulinism might look like today. I lift my hands to them.

I acknowledge my brothers, Joshua, Judah, and Abram, who have shown me how wonderful, transformative, and good sibling relationships can be. And my nephews and nieces—Evan and Wyatt, Emery and Selah, Ben and Chris and Daniella—who gave me life at a time when I was separated from my own children. Without their love, the joy they experienced playing silly games with me, and the ways that made me feel okay in the midst of a very not-okay time, this project would never have been completed.

I acknowledge all of those who encouraged me to complete this project at various times over these years. Apart from those already mentioned, thank you, Daniel Imburgia, Chris Graham, Nathan Colquhoun, Daniel Slade, Danielle Firholz, Chris Tilling, Nicole Luongo, Mark Van Steenwyk, John Stackhouse, Christian Amondson, Audrey Molina, Larry Welborn, Ward Blanton, Roland Boer, and my ever loving, ever gentle, ever patient mother (I love you, mama!). Thank you, Neil Elliott, for agreeing to be the first reader of this project. It is a great joy to be able to work with you (it is like a dream come true for me after I first read *Liberating Paul* all those years ago). And thank you, Regent College (Vancouver) for allowing me to bring this project to completion after all this time and all these words. I appreciate the graciousness you have shown me. Thank you, also, to Steve Thomson (the Silver Fox), for making me read Paul in new and suddenly exciting ways when I was first an undergraduate student, and to Ms. Lane, my high school writing teacher, who believed I had a special gift for writing at a time when I had recently been deprived of housing (i.e., made homeless) by my parents and did not believe anything good about myself.

Finally, I also acknowledge the great multitude of those whom I have known who lost their homes, health, happiness, well-being, children, and, in many cases, their lives, because the Law of Sin and of Death continues to be enforced by the blind and corrupt rulers of this present evil age. I miss you and love you all. You are the song in my heart and the fire in my blood. And, since the system that killed you or left you for dead will not burn down by itself, I offer the following work as a spark.

1

INTRODUCTION: IMPERIAL ENCLOSURES AND THOSE WHO REFUSE THEM

AS AN ACADEMIC, I came of age at a time when anyone interested in contemporary politics, social theory, and economics was talking about (or, at least, demonstrating their awareness of) Francis Fukuyama's thesis about the end of history.[1] With the collapse of the Soviet Union, Fukuyama declared that the world was once and for all left with no alternatives to free market capitalism. History had ended. Capitalism had won and it was here to stay. It was the best and only option. Reflecting on Fukuyama's thesis at that time, I concluded that imperialism (in this case, the increasingly global form of transnational "free market" capitalism) not only tries to present itself as the culmination of past history but also tries to close the future to any alternatives. If we accept this, all of us become trapped within the perpetuation of the eternal now of empire. If we believe history to be a commons that was shared (albeit always in a conflicting and contested manner) among various peoples, Fukuyama's thesis demonstrates one of the ways in which capitalism engages in an enclosure of the commons in order to dispossess the many and further enrich an already wealthy few.[2] Universal history, as with everything else that was once held in common, becomes the private property of those who benefit most from the trajectory of the

1. See Fukuyama, *End of History*.

2. On commoning and the ways in which capitalism encloses the commons—both at capitalism's inception and in our present moment—see Federici, *Caliban and the Witch*; *Re-Enchanting the World*; *Witches, Witch-Hunting, and Women*.

1

status quo and who are, thus, most invested in perpetuating and further entrenching that trajectory.

Given that I was a Religious Studies student at that time, I also understood all of this to be profoundly eschatological (and I rejected a lot of the language games that people played in order to distinguish "eschatology" from "teleology," or "theology" from "ideology," or "philosophy" from "theology" from "history," and so on). Specifically, I came to the conclusion that imperialism is heavily invested in promoting a realized form of eschatology. I have always been skeptical about claims that secularism takes us into an age that is post-ideological or, for that matter, fundamentally different than a world defined by religious beliefs. It seems to me that many of the most prominent adherents of seemingly secular economic systems—folks like Friedrich Hayek or Milton Friedman and their heirs from the Chicago School, who paved the way for capitalism as we know it—have simply taken categories that were historically associated with religion (and, historically, religion was always interwoven with politics and economics) and reworked them around the valorization of wealth accumulation and the degradation of life (regardless of quasi-mystical claims that are made about "the invisible hand of the market" and all boats rising).[3] Capitalism, it seems to me, is not so much post-religious as it is a new religion with its own ethics, values, core beliefs, and eschatology.[4]

Viewed in this way, neoliberal capitalism has some remarkable similarities to the imperial cult(s) spreading through the eastern portion of the Roman Empire during the first century CE.[5] Like the Roman imperial cult(s), capitalism is very happy to have people continue to worship a great variety of gods so long as, along the way, they pinch a little incense to Caesar, respect the rule of law, and pay their taxes. Thus, in the first century, images of the divine Caesars were venerated alongside local deities, and in the twenty-first century, the Christian festival of Christmas becomes a festival of consumption and the time of year when the greatest amount of credit-debt is accumulated (approximately one-third of all retail sales in

---

3. See Hayek, *Road to Serfdom*; Friedman, *Capitalism and Freedom*.

4. On this point, see Loy, "Religion of the Market," 275–90; Hopkins, "Religion of Globalization"; Derrida, *Specters of Marx*, 70–85. Also Horsley, *Religion and Empire*, 133; Brueggemann, *Mandate to Difference*, 63; Wright, *New Tasks*, 36; Moltmann, *Way of Jesus Christ*, 100.

5. The reason why I prefer to speak of "the imperial cult(s)" rather than "the imperial cult" or "imperial cults" will become apparent in chapter 3.

the US take place at this time).[6] It seems to me, then, that capitalism isn't so much "secular" as it is a contemporary manifestation of the ideo-theology that is favored by imperial rulers. Consequently, I have also come to suspect that a sustained study of any manifestation of imperialism—its ideology, its political structures, its economic practices, its propaganda, and so on—can help shed light on our current situation.

In volume 1 of this series, I examined four main positions pertaining to Paulinism and politics and spent a considerable amount of time exploring the background material that is used to justify those positions. It seems to me that it is impossible to evaluate the plausibility of the various perspectives proposed without that kind of sustained examination. It is especially critical to do this if one wants to enter into challenging but thoughtful conversations with those on the other side of the barricades that we erect to entrench ourselves within self-affirming echo chambers. As I stated in volume 1, I am not interested in "preaching to the choir." I want to expand the membership of a certain choir while also diminishing the membership of certain other choirs. This, I believe, is the sort of partisanship required of the contemporary Paulinist.

By the end of volume 1, certain understandings of the Pauline faction seemed far less plausible than others. Notably, both conservative and liberal understandings of Paulinism seemed to be either refuted by the evidence or seemed to be based upon assumptions that were highly unlikely in light of the evidence. What came to the fore was an understanding of the Pauline faction as a politically persecuted movement that arose among oppressed, dispossessed, enslaved, and colonized peoples in the eastern portion of the Roman Empire. Granted, there was diversity within the assemblies of Jesus loyalists associated with the Pauline faction, but this diversity had much more in common with the diversity that one finds in a single-room occupancy hotel in Vancouver's downtown eastside, or in a favela in Rio, or in the dorms of an Apple sweatshop in Korea than the diversity one finds in a suburban church in the territories colonized and occupied by Canada or the US.

However, this study of background material, while covering most of the traditional subjects used as foundations for the study of Paulinism and

6. Of course, for the last two millennia, Christianity has had a privileged position within occidental forms of imperialism, so it is no surprise to find it working hand-in-glove with capitalism since the first days thereof; but capitalism, like the imperial cult(s), embraces and profits from multiculturalism so long as capitalism (like Roman imperialism) is permitted to be the central formative structure within society.

politics, is incomplete in two significant ways. First of all, our initial examination of Pauline apocalyptic eschatology is deficient on two points: it does not give sufficient attention to apocalyptic movements (versus apocalyptic literary features) and it does not examine the perspective of the Pauline faction in light of the Roman imperial eschatology that was aggressively propagated throughout all the locations visited by Paul and his coworkers. Second, our prior examination does not dwell in detail on the ideo-theology of Roman imperialism, its key values, and the language and practices associated with the spread of the imperial cult(s)—the fastest growing religion in the eastern portion of the Roman Empire when the Pauline faction was active. This is a major gap. In my opinion, it is impossible to make sense of what the Pauline faction was doing if we do not examine these matters in detail. Ignoring this while talking about Paulinism would be akin to trying to make sense of the incarceration rates of young Black men in territories colonized by the US or of Indigenous peoples in Canada-occupied territories without paying any attention to the ongoing American and Canadian histories of racism, white supremacy, and settler colonialism.[7] Studying those incarceration rates without an understanding of that ongoing history will almost certainly lead to not just inaccurate but actively harmful conclusions that would only further incite violence against oppressed peoples. The same, I suspect, takes place when Paulinism is studied without being understood within the ongoing history of Roman imperialism. This may seem like a bold assertion to those unfamiliar with this history and how Paulinism looks and sounds when situated within this context, but it is a conclusion that I have come to hold with increasing certainty over the years that it took me to complete this study. Therefore, in this volume, I will address these two deficiencies. Chapter 2 will pick up our study of Pauline apocalyptic eschatology understood in relation to the history of apocalyptic movements and the realized eschatology of Rome. Chapter 3 will then engage in a detailed examination of the ideo-theology of Rome, its four cornerstones, and the significance of the imperial cult(s). Upon completing this volume, we will finally be well-situated to evaluate

7. Thankfully, there is a very rich area of scholarship that explores this carefully. See, for example, in the context of the US, Alexander, *New Jim Crow*; Anderson, *White Rage*; Taylor, *From #BlackLivesMatter to Black Liberation*. Going back to the origins of the American State, see Horne, *Counter-Revolution of 1776*. In the Canadian context, see Razack, *Dying from Improvement*; *Race, Space, and the Law*; Kaye, *Responding to Human Trafficking*; Maynard, *Policing Black Lives*; Comack, *Racialized Policing*; Oudshoorn, *Trauma-Informed Youth Justice*.

the values, practices, theory, ideology, and work of the Pauline faction. That will be the work of volume 3.

This volume provides us with an in-depth look at the multifaceted dynamics of Roman imperialism. We will see how it co-opts traditional beliefs and values, attempts to regulate, bleach, or eliminate non-compliant elements, and inserts itself so powerfully and ubiquitously into all areas of life, that life without it seems (almost but not quite) unimaginable. In order to discipline the imaginations of vanquished peoples in this way, a significant amount of imperial capital is invested in reformulating how people understand, mark, and experience not only history but time itself. In particular, the domain of the future—experienced as an in-breaking *novum* or as the domain where radical change might be possible—is closed off, and the inhabitants of the empire are enclosed within the eternal now of imperialism. For those who experience empire as a burden rather than as a golden age of abundance, there is no hope of an alternative. The only choice is between accommodation and submission or death. Accommodation for local elites, of course, was not often all that burdensome. It was an easy choice. Yet for those looking at living a life of slavery, experiencing sexual violence regularly, and never knowing if one will have enough food to eat tomorrow, accommodation is not always more appealing than death—even death on a cross.

Thus, although empires attempt to eliminate the future as a domain of radical new possibilities that disrupt, overturn, or destroy the status quo and its trajectory, they never fully succeed.[8] There is more to this statement than the obvious truism that all empires eventually end (and this will be just as true of the empire of global capital as it was of capitalism's predecessors—even if, contra Marx and Engels, the fall of capitalism does not give rise to communism but, instead, is replaced by a new feudalism). Rather, it means that in every moment of empire, there are always those who reject imperialism's realized eschatology in order to not only claim a different future but also try and live within that counter-imperial future now—because the time is short, the old is passing, and, behold, the new day is already at hand. It is here that one finds various apocalyptic movements in the ancient

8. Even Fukuyama himself changed his tune in October 2018, when he acknowledged this and declared, "Socialism ought to come back" (see Eaton, "Francis Fukuyama Interview"). Of course, it should be observed that Fukuyama is not really calling for socialism qua socialism; rather, he is calling for an increase in the kind of philanthrocapitalism necessary to maintain the power imbalances of neoliberalism and prevent society from collapsing completely into chaos and open revolt.

Near East, and it is here, I believe, that we find the Pauline faction. They make good company. I'd like to join that company and hope by the end of this series that you will, too.

2

APOCALYPTIC ESCHATOLOGY AND THE FOUNDING NARRATIVES OF EMPIRE: HISTORY AND RESISTANCE

> Allow me, citizens, to do at this point what poets who write about Roman history do, and pass over our disaster.
>
> —Cicero, *De Imperio Cn. Pompei* 25

> God chose the stillbirths, the low-born and despised things of the world, things that are not, to invalidate, to inactivate, to annihilate, and to reduce to nothing, the things that are.
>
> —1 Corinthians 1:28 (my translation)

Introduction: Making History

HISTORY, LIKE ANY DISCOURSE where "truths" and "facts" are formulated within the context of unequal distributions of power and knowledge, has always been a contested terrain. How a collective marks time, what beginnings and endings it recognizes, what festivals cycle through its calendar, who is remembered and who is forgotten, what is or is not hoped for—all of these things are ways of giving expression and embodiment to particular historical narratives. Over the last few centuries within Western "civilization," the dominant historical narratives were critical elements of the ideological state apparatus.[1] In this context, history is ideology in at least two ways in which that word is used. It is ideology in the strict, definitional sense of being a core component of the set of beliefs deployed by a group in order to make time, space, and one's life therein intelligible and meaningful. It is also ideology in the more popular sense of being a discourse that is manipulated by certain parties in order to impose their view of the world onto others and to ensure those others remain properly situated within that world.

To understand history as ideology is not to suggest that history is disconnected from memory. "Memory," as Jacob Taubes asserts, "is the foundation of history," and different histories have varying degrees of force or compulsion based upon how they resonate with what people remember.[2] Various tools assist the act of remembrance—texts, archives, images, even language itself—but none of those tools are neutral, purely objective, or outside of the domain of ideological influence and constitution themselves. However, memories are critical for the constitution of both individual and collective identities (and for the ways in which the distance between individuals and collectivities are enforced or collapsed).[3] But these memories, like these identities, are always in motion, they are constantly contested, reinterpreted, shuffled, and remembered in slightly modified or entirely new ways. As Elizabeth Schüssler-Fiorenza says, history "seeks to articulate a living memory."[4] And people and communities live those memories. As William Faulkner observes, "The past is never dead. It's not even past."[5]

However, the effort to present history as dead and past, as an "objective" or "scientific" discourse strictly populated by "facts" that are devoid of any strict (moral, eschatological, other) judgments or meanings, has always

1. As per Althusser, "Ideology and Ideological State Apparatus," 85–126. Of course, in the postmodern world of globalization and transnational financial institutions and corporations, the primacy of the nation state has become increasingly challenged. However, as the resurgence of neo-fascist nationalism in Europe, South America, and the territories colonized by the US demonstrates, the nation state is far from being a thing of the past.

2. Taubes, *Occidental Eschatology*, 13.

3. See Esler, *New Testament Theology*, 68–69; Moltmann, *Experiences in Theology*, 32–33, 104.

4. Schüssler-Fiorenza, *In Memory of Her*, xxii, xxvi.

5. Faulkner, *Requiem for a Nun*, 73.

been a performance imposed by those who have enough access to power/ knowledge and wealth to try to universalize their understanding of history.[6] One of the most prevalent ways of going about doing this is to attempt to "naturalize" one's own understanding of history and make it appear non-ideological. This is often accomplished through a discursive transition from a focus on "history" to a focus on "time."[7] This transition is often treated as a particularly modern phenomenon (Moltmann traces a line from Daniel Bell's end of ideology, through Joachim Fest's end of utopian socialism, to Francis Fukuyama's end of history), but, as we will see below, this approach is already well developed by Roman imperialism in the calendar developed by Julius Caesar and further perfected by Augustus.[8] This includes what we take to be the modern story of progress, which Moltmann describes as a tool of domination used by current rulers.[9] Progress here is understood in a twofold sense—time is moving forward and things are getting better. History and the naturalization of a particular conception of time and its progression are not so much ideological tools of modernity as they are ideological tools of imperialism.

In order for this model of history to become hegemonic, a considerable amount of forgetting is necessary.[10] In such an anamnestic space, people can resort to "timeless philosophies or mystical eternities" in order to experience comfort and meaning.[11] It is no wonder then, in the context of the Pauline faction (wherein the Roman Empire was aggressively pursuing their own closure of history), mystery cults and timeless philosophies like Stoicism were thriving. A fundamental part of this is disarming apocalypticism with hopelessness, cynicism, and an inhuman determinism that is impervious to actions performed by individuals or groups.[12] When

6. On power/knowledge, see Foucault, *Power/Knowledge*, 51–52.

7. See Bauckham, "Time and Eternity," 170. As Kierkegaard already recognized, "The misfortune of our time is precisely that it has become only 'time'" (quoted in Taubes, *Occidental Eschatology*, 172).

8. For Moltmann, see *Coming of God*, 223–25. Also Bell, *End of Ideology*; Fukuyama, *End of History*.

9. Moltmann, *God in Creation*, 125.

10. To live without history is to live without memory, and any culture where history is closed is necessarily an anamnestic culture (Moltmann, *Coming of God*, 221; *Experiences in Theology*, 41).

11. Balthasar, *Theology of History*, 41.

12. See Moltmann, "What Has Happened," 119–21; *Coming of God*, 226–30. The violence and betrayal of Barack Obama's two-term presidential administration in the

the empire seems all-powerful, even the apocalyptic can be thoroughly de-politicized, individualized, and privatized.[13] In this way, apocalypticism is rendered incapable of hope, let alone the kind of active resistance that is willing to endure suffering and death in conflicts with imperial powers who try to entrap all others within their eternal dominion.

I believe it is important to state this at the outset because, when looking at older conceptions of history, the contemporary reader may be tempted to think condescendingly of "ancient history," caught up as it is with mythology, religion, and other fantastic elements that we claim to have purged in our much more objective history-making. I believe that it is a mistake to think this way. Our histories are as ideological as Greek, Roman, or Judean histories. That they appear otherwise to us helps us to see how deeply enmeshed we are in the ideologies that dominate us.[14] Therefore, when we approach history and consider legitimate ways of doing history or marking time, a Foucauldian lens is useful: why does this approach count and other approaches do not?[15] Whose interests does this conception of time and history support? Whose lives are lost or forgotten here? What socioeconomic or political structures are masked or naturalized? Who speaks and who does not? What dates are remembered and what dates are forgotten? What is remembered on those dates and what is forgotten?[16]

US shows how this cynicism is capable of even overtaking and deploying the discourse of hope in order to prevent anything but spectacular change (as per Guy Debord) from taking place.

13. See Elliott, "Disciplining the Hope," 193–96; Carter, "Paul and the Roman Empire," 9.

14. As Žižek has often noted, "nature" is simply ideology operating at its finest. That is to say, whatever seems most natural, normal, and obvious to us shows where we have bought so fully into a system of beliefs that the beliefs no longer seem like beliefs—they seem real.

15. As in much of his work, but especially Foucault, *Archaeology of Knowledge*.

16. American rituals related to the remembrance of "9/11" are instructive here. On September 11, 2001, planes were flown into the twin towers in New York and the Pentagon. This prompted annual commemorative events that have become a staple of American warmongering, righteousness (or justice), and greed. This event is universalized as the year (2001) is dropped and "9/11" becomes every 9/11 forever after. It is interesting to observe this because on September 11, 1973, Pinochet's coup (with the support of the Americans) toppled the democratically elected Allende government in Chile and prompted decades of terror, torture, and disappearances there. This event was never commemorated or memorialized in the American calendar. Thus, 9/11 is remembered in one way (to meet certain ends) and forgotten in another (to avoid certain other ends).

In this chapter, I will first examine Roman ways of marking time and how that was developed by the Caesars—especially Augustus—in order to promote a form of realized eschatology that is focused upon the endless rule of those Caesars. I will then turn to examining apocalypticism, paying special attention to how Paul and his coworkers formulated apocalyptic beliefs and practices that intentionally and directly conflicted with Roman eschatology.

The Time of Empire: A Golden Age

Cyclical and Linear Time

In the 1960s, it was common for scholars to assert that the Judeo-Christian tradition (with the emphasis usually falling on the Christian side of the hyphen) was responsible for providing the Western world with a linear rather than cyclical conception of time.[17] The world of pre-Christian or non-Jewish "paganisms" was taken to be experienced and interpreted through the eternally recurring cycles of seasons, the lunar phases, and the rise and fall of various ages. Thus, for example, it is argued that the Greeks (who provided the philosophical foundation for much of Roman society) saw cyclical time as bondage and instead of seeking freedom in time, sought freedom from time in eternity.[18] In contrast to these cycles, scholars like Paul Merkley argue that Judaism posited a unique beginning to time, which, along with YHWH's involvement in history, created a calendar that the people followed instead of the cycles of nature.[19] This then finds its fullest expression in the Jesus-event, which becomes the cornerstone for the creation of the Christian calendar, providing the foundation for the linear time of the Western world that has now become the 24/7 of global capitalism.[20]

However, more recent studies have demonstrated that the cyclical-linear divide created in relation to the Judeo-Christian tradition and so-called paganism is inaccurate. As Denis Feeney observes, positing Greek time

17. See, for example, Cullman, *Christ and Time*, 51–60; Merkley, *Greek and Hebrew Origins*, 45–46, 60–66; Jensen, *Subversive Spirituality*, 33–34.

18. Cullman, *Christ and Time*, 52–55; Merkley, *Greek and Hebrew Origins*, 60–63.

19. Merkley, *Greek and Hebrew Origins*, 93.

20. On this point, see Crary, *24/7*. On the ways in which Christian monasticism gave rise to the clock and contemporary time-keeping, see Mumford, *Technics and Civilization*, 12–18.

as cyclical and Judean time as linear or teleological misrepresents both.[21] For example, the Judean lunar calendar, which likely originated during the Babylonian captivity, was marked by cycles and recurring festivals (and, of course, much of the Christian calendar operates cyclically). Conversely, the very idea of creating a universal history that accounts for all peoples in all places is frequently accredited to Herodotus, an aristocratic Greek, and Greek history also recognizes a beginning and not simply a cycle but a succession of ages.[22] This combination of linear and cyclical conceptions of time and history is especially prominent in imperial Roman ideology.[23] Furthermore, this approach to history is markedly eschatological, and it is difficult to properly understand the apocalyptic eschatology of the Pauline faction without some understanding of this.

Roman Markers of Time

Within Roman conceptions of history, there are frequent references to cosmic cycles, the recurrence of ages, and a certain astrological determinism that leads some, especially the Stoics, to view history as meaningless.[24] Thus, Seneca observes, "All things fall into the same abyss" and "whatever years lie behind us are in death's hands."[25] However, as Feeney emphasizes,

21. Feeney, *Caesar's Calendar*, 2–3.

22. See Merkley, *Greek and Hebrew Origins*, 15–17, 27, 31–32. Merkley notes that Herodotus did not win many over to his view and so focuses on Greek philosophies that deal with eternity and timeless truths as a means of escaping the meaningless cycle of history (*Greek and Hebrew Origins*, 51–59).

23. Which, it should be recalled, we find in documents written by elite members of society, which are intended to serve the interests of those people. See Koester, *History, Culture, and Religion*, 331–35. (NB: It was only after I was in the final stages of editing this manuscript for publication that I learned about Elaine Pagels's report about the ways in which Koester sexually abused her and other students [see Pagels, *Why Religion?*]. I would have preferred to have scrubbed him from my manuscript [as I also have done in the past with John Howard Yoder and then Stanley Hauerwas after Hauerwas published his rape apologist letter on behalf of his eternally unapologetic rapist friend in October 2017], given that I think that men who exploited their power to get away with serially abusing women should be remembered for what they did and not for what they said, but instead of reworking my manuscript at this late stage, I have chosen to note this matter here.)

24. See Kee, *Beginnings of Christianity*, 472–74; Vos, *Pauline Eschatology*, 316n21.

25. Seneca quoted in Meeks, *First Urban Christians*, 174–75.

"Roman time structures . . . are premodern and modern at once."[26] While cyclical elements are present, there are also a number of ways in which Romans marked a linear progression through time. For example, the Romans marked time with honorific eras, with *saeculum* (marking a generation according to its oldest living member), and with anniversaries of years.[27] Sometimes events marked a shift to a new moment in history. The founding and refounding of (a new, better, truer) Rome by people like Romulus, Augustus, and Nero is one example of this.[28] The Roman *fasti* are another. The *fasti* were annual calendars that were named after the chief magistrate of that year, and so the *Fasti Consulares*, the calendar of the consuls, marks a trajectory through time, even as the *Fasti Anni*, which lists the days of the year and when festivals are celebrated, marks the cycle of time.[29] The significance of a year being named after its consul should not be underestimated. As Feeney notes, "The original purpose of the *fasti* was not to facilitate chronological reckoning," but to track succession, collegiality, offices of prestige, and in the process of doing so, "the consuls *were* the particular year."[30] In all these ways, then, the Romans attempted to "impose *meaningful* shape on the flux of past time and create a sensation of *monitored progress* through time."[31]

All of this is brought to something of a climax with the calendrical reforms performed by Julius Caesar and perfected by his heir, Caesar Augustus.[32] The reforms demoted the significance of the consuls while promoting the significance of the emperor—especially Augustus. Thus, for example, Augustus changes the beginning of the *Fasti Consulares* from the beginning of the republic to the founding of the city of Rome by Romulus (whom Augustus is said to parallel in many ways). He shifts the cultic center for the rites involved with the *fasti* from the cult of Jupiter to a temple he, Augustus, built and dedicated to Mars Ultor (Mars the Avenger), an ancestor of his adoptive father, Julius Caesar (who had been assassinated by Roman

26. Feeney, *Caesar's Calendar*, 2.

27. Feeney, *Caesar's Calendar*, 14–45, 139–41, 145–46.

28. Feeney, *Caesar's Calendar*, 68–70, 86–95, 100–106.

29. Feeney, *Caesar's Calendar*, 167–69. Feeney also notes that the *Fasti Consulares* and the *Fasti Anni* should not be treated as completely separate entities.

30. Feeney, *Caesar's Calendar*, 171.

31. Feeney, *Caesar's Calendar*, 147, 157.

32. See Suetonius, *Twelve Caesars*, 28, 69; Plutarch, *Lives of the Noble*, 59.

senators and consuls).[33] The *fasti* also eventually shift from tracking magistracies to tracking the high priesthood of the imperial cult.[34] Furthermore, Julius Caesar renamed two months after his divine ancestors Mars (March) and Venus (April), and Augustus named the month of July after Julius and the month of August after himself.[35] Thus, the role of the consuls is increasingly reduced (from that of representational historical actors to that of ciphers for dates) even as the role of the emperor becomes increasingly important to Roman ways of marking time and defining one's identity and world as Roman.[36]

Furthermore, Caesar's calendar was intended to be a universal calendar—the calendar deployed by *all* people. Prior to the Caesars, cities and regions had their own calendars and ways of marking time.[37] Julius Caesar and then Augustus (and the Julio-Claudian emperors who came after them), tried to synchronize other histories, festivals, and significant dates into their own calendar, thereby making all of history into a single entity dominated by the Caesar.[38] This act of synchronization was performed in a way that tied Romans to what was best about other cultures while also maintaining Roman superiority over all others—it was, by no means, a neutral or apolitical effort.[39] Instead, it was a way in which the Romans worked to colonize not only the territories but also the temporality and subjectivity of those whom they conquered. As such, Roman officials actively spread their calendars and versions of history among those whom they had defeated.[40] Clifford Ando summarizes this well: "The Roman imperial government advertised to its subjects the existence of a shared history and a common political theology: the history was that of Rome in the era of her empire, and the one constant in the religious firmament was

33. Feeney, *Caesar's Calendar*, 174–81.

34. Price, *Rituals and Power*, 106.

35. Feeney, *Caesar's Calendar*, 184–88. Nero later renames the month of April (which was named for Venus) after himself and calls it Neroneus (Suetonius, *Twelve Caesars*, 241). Thus, the man who murdered his own mother to gain greater power (and who later murdered his own wife) also had his female ancestor eliminated from the calendar and replaced with himself.

36. Feeney, *Caesar's Calendar*, 191.

37. Feeney, *Caesar's Calendar*, 9–25.

38. Feeney, *Caesar's Calendar*, 13–16, 65–66. However, as Feeney notes, not everyone adopted Caesar's calendar (*Caesar's Calendar*, 209–11).

39. Feeney, *Caesar's Calendar*, 13–16, 23–42.

40. See Zanker, *Power of Images*, 237.

the emperor."[41] Indeed, that Julius Caesar and Augustus were able to create a calendar that synchronized with natural rhythms and cycles gave further credibility to their claims that they were presenting or unveiling a universal history—it appeared to both validate their claims to divine or semi-divine powers (given their ability to coordinate the movement of celestial bodies with their calendar) while simultaneously naturalizing their power, making it appear as if the world they ruled was simply the world as it was.[42]

Julius Caesar may have done most of the work to create the calendar, but Augustus became the true focus of it. Many holidays around the empire were celebrated in relation to him. The day he assumed the *toga virilis* (marking his transition from a boy to a man), the day he took the *fasces*, when he became *Pontifex Maximus* (high priest), when he held his first consulship, when he had his first victory, when Lepidus's army went over to Augustus, when Augustus was first hailed as emperor, when he returned to Rome from overseas, when he was given the name Augustus, when he dedicated the *Ara Pacis* (the altar of peace) at Rome, and when he dedicated the Temple of Mars were all made into public holidays and festivals.[43] Indeed, the first Roman festival named after a living person occurred in 19 BCE with the *Augustalia*.[44] Additionally, in a manner further demonstrating the cyclical and linear nature of the Roman conception of time, Virgil's history ensures that Aeneas arrived before Rome on "the same day" that Augustus arrives at Rome. The subsequent day, Aeneas receives the shield of Vulcan and Augustus celebrates a triple triumph.[45] Prior to this, Augustus had already ensured that his birthday—another public holiday—was celebrated on the day of the festival of Apollo (a god to whom Augustus claimed a particularly strong attachment, as the next chapter shows), but eventually his birthday is made into the starting point of the year. This comes about as a result of a competition in the province of Asia in 29 BCE, wherein various cities and individuals competed to find the best way of honoring Augustus.[46] This carries very significant theological and political (i.e., ideological)

41. Ando, *Imperial Ideology*, 23.

42. See Feeney, *Caesar's Calendar*, 193–97, 202, 209.

43. Hardin, *Galatians and the Imperial Cult*, 27; Winter, *Divine Honours for the Caesars*, 26–27. Other members of the imperial family are quickly added and Winter observes that the birthday of Drusus, the birthday of Tiberius, and the birthday of Germanicus are celebrated as holidays (*Divine Honours for the Caesars*, 26–27).

44. Feeney, *Caesar's Calendar*, 189.

45. Feeney, *Caesar's Calendar*, 161–62.

46. Although some cities in Italy also began their official year on the birthday of

implications, much of which are captured in the famous Priene inscription (fragments of which have been found at several other locations), describing the decision to change the calendar in this way:

> (It is difficult to tell) whether the birthday of the most divine Caesar is something of greater pleasure or benefit, which we could rightly accept to be equivalent to the beginning of all things; and he [Augustus] restored, if not to nature, at least to serviceability, every form, which was falling away and had carried over into misfortune; and he has given a different look to the whole world, which gladly would have accepted destruction had not Caesar been born for the common good of all things.[47]

Twenty years later, in 9 BCE, a further decree goes out from the Asian Kionon (league of cities):

> Since the Providence that has [divinely] ordained our life, having harnessed her energy and liberality, has brought to life the most perfect good, Augustus, whom she filled with virtue for the service of mankind, giving him, as it were, to us and our descendants a savior, he who brings an end to war and will order [peace], Caesar, who by his [epiphany] surpassed the hopes of all those who anticipated [good news] not only [outstripping the benefactors] coming after him, but also leaving no hope of greater benefaction in the future; (And since) the [birthday] of the god initiated to the world the good news resulting in him . . . (and since) Paullus Fabius Maximus . . . has invented an honor for Augustus that until now has been unknown to the Greeks—to begin time from his birthday—for that reason, with good fortune, and safety, the Greeks of Asia have decided in all the cities to begin the New Year with the 23rd September, which is the birthday of Augustus.[48]

Much of the content of these inscriptions will be explored in more detail in the next chapter, but this makes sufficiently clear that history-making is a political act. Time, the year, all things begin with Augustus, the universal benefactor, descended from heaven, whose gospel of peace and salvation goes out to the ends of the earth in the ever-expanding imperial body

---

Augustus (see Suetonius, *Twelve Caesars*, 85).

47. As per Hardin, *Galatians and the Imperial Cult*, 32. See also the translation in Lietzmann, *Beginnings of the Christian Church*, 167.

48. Again, as per Hardin, *Galatians and the Imperial Cult*, 32–33.

politic—and all of this becomes routinized and institutionalized through the calendar in order to create a sense of natural permanence.[49]

It is interesting to note that the decree quoted from 9 BCE says that beginning time from the birthday of Augustus is a novelty to the Greeks—because this move would not be a novelty to Judeans. At the same time as apocalyptic "theologies of resistance" were cropping up in Palestine in response to the conquests accomplished by Alexander and the Diadochi, Seleucus I Nikator (Victor) had declared that the first day of the calendar was to be the day when he reconquered Babylon in 312 BCE.[50] The reign of Seleucus I was to be the beginning of all things, and his reign was to be as lasting as time itself. As Anathea Portier-Young observes: "All past, all present, all future unfolds from the empire's beginning. The ordering of human life in time is now guaranteed by the structures of empire and depends on the empire for its stability."[51] Furthermore, in 167 BCE, Antiochus IV Epiphanes (God Manifest) sought to further universalize the Seleucid calendar by mandating an end to Judean calendar observations.[52] Here, "Antoichus's intervention into times and the law challenged divine sovereignty and sought to restructure the very order of the cosmos and human life within it."[53] As a part of this effort, Antiochus also required Judeans to celebrate his birthday every month within their temple in Jerusalem. Portier-Young comments on this in a way that directly relates to the Augustan calendar and the celebration of Augustus's birthday as the birth of all things:

> A mandated celebration of the king's birthday, would merge the religious and political in a state-sponsored and mandated ritual that repeatedly drew its participants into the very life of the king. His birth would become a beginning made ever present, a past that would keep repeating, and a future that awaited them as surely as the moon waxed and waned. . . . The birthday celebration enacted a novel ordering of life according to the life of the king. It also made the Judean people participants in this new order.[54]

---

49. See Crossan and Reed, *In Search of Paul*, 241; Price, *Rituals and Power*, 54–61.

50. The term "theologies of resistance" comes from Anathea E. Portier-Young's excellent book, *Apocalypse Against Empire*.

51. Portier-Young, *Apocalypse Against Empire*, 81.

52. Portier-Young, *Apocalypse Against Empire*, 181.

53. Portier-Young, *Apocalypse Against Empire*, 182.

54. Portier-Young, *Apocalypse Against Empire*, 197. Thus, Antiochus IV, like Augustus after him, marks both time and space and creates new memories (of festivals that are celebrated and the stories that go with them) and new identities (Portier-Young,

The Judeans, however, did not always take kindly to this, so they developed apocalyptic literatures and communities of resistance and, in doing so, provided the Pauline faction with a strong basis for their apocalyptic and eschatological confrontation with Rome.

Thus, although the reorientation of the calendar around Augustus may have been new to the Greeks, the idea was not new to those who had traveled farther east to Antioch or into Palestine, and it is likely from these regions that Paullus Fabius Maximus came up with his winning suggestion to honor Augustus by making history (literally and figuratively) by re-creating the Greek calendar. Along with this came all of the festivities and holy days already mentioned (and, it should be recalled, the events mentioned were considered religious festivals). Bruce Winter is correct in observing that "the veneration of the emperors, living and dead, through games held for imperial festivals and through the procession and presence of their images at games is well attested in the provinces by inscriptions, texts and archaeology."[55] This is already true by the time of the Pauline faction. Thus, Simon Price is correct to conclude that "time itself was changed by the imperial cult."[56]

Two final points about these political, holy days deserve mention. First, many festivals were designated as "no work" days for the populace and they were often accompanied by parades, processions, feasts, and games—they were spectacular and they were fun.[57] As Horace says, "Tomorrow, a festal day on account of Caesar's birth, admits of indulgence and repose."[58] The festivals, in other words, were designed to appeal to a large number of people and, in fact, much about them was genuinely appealing. However, among people who were vanquished and enslaved, this appeal may have gone only so far. One does not expect slaves to be granted no work days for all of these events (although perhaps some favored slaves in higher ranking households would be granted this), but a good many wealthy and influential provincials not only participated enthusiastically in these imperial cultic celebrations, they also actively worked to advance

---

Apocalypse Against Empire, 198–200).

55. Winter, *Divine Honours for the Caesars*, 24. Winter notes how sacrifices were made *on behalf of* Augustus at all of these holy day celebrations; additionally, on Augustus's birthday and on the anniversary of when he was named Augustus, sacrifices were made directly *to* Augustus (*Divine Honours for the Caesars*, 27).

56. Price, *Rituals and Power*, 106.

57. See Winter, *Divine Honours for the Caesars*, 139; Sanders, *Paul*, 114–15.

58. Horace, *Epistles* 1.5.1.

them (as demonstrated by the competition between the cities in Achaea). Second, all members of a civic population were expected to participate in these festivals whenever they were held. Cities ordered all citizens to participate and took steps to ensure that those who were not attending the main festival were, for example, sacrificing to Caesar outside the doors of their homes when the procession passed or were at least wearing a wreath to mark their participation.[59] This was critical to a city's efforts to demonstrate loyalty and thereby advance itself over its rivals by gaining greater approval from the emperor.[60] One of the results of this was that any who refused to participate without receiving express imperial permission to do so (as the Judeans had received) potentially jeopardized the well-being of the whole city and faced very serious—potentially fatal—repercussions.[61]

This mandated voluntary participation was critical from the Roman perspective because Rome wanted to justify her rule by manufacturing a consensus that could be ritualized and documented.[62] Thus, Augustus consistently narrates his personal rise to power as something granted to him by universal consent, and it is this consent that sets him apart as a true first among equals (*Princeps*) rather than an authoritarian dictator.[63] Romans viewed those who violated this consensus as an "infection" or a "poison" that threatened the well-being of everyone, understood as a single body, with the emperor as the head.[64] As the head, any attack on the emperor was considered an attack on all. Within this vision of the fleshy imperial body politic, piety towards the gods (who ensured the well-being of the State) could then also be expressed in piety toward the emperor (as the head of that State).[65] Having vanquished cities adopt the Roman calendar and celebrate officially sanctioned holidays and festivals was one of the key tools used to develop transnational consensus.[66] Furthermore, any who were members of a Roman household (even as slaves) were required to worship the gods of that household. Simple avoidance was impossible, and if any noticeably refused to participate in the worship of household gods, of civic deities, and in the religious festivals of Rome, they would immediately

59. See Winter, *Divine Honours for the Caesars*, 26.

60. Winter, *Divine Honours for the Caesars*, 78.

61. See Winter, *Divine Honours for the Caesars*, 5, 53.

62. Ando, *Imperial Ideology*, 5–7.

63. Ando, *Imperial Ideology*, 146–47.

64. Ando, *Imperial Ideology*, 393.

65. Ando, *Imperial Ideology*, 393.

66. Ando, *Imperial Ideology*, 407–8.

be considered a deeply worrying threat to the physical, moral, economic, spiritual, and political well-being of everyone else.[67]

Of all of these festivals, the most important event celebrated during the reign of Augustus (or any subsequent Julio-Claudian Caesars) was the *Ludi Saeculares*—the Secular Games, which marked the birth of a new age.[68] After ten years of preparation, the Secular Games were celebrated in 17 BCE, timed to coincide with the passage of a comet.[69] Prior to the games, which took place from May 30 until June 3, heralds announced the event for several months, new coins were minted, and instruments of purification were distributed to citizens so that they could adequately prepare themselves.[70] The recovery of lost standards from the Parthians in 20 BCE was presented as an anticipatory event that restored honor to Rome and showed that the gods sided with them and their claim to be the agents of universal rule, justice, and peace.[71] Horace also composed his *Carmen saeculare* for the event, presenting himself as a *vates*, a seer and magician capable of speaking with power among gods and men.[72] The Secular Games were said to usher in a new Golden Age, a new Saturnian Age, which was thoroughly and overwhelmingly Augustan.[73]

Realized Eschatology and the Return of the Golden Age

Talking about a golden age is eschatological language, and as Dieter Georgi observed more than twenty years ago, many of the central Roman texts

---

67. See Hurtado, *Destroyer of the Gods*, 49, 53–54, 56–57. While it is useful to cite Hurtado on this point, his general presentation of the Roman imperial cult is deeply problematical for reasons I outline in Oudshoorn, "Response to Larry Hurtado's *Destroyer*." Hurtado's response to those objections can be found in Oudshoorn, "Hurtado Responds."

68. The Latin word *saecular* designates an "age" or "generation," defined as a one-hundred-year period (with the premise being that no one who had attended the last *saecular* games would be alive after one hundred years).

69. Zanker, *Power of Images*, 167.

70. Zanker, *Power of Images*, 167–68.

71. Zanker, *Power of Images*, 183–92.

72. See Georgi, "God Turned Upside Down," 37, 41; Beacham, "Emperor as Impresario," 162; Zanker, *Power of Images*, 167.

73. Feeney, *Caesar's Calendar*, 181–82. See also Virgil, *Aeneid* 8.459–61; Horace, *Odes* 4.2.37–40.

from the age of Augustus are "highly eschatological."[74] What was widely disseminated throughout the Roman Empire—notably in cities where the Pauline faction was active—was a realized eschatology associated with the imperial cult(s).[75] A realized eschatology posits the presence of the *telos* of history in the now time. There is no more waiting, there is no more to come—already we have arrived at the end and fulfillment of all things. Hence, history is read as a story destined for the outcome fulfilled by the Caesars who have become "the instruments of destiny."[76] Here, all things everywhere are incorporated into this vision of fulfillment—this is an eschatology that makes universal claims. Hence, Virgil writes:

> Here is Caesar of the line of Iulus,
> All who shall one day pass under the dome
> Of the great sky: this is the man, this one,
> Of whom so often you have heard the promise,
> Caesar Augustus, son of the deified,
> Who shall bring once again an Age of Gold
> To Latium, to the land where Saturn reigned,
> In early times. He will extend his power
> Beyond the Garamants and Indians,
> Over far territories north and south
> Of the zodiacal stars, the solar way,
> Where Atlas, heaven-bearing, on his shoulder
> Turns the night-sphere, studded with burning stars.
> At that man's coming even now the realms of Caspia and Maeotia
> tremble, warned
> By oracles and the seven mouths of Nile
> Go dark with fear. The truth is, even [Heracles]
> Never traversed so much earth.[77]

74. Georgi, "God Turned Upside Down," 36. I'm surprised by how little follow-up New Testament scholars seem to have done on this observation, but I may have simply missed those who have. Hardin does pick up on this (Hardin, *Galatians*, 34–46).

75. Georgi, *Theocracy*, 29, 46. Carter, *John and Empire*, 204–8; Wright, *Paul*, 64; Eder, "Augustus and the Power of Tradition," 16. This cult will be explored in more detail in the next chapter. Here, the focus will be on its eschatological component.

76. Dewey, *Spirit and Letter in Paul*, 104.

77. Virgil, *Aeneid* 6.1060–77.

There is a messianism to this eschatology, and as much as Rome's perception of Augustus may have tempered Pauline perceptions of Jesus, it may be that strands of apocalyptic Judean messianism also influenced the formation of Roman imperial eschatology.[78] However, what is of special significance about this as a realized eschatology—and what makes it (and most realized eschatologies) so useful to an imperial ideology—is that it posits the future as an endless extension of the present.[79] Zanker summarizes this well: "The fusion of myth and history was realized in the creation of a timeless present. A concept of the future, in the sense of a further development, did not exist in this system. The *saeculum aureum* had dawned, and it was only a question of maintaining and repeating it."[80] Thus, we see that the collapse of history into "mere time" existed well before the invention of the clock or the rise of modernity. For as much as the imperial Roman presentation of history is eschatological, it also aggressively naturalized this eschatology and made it the de facto way in which people experienced time itself.[81]

Part of the process of naturalizing this particular eschatology was the construction of an original historical Golden Age from which this new golden age gains its meaning and its central themes. The motif of a primal golden age had already gained considerable attention during the Roman civil wars when violence, decline, and "unabated longing" defined the Roman context—and this was heavily exploited by the Augustan poets.[82] This first Golden Age was said to be a Saturnian age because it was then, as Virgil writes, that Saturn fled from Jove and founded Latium, giving laws, peace, justice, and security to those who lived there during the "golden centuries" when gods lived among people.[83] Ovid also describes this age in detail:

> In the beginning was the Golden Age, when men of their own accord, without threat of punishment, without laws, maintained good faith and did what was right. There were no penalties to be afraid of, no bronze tablets were erected, carrying threats of legal

78. See Merkley, *Greek and Hebrew Origins*, 149, 163–65, 170–75, 180–81, 185–91.

79. Elliott, *Arrogance of Nations*, 143–45; Carter, *John and Empire*, 206–8.

80. Zanker, *Power of Images*, 215.

81. As Moltmann says, "History and eschatology can neither be totally divided nor totally integrated but the eschatological does become historical, and so the historical also becomes eschatological" (*Church in the Power of the Spirit*, 192).

82. See Kautsky, *Foundations of Christianity*, 49–50. These poets, it should be noted, were responsible for crafting the central stories, motifs, and performances of the imperial Roman ideology.

83. See Virgil, *Aeneid* 8.423–44.

action, no crowd of wrong-doers, anxious for mercy, trembled before the face of their judge: indeed, there were no judges, men lived securely without them. Never yet had any pine tree, cut down from its home on the mountains, been launched on ocean's waves, to visit foreign lands: men knew only their own shores. Their cities were not yet surrounded by sheer moats, they had no straight brass trumpets, no coiling brass horns, no helmets and no swords. The people of the world, untroubled by any fears, enjoyed a leisurely and peaceful existence, and had no use for soldiers. The earth itself without compulsion, untouched by the hoe, unfurrowed by any share, produced all things spontaneously, and men were content with foods that grew without cultivation. They gathered arbute berries and mountain strawberries, wild cherries and blackberries that cling to thorny bramble bushes: or acorns, fallen from Jupiter's spreading oak. It was a season of everlasting spring, when peaceful zephyrs, with their warm breath, caressed the flowers that sprang up without having been planted. In time the earth, though untilled, produced corn too, and fields that never lay fallow whitened with heavy ears of grain. Then there flowed rivers of milk and rivers of nectar, and golden honey dripped from the green holm-oak.[84]

This original Golden Age is followed by a Silver Age when labor first appears—from spring the four seasons develop and it is necessary to build shelters, people must begin to work the land in order to produce crops, and war (but, notably, not wickedness) appears.[85] A fall takes place with the transition from the Silver Age to the Iron Age when all kinds of wickedness, bloodshed, struggle, incest, patricide, and impiety become present and prominent. In the Iron Age, "all proper affection lay vanquished and, last of the immortals, the maid Justice left the blood-soaked earth."[86] This Iron Age then dominates human history, and as crises pile upon crises and the Roman people go through years of devastating civil wars, people begin

84. Ovid, *Metamorphoses* 1. Most of the images used here are self-explanatory in their meanings. The reference to ships refers to the ways in which the Romans saw technological developments as corruptions from a purer primal state of nature that was now being destroyed (see Feeney, *Caesar's Calendar*, 118–30). It is interesting to note the difference between Virgil and Ovid as to when the law appears or becomes necessary. Even imperial ideologues have differences, and these differences can have significant implications. For more on the differences between Virgil, Horace, Ovid, and Tacitus, see Feeney, *Caesar's Calendar*, 131–36.

85. Ovid, *Metamorphoses* 1.

86. Ovid, *Metamorphoses* 1.

to wonder where hope can be found. Augustus presents himself as the answer to this.

In part, after the trauma of the civil wars, the Golden Age had to be resurrected in order to forget some of what had been done and to reframe those who came out on top (largely due to their ability to slaughter their enemies).[87] This forgetting and reframing was presented as a significant religious revival that would get to the root of the religious, spiritual, and moral problems that prompted the civil wars and thereby heal Rome so that peace, justice, and plenty could return to earth.[88] All of this becomes possible through a restored intimacy between gods and people, facilitated by the person of the emperor. Thus, a return to a golden age is also a call to a renewed morality and spirituality.[89] All of these themes are repeatedly emphasized and interwoven by the Roman poet-propagandists. Interweaving the return of Justice with the epiphany of Augustus as elements of the arrival of the Golden Age, Virgil writes:

> Ours is the crowning era foretold in prophecy:
> Born of Time, a great new cycle of centuries
> Begins. Justice returns to earth, the Golden Age,
> Returns, and its first-born comes down from heaven above.
> Look kindly, chaste Lucinda, upon this infant's birth,
> For with him shall hearts of iron cease, and hearts of gold
> Inherit the whole earth—yes, Apollo reigns now.[90]

Virgil then draws upon themes of virtue, piety, peace, and abundance as he continues to describe this age:

> This child shall enter into the life of the gods, and behold them
> Walking with antique heroes, and himself be seen of them,
> And rule a world made peaceful by his father's virtuous acts.
> Child your first birthday present will come from nature's wild
> . . . earth will shower you with romping ivy . . .
> Goats shall walk home, their udders taut with milk . . .

---

87. See Zanker, *Power of Images*, 33.

88. See Zanker, *Power of Images*, 101–2. Other synopses of themes related to the Golden Age are offered in Howard-Brook and Gwyther, *Unveiling Empire*, 115; Crossan and Borg, *First Paul*, 178.

89. Georgi, "Turning God Upside Down," 41.

90. Virgil, *Eclogues* 4.4–10.

> The ox will have no fear of the lion . . .
> But snakes will die, and so will fair-seeming poisonous plants.
> Everywhere the commons will breathe of spice and incense.[91]

To this are added further images of abundance arising from nature without any need for human labor:

> But when you [Augustus] are old enough to read about famous men
> And your father's deed, to comprehend what manhood means,
> Then a slow flush of tender gold shall mantle the great plains,
> Then shall grapes hang wild and reddening on thorn tress,
> And honey sweat like dew from the hard bark of oaks.[92]

This then puts an end to unnatural technological developments:

> Later, when the years have confirmed you in full manhood,
> Traders will retire from the sea . . .
> Every land will be self-supporting.
> The soil will need no harrowing, the vine no pruning-knife;
> And the tough ploughman may at last unyoke his oxen.
> We shall stop treating wool with artificial dyes,
> For the ram himself in his pasture will change his fleece's colour
> Now to a charming purple, now to a saffron hue,
> And grazing lambs will dress themselves in coats of scarlet.[93]

This, in turn, leads to a cry of longing for the coming of Augustus, although, of course, Virgil is writing after Augustus has already become well established as the sole authority in Rome and throughout the empire:

> Come soon, dear child of the gods, Jupiter's great viceroy!
> Come soon—the time is near—to begin your life illustrious!
> Look how the round and ponderous globe bows to salute you,
> The lands, the stretching leagues of sea, the unplumbed sky!
> Look how the whole creation exults in the age to come![94]

Other poets write similar things. Calpurnius Sicilus writes about the "untroubled peace" that arose when the Golden Age was born again and a "very

91. Virgil, *Eclogues* 4.18–25.
92. Virgil, *Eclogues* 4.26–30.
93. Virgil, *Eclogues* 4.37–45.
94. Virgil, *Eclogues* 4.48–52.

God" ruled the nations.[95] And in the *Carmen Saeculare* and various odes, essays, epistles, and epodes, Horace discusses the abundance in wealth, nature, and honor that is a part of the Golden Age, which is equally defined by peace, lawfulness, piety, family values, blessings on families, salvation, good luck, loyalty (*pistis*), truth, and virtue.[96]

Part of the purpose of repeating and ritualizing this narrative was to systematize the imperial trajectory established by Augustus so that subsequent Julio-Claudian Caesars could deploy this imagery. However, they are never as convincing as Augustus. Thus, Suetonius mentions a public satire mocking Tiberius's rule in relation to a golden age: "Saturn's golden age has passed, / Saturn's age could never last; / Now while Caesar holds the stage / This must be an iron age."[97] Claudius is subjected to even greater mockery because he recreated the Secular Games in 47 CE, claiming that Augustus calculated the date wrongly. This inspired considerable amusement because part of the claim made about the Secular Games was that no one alive would have been present at the last one (but, of course, people who had attended the Augustan Games were still alive to attend the version offered by Claudius).[98] Other Augustan parallels ascribed to Claudius, like his deification, are thoroughly mocked by the Roman elite who gathered around Nero.[99] However, the ideology of the Golden Age reborn gained considerable traction during the reign of Nero, precisely when the Pauline faction was active. After the violence of Claudius and Caligula raised the specter of another civil war, Nero is praised as a long-awaited savior who will restore peace to the world in a new (or renewed) Golden Age.[100] Thus, according to Seneca, the reign of Nero was to be a time defined by justice, goodness, piety, integrity, honor, moderation, happiness, virtue, and the banishment of evil.[101] Like many others, Seneca believed that there was a great need for a return to the halcyon state of the original Golden Age:

95. Sicilus quoted in Crossan and Borg, *First Paul*, 178.

96. See Horace, *Odes* 4.5.1–40; 4.15.1–32; 4.5.41–44; *To Augustus*; *Epodes* 16.27–34, 41–56; *Carmen saeculare* 13–20, 29–32, 45–48, 57–60; *Epistles* 1.12.3. Zanker explores how these themes are reinforced and distributed in imperial architecture, like the reliefs on the *Ara Pacis* (Zanker, *Power of Images*, 172–82).

97. Suetonius, *Twelve Caesars*, 139.

98. Suetonius, *Twelve Caesars*, 195.

99. See Seneca, *Apocolocyntosis*. Elliott refers to this as an example of a hidden transcript of the powerful (*Arrogance of Nations*, 66–70).

100. Stauffer, *New Testament Theology*, 139; Jewett, *Romans*, 47–48.

101. Seneca, *De clementia* 2.1–2.

Then must come
Once more upon the world a day of death,
When skies must fall and our unworthy race
Be blotted out, until a brighter dawn
Bring in a new and better generation
Like that which walked upon a younger world
When Saturn was the ruler of the sky.
That was the age when the most potent goddess,
Justice, sent down from heaven with Faith divine,
Governed the human race in gentleness.
War was unknown among the nations; arms,
Shrill trumpets, cities guarded by strong walls,
Were things unheard of; roads were free for all,
And all earth's goods were common property.
Nay, Earth herself was happy to extend
Her bounteous fertility like a joyful parent
Sure in the trust of her devoted sons.
. . . We are crushed down
Under our own intolerable age
When crime is king,
Impiety let loose,
And lawless love gives reign to Lechery.
All-conquering Lust with hands long used to rapine
Plunders the boundless wealth of all the world
To squander it for nothing.[102]

In his *Apocolocyntosis*, Seneca described this Age arriving with Nero:

[One of the Fates] teases the fleeces of white to pure bright yarn,
Guiding with golden touch; new colours now dawn.
The sisters look at their work in awed surprise,
To see cheap wool turn into a mass of gold.
The golden years spin out in a lovely line.
No limits are set. They tease the favoured fleece,
Filling their hands in joy, so sweet is their task . . .
Says Apollo, 'Let [Nero] see more than a mortal span,
Image of me in looks and beauty as well,

102. Seneca, *Octavia* 394–411, 427–33.

27

In song and voice no worse.

To a weary folks

He brings the glad days, to muted law a tongue,

As the Morning Star sets the stars to flight,

As the shining sun, when his chariot moves first from the line,

So Caesar comes, so Nero appears to Rome,

His bright face flowing with gentle radiance,

His neck all beauty under his flowing hair.[103]

Part of the argument made on behalf of Nero was that his Golden Age would be superior to the Golden Age of Augustus because Nero came to rule peacefully and not as a result of a civil war. Thus, Seneca writes:

[Augustus] had been some time the sport of Fortune

In many grievous accidents of war

On land and sea, until he had brought down

His father's enemies; you [Nero] the goddess

Has with a willing and a bloodless hand

Bestowed her sovereignty; placed in your grasp

The rein of government, made earth and sea

Your subjects. Then all jealous rivalry

Cease, overruled by dutiful accord.

The zeal of senators and knights was kindled

To serve you; common people in their prayers

And senators in proclamations named you

Giver of peace. Of all the human race

Elected arbiter, you rule a world

In peace and hope, the Father of our Country.[104]

Lucan makes a similar point.[105] As does Calpurnius Siculus in 57 CE, while also emphasizing the abundance that comes with the Golden Age:

Amid the untroubled peace, the Golden Age springs to a second birth; at least kindly Themis, throwing off the gathered dust of her mourning, returns to earth; blissful ages attend the youthful prince. . . . For long, Meliboeus, have I been pondering verse, verses of no woodland ring but fit to celebrate the golden age, to

103. Seneca, *Apocolocyntosis*.

104. Seneca, *Octavia* 478–92.

105. Lucan, *Civil War* 7.122–23.

praise even the very god who is sovereign over the nations and cities and toga-clad peace? Do you see how the green woods are hushed at the sound of Caesar's name? . . . Yes, all the earth and every nation adores him. He is beloved of the gods; as you see, the arbutus-tree pays him silent homage; at the sound of his name the sluggish earth has warmed to life and yielded flowers; invoke him, and in his honor the wood spreads its thick, perfumed foliage, and the spellbound tree breaks into bud again. As soon as the earth felt his divine influence, crops began to come in rich abundance, where furrows previously disappointed hope; at length the beans scarcely rattle in their well-filled pods: no harvest is choked with the spread of barren tare, or whitens with unproductive oats.

O you gods, I pray recall only after a long span of life this youth, whom you, I know it well, have sent us from heaven itself . . . let him be a god and yet loath to exchange his place for the sky.[106]

Initially, it appears that Nero attempts to live up to these expectations, notably in terms of replacing corruption with virtue, but well after things have fallen apart, in 65 CE, Nero is still claiming that "the earth now teemed with a new abundance, and wealth was thrust on [people] by the bounty of the gods."[107]

The Reality of the Golden Age: Conquest, Plunder, Enmity

It is important to remember that it is the emperors and their beneficiaries who were most interested in disseminating this narrative pertaining to a realized eschatology and the conception of time and history that comes with it. For Augustus and his heirs, it seems natural to view the age as golden, but as Klaus Wengst points out, this age was only golden for the triumphant and the very small minority of people situated in places of wealth and power which gave them access to the plunder that went to the victorious.[108] Granted, the general populace of Rome also benefited from these things—the daily allotment of bread, the provision of fresh water to the city, and various renovations and building projects would add to the lives of some non-elite members in positive ways. Apart from being paid

---

106. See Winter, *Divine Honours for the Caesars*, 44–47.

107. Tacitus, *Annals* 8.4–5; 16.2.

108. Wengst, *Pax Romana*, 10–13. See also Carter, *John and Empire*, 205, 223; Horsley, "Gospel of Imperial Salvation" 17–18.

for by the emperor himself, the cost for these things was downloaded to the provinces via taxes on agricultural (and other) production.[109] Already before the Augustan expansion of the empire brought conquest and plunder to a new level, Cicero commented on this massive transfer of wealth from the peripheries of the empire to the centralized Roman elite: "Where do you imagine the wealth of all those foreign countries has gone, countries that are now so poor, when you observe that all Athens, Pergamum, Cyzicus, Miletus, Chios, Samos, and indeed all Asia, Achaea, Greece, and Sicily are now crammed inside a tiny number of country houses?"[110] This then becomes a critical component of Cicero's plea to actively engage in the military defense of Asia (where the Pauline faction would spend much of their time). Cicero says:

> Just think how eager you ought to be to defend the safety of your allies and the prestige of your empire when you *have been* injured—and especially when your most important revenues are at stake! The revenues of the other provinces, citizens, are scarcely large enough to make it worth our governing those provinces; but Asia, on the other hand, is so rich and fertile that it easily surpasses all other territories in the productiveness of its soil, the variety of its crops, the extent of its pasturage, and the size of its exports. Therefore, citizens, if you wish to hold on to something that is useful in time of war and desirable in time of peace, you must defend this province. . . . The whole system of credit and finance which operates here in Rome, here in this very forum, is tied up with and inseparable from the money invested in Asia: if that is lost, then our finances here are inevitably involved in the same general collapse.[111]

Having noted how the wealth of the Roman elite was directly tied to the exploitation of the provinces, Cicero speaks more forthrightly about the growth of Roman wealth than those who sing the praises of the Golden Age:

> It is impossible to exaggerate, citizens, the degree to which we are detested by foreign peoples, because of the greed and corruption of the men we have sent out to govern them in recent years. In all those lands, do you think there is any shrine that our magistrates have treated as sacred, any state they have treated as inviolable, or

109. Garnsey and Saller, *Roman Empire*, 56–57.
110. Cicero, *In Verrem* 2.5.127.
111. Cicero, *De Imperio Cn. Pompei*, 14, 19.

any private home they have treated as closed and barren to them? On the contrary, they actually go searching for rich and flourishing cities that they can find an excuse for declaring war on: that gives them their opportunity of plundering them. . . . When you sent out armies, do you think it is to defend your allies from the enemy, or to use the enemy as an excuse for attacking your friends and allies? . . . Do you imagine that there is any state at peace with Rome that remains rich? Do our opponents consider any state that remains rich to be at peace with Rome?[112]

Now, granted, Cicero writes prior to the rise of Augustus (and Augustus did try to control some of the more rapacious practices of provincial governors), but plunder, greed, and exploitation continued all throughout the early empire. For example, because of this, Tiberius tried to improve upon Augustus's controls by permitting governors to remain in power for longer periods of time so that they would eventually become gorged and satiated and slow down their acts of violence, whereas new governors were constantly stirring up the local peoples because they were not yet sated.[113] No wonder, then, Cicero also remarks: "What a wretched business it is, not simply running the country, but even saving it."[114]

For most people, the Golden Age was a lie, and instead of the arrival of a savior, the Romans came in to plunder, enslave, colonize, and rob the peoples whom they conquered in war. This is why the supposed peace of the Golden Age(s) of Augustus through Nero was maintained by a constant state of war—the arrival of the eschatological peace proclaimed by Rome required the military and local rulers to ensure the ongoing pacification of the vanquished.[115] But the vanquished are never fully conquered ("We have more reason to be afraid," Cicero says, "of silent, hidden enemies than

112. Cicero, *De Imperio Cn. Pompei*, 65–67.

113. See Carter, *John and Empire*, 296.

114. Cicero, *In Catilinam* 2.14. Here, the Roman emperors simply continue the older practices of the kings, of whom Polybius says, "Perhaps all kings, at the beginning of their rule, hold out the word 'freedom' and address those who share their goals as friends and allies; but when it comes to administrating affairs, they no longer treat them as allies, but instead in the manner of a despot" (Polybius quoted in Portier-Young, *Apocalypse Against Empire*, 188–89).

115. See Crossan and Reed, *In Search of Paul*, 141. One thinks, here, of George W. Bush's words about Iraq II: "I just want you to know that when we talk about war, we're really talking about peace" (Speech delivered in Washington, DC, June 18, 2002). Talk of the Golden Age also resonates with the neoliberal economic aphorism that "a rising tide lifts all boats."

open and declared ones").[116] Furthermore, the universal scope of the claims made about the reign of the Caesars is also undermined by the ongoing wars the Romans fought with peoples whom they did not conquer. In light of the conflict this might create for their proclamation of eschatological peace, the Romans argued that the unconquered were not worth conquering because they were too uncivilized, savage, stupid, and useless.[117] It is to such people, often also persisting among the vanquished, that we owe the apocalyptic tradition.

Apocalypticism: Resisting History and Histories of Resistance

Background and Context

Apocalypticism, the apocalyptic movements that inspired apocalyptic literature and the apocalyptic literature that inspired apocalyptic movements, arose during the reign of Alexander the Great and continued to develop and expand during the centuries of the Diadochoi. The Romans tried to control apocalypticism—Augustus had 2,800 compilations of apocalyptic texts collected and burned in 12 BCE, private ownership of oracle collections became illegal, and the Sybilline Oracles were edited and then hidden beneath the statue of the Palatine Apollo at Rome—but still apocalypticism persisted.[118] Its influence was significant and its mark can be found on Roman writers like Virgil and Plutarch. Key Roman themes of a concern for maintaining cosmic order, moral accountability before the gods, confidence in divinely inspired oracles, belief in a divinely-chosen human agent to fulfill the will of the gods, and the use of traditional mythic imagery to communicate these things demonstrate an interaction with apocalypticism.[119]

Apocalypticism was not unique to Palestine or to Judean writers and movements in the diaspora. The work of Berossus, a Babylonian writing in Greek under Alexander, fits within apocalypticism at times, and other

116. Cicero, *In Verrem* 2.5.182.

117. See Ando, *Imperial Ideology*, 324–26.

118. See Aune, *Prophecy in Early Christianity*, 73, 79; Zanker, *Power of Images*, 121.

119. See Kee, *Beginnings of Christianity*, 464–69. Kee argues that these themes show the influence of apocalypticism upon Roman ideology, but, as we will see, there is far more of a give-and-take relationship between apocalypticism and the dominant ideologies of the ruling powers. Both counteract and co-opt each other and so each is critical to the development of the other.

Hellenistic Egyptian apocalyptic texts date to around the same time.[120] Greek and Roman societies also had a history of oracles of doom and (sometimes) deliverance that would circulate among the public.[121] These were especially prominent during the times of crisis, disaster, and prolonged war that either nullified or significantly problematized prior systems of meaning.[122] Palestine was going through such a period from the third century BCE through to the end of the first century CE.[123]

In 332 BCE, Alexander conquered Jerusalem, and his successors, the Diadochoi, who defined themselves as conquerors and militaristic warrior kings, fought over the region from 323 BCE through to 281 BCE.[124] Between 274 BCE and 168 BCE alone, there are six "Syrian Wars" between the Ptolemies and Seleucids. During this time, Jerusalem was conquered multiple times, the temple desecrated and plundered, and countless people were slaughtered, raped, enslaved, dispossessed, and scattered.[125] Even after the Romans intervene in 168 BCE to settle the conflict, they were unconcerned when, in 167 BCE, Antiochus IV Epiphanes set up a deadly reign of terror in Jerusalem in response to a revolt (which, conveniently, allowed him to reassert himself as a conquering king in the tradition of Alexander and the Diadochoi).[126] This prompted the Maccabean revolt, which resulted in semi-autonomous Hasmonean rule before a more independent kingdom was established in 110 BCE. This kingdom was short-lived. In 63 BCE, Pompey conquered Palestine and, like the conquerors before him, besieged the temple, proclaimed himself the liberator of Palestine, and immediately desecrated the holy of holies by walking in and out of it unscathed.[127] Rome

---

120. See Kee, *Beginnings of Christianity*, 463–64.

121. See Aune, *Prophecy in Early Christianity*, 43, 73–77.

122. Aune, *Prophecy in Early Christianity*, 73–77; Howard-Brook and Gwyther, *Unveiling Empire*, 16–18; Vos, *Pauline Eschatology*, v.

123. This continues, of course, into the second century CE, but that takes us well past the time of Paul and his coworkers.

124. Portier-Young, *Apocalypse Against Empire*, 49–51.

125. Portier-Young, *Apocalypse Against Empire*, 67–69.

126. Portier-Young, *Apocalypse Against Empire*, 115–16, 133, 158–68.

127. See Wright, *New Testament and the People of God*, 159. This was done as a part of the Third Mithridatic War, which Cicero urged the Romans to engage in because of the impact it would have on their revenues. He called it: "A war in which the largest and most reliable revenues of the Roman people are at stake, the loss of which would entail the loss of both the means of enjoying peace and the means of making war" (*De Imperio Cn. Pompei* 6). On Pompey as a ruler who liberated the people from Hasmonean rule, see Horsley, "Jesus and Empire," 78.

wanted Palestine, in part for her corn supply and in part to safeguard a much larger supplier—Egypt—from the threat of Parthia.[128] Therefore, Herod the Great, a critical ally of Augustus (then known as Octavian) during the wars that followed the assassination of Julius Caesar, was given control of Palestine in 37 BCE, completed the subjugation of the territories on behalf of Rome, while also actively working to romanize the region. One consequence of this was that after the death of Herod in 4 BCE, a series of major revolts occurred throughout the region (which Rome then turns into a Roman province in order to increase imperial supervision). The response to these revolts was a Roman military campaign defined by massive violence, rape, slaughter, and slavery.[129] At one point, Emmaus was totally destroyed, two thousand revolutionaries (or terrorists from the Roman perspective) were crucified in the hills of Judea and near Magdala, and tens of thousands of people were collected and sold into slavery in Rome and elsewhere throughout the empire.[130] These events took place in remarkable proximity (in both space and time) to the first members of the Jesus movement. As Richard Horsley writes:

> The Roman consistently practiced a scorched-earth policy: they burned villages and slaughtered or enslaved the inhabitants and crucified any who resisted as a way of terrorizing the remaining populace into acquiescence to Roman domination. Galilee was hit particularly hard repeatedly by the Roman armies moving through the district to put down minor insurrections or major revolts.[131]

Pilate arrived as governor in 26 CE. He was considered an "aggressive, no-nonsense promoter of Roman power" and spread the imperial cult, collected taxes, administered justice, oversaw the Roman troops, and plundered the treasury in the temple in order to build an aqueduct.[132] He also crucified Jesus of Nazareth, mocking him as a failed revolutionary.[133]

128. Wright, *New Testament and the People of God*, 154. Horsley argues that about 12.5 percent of the Palestinian Jewish crop went to Caesar—a heavy burden to bear, especially when it is remembered that this does not account for tithes for priests and for the temple-based aristocracy (*Liberation of Christmas*, 36–37).

129. See Horsley, *Liberation of Christmas*, 30–31; "Jesus and Empire," 78–79.

130. Horsley, "Jesus and Empire," 79.

131. Horsley, *Covenant Economics*, 82.

132. Horsley and Silberman, *Message and the Kingdom*, 66–67; Carter, *John and Empire*, 291–92.

133. The sign "King of the Jews" that Roman soldiers placed on Jesus's cross is an act of imperial and colonial mockery akin to the American soldiers who took pictures of

It is not surprising to discover that apocalypticism flourished in this context. Over against the totalizing claims of the empire, apocalypticism offered a contradictory but "equally totalizing counterdiscourse" dealing with themes of universalism, moral and ontological dualisms, vindication, imminence, judgment, and inspiration.[134] However, these themes are all presented differently than the ways in which they are presented in the imperial ideology. These differences are said to arise from a revelation (an apocalypse) that permits people to see things as they actually are and not merely as they appear to be.[135] Much of this apocalyptic seeing is facilitated by an engagement with texts that the Judeans held as sacred.[136] However, some sort of divine or heavenly agent is often needed to assist the seer in understanding these texts correctly—especially when it comes to how they are relevant to the present moment of crisis, oppression, and death. The divine agent helps the seer to remember the history of "the mighty acts of God," thereby tearing open a closed history (the realized eschatology of empire) and revealing a future that is open to the fulfillment of divine promises repressed by imperial history-making.[137] This accomplishes the "liberation of the future from the power of history."[138]

---

themselves urinating on the corpses of Afghani civilians whom they had killed and then branded as terrorists.

134. Portier-Young, *Apocalypse Against Empire*, 35; see also 2, 26, and from the introduction by John J. Collins, xii–xiii. See also Ramsaran, "Resisting Imperial Domination," 93–94; Beker, *Paul's Apocalyptic Gospel*, 30; Howard-Brook and Gwyther, *Unveiling Empire*, 4, 46–86.

135. See Howard-Brook and Gwyther, *Unveiling Empire*, 4, 29, 44.

136. See Portier-Young, *Apocalypse Against Empire*, 218–21. However, as she notes, this encapsulates multiple traditions where no universal agreement exists on what counts as a sacred text or Scripture.

137. See Moltmann, *Experiences in Theology*, 56; *Theology of Hope*, 92, 103–4.

138. Moltmann, "Liberation of the Future," 267. It is also, as has now been widely noted, a course of action that goes against a belief in progress (which is tied to the perpetuation of the trajectory of the status quo). As Emil Brunner noted well before the recent revival of apocalyptic themes in Pauline studies: "The life of the world to come is distinct from *futurum* . . . it suggests the realization of hope through an event which springs from the beyond, from the transcendent; not like *futurum*, something which grows out of what already exists" (Brunner, *Eternal Hope*, 25). I think Brunner's comment is helpful, but it also contains the seeds of some problematic elements of contemporary apocalyptic Paulinism which seems paralyzed by its desire for an apocalypse that never quite seems to come (since any action prior to that apocalypse will only be complicit in the old, as it is the apocalypse itself which creates or opens the way to a *novum* that is genuinely liberatory). Here, it seems to me, these scholars end up becoming as passive and inconsequential as Marxists awaiting the industrialization of the working-class, radicals awaiting

This liberation of historical time is intimately connected to action. Right seeing was necessarily accompanied by right doing. As Portier-Young observes, "The image of open eyes vividly captures the insistence in each apocalypse on the interrelation of knowledge and obedience, vision and praxis, that formed the heart of apocalyptic theologies of resistance to empire in early Judaism."[139] In this regard, apocalyptic texts can be understood as "militant documents" and "*interventions*."[140] Apocalypticism is "a speech of rupture" where words are not always necessary.[141] It is resistance literature that answers and counters empire, not only by what it says, but also (and most importantly) by what its proponents do, and urge others to do.[142] Revelations that reveal the imminent fulfillment of divine promises inspire engagement instead of withdrawal and "the relocation of ultimate power from earth to heaven makes it possible both to imagine and engage in effective resistance" in the here and now.[143]

The concept of rupture is critical to this. Belief in a dualism between ages, an old age (like an age of iron), and a new age (like an age of gold), can cripple action—unless one receives a revelation declaring that the old age is passing (even if that old age is officially declared to be the Golden Age by imperial propaganda) and the new age is being born. Apocalypticism emphasizes this.[144] Things are being revealed *now* because time and space and subjectivities are being ruptured *now*. *Chronos* is being eclipsed as *Kairos* is apocalypsed, and now is the time to act.[145] And to whom do we ascribe the most enduring legacy of a life that embodies the proclamation of the end of one age and the birth of another? Paul. It is no wonder, then,

the revolution, or Christians awaiting the second coming.

139. Portier-Young, *Apocalypse Against Empire*, 389.

140. This is from Badiou's description of Paul's letters (*St. Paul*, 31).

141. Badiou, *St. Paul*, 31. An apocalypse is, thus, like a truth-event. Geoffrey Holsclaw describes it in this way: "The coming-forth of a new being within the situation creates a truth procedure that transforms the original situation and its corresponding knowledge" (Holsclaw, "Subjects between Death and Resurrection," 157). As Badiou says, "A truth is always that which makes a hole in a knowledge" (*Being and Event*, 345).

142. See Portier-Young, *Apocalypse Against Empire*, 217.

143. Portier-Young, *Apocalypse Against Empire*, 8; see also 4, 44.

144. Pate, *End of the Age Has Come*, 29–30.

145. Mikhail Bakunin sounded particularly apocalyptic when, upon quitting the Jura Federation in 1873, he said, "During the last nine years, more than enough ideas for the salvation of the world have been developed by the International (if the world can be saved by ideas) and I defy anyone to come up with a new one. This is the time not for ideas but for actions, for deeds" (Bakunin, "Letter to the Comrades").

that Alain Badiou describes Paul as "the poet-thinker of the event ... a new militant figure."[146]

Pauline Apocalypticism

In Rom 11:25, the Pauline faction writes as those unveiling a mystery about various historical stages, and in 16:25–26a, they conclude the letter by speaking of their being established in the gospel and the *kerygma* of Jesus Anointed, "according to the revelation [*apocalupsin*] of the mystery that was kept secret for long ages but is now disclosed." In 1 Cor 2:1, the Pauline faction writes about the "mystery of God" to the Corinthians, and in 1 Cor 15:15, they again claim to be disclosing a mystery related to God's plan, the transformation of the living, and the resurrection of the dead. This language roots Paulinism within the tradition of the apocalypticists.[147] The Pauline faction also presents the events in which they participate, and which define history, as an "apocalyptic moral drama" with larger-than-life agents like Sin, Flesh, Law, Spirit, God, the Anointed, Creation, Israel, anti-God Powers, Humanity, Ambassadors, Rulers, Life, and Death, all included as participants.[148] The alignment of the participants is apocalypsed in a way that contradicts the alignments heralded by imperial Roman ideology.[149] As Wayne Meeks says, the Pauline faction "disestablishes the world ... [because] eschatological scenarios undermine the cultural system that masquerades as common sense."[150] Thus, apocalypticism and its themes are central to the Pauline faction. Rollin Ramsaran, for example, shows how other prominent apocalyptic themes like the divine judgment of wicked

146. See Badiou, *St. Paul*, 2.

147. See Cousar, *Introduction*, 8, 188n13; Collins, *Apocalyptic Imagination*, 256; Cullmann, *Christ and Time*, 77; Sampley, *Walking Between the Times*, 1; Elias, *Remember the Future*, 252. Roetzel suggests that apocalypticism would be particularly appealing to Paul (*Paul*, 23). While this is true—on the whole, revolutionary ways tend to appeal more to those experiencing marginality or oppression—one should be cautious about overemphasizing this point without using a properly intersectional approach that recognizes how those with relatively higher status among a more generally colonized population were also key proponents of both apocalypticism and imperialism.

148. See Martyn, "Gospel Invades Philosophy," 27–28; Jennings, *Outlaw Justice*, 137; Moltmann, *God in Creation*, 121–24.

149. See Carter, "Vulnerable Power," 471–72; Schweitzer, *Mysticism of Paul the Apostle*, 99.

150. Meeks, *First Urban Christians*, 180.

rulers and the restoration of rule to the just, along with the vindication of those who died in the struggle for justice, guide the flow of the argument of 1 Corinthians.[151] Another central theme, the conception of history split into (multiple but essentially) two ages, is also prominent. As Jacques-Louis Martyn demonstrates, this theme is especially strong in Galatians, although it is found throughout the Pauline corpus.[152] Thus, Paul and his coworkers speak of being liberated from the "present evil age" in Gal 1:4 and in 1 Cor 2:6–8, highlight how divine wisdom confounds that of the doomed and perishing rulers of this age—rulers whose ideology, they add in 2 Cor 4:4, has veiled the eyes and blinded the minds of those whom they rule, and who proclaim *pax et securitas* (as per 1 Thess 5:4) while remaining unaware that they are doomed to destruction.

For the Pauline faction, the pivotal turning point between the ages, which also reveals where all the various agents are situated in the apocalyptic drama, is the Jesus-event. As J. Christiaan Becker states, "The coherent centre of Paul's gospel is constituted in the apocalyptic interpretation of the Christ-event." Douglas Harink waxes more eloquent:

> For Paul, all apocalyptic reflection and hope comes to this, that God has acted critically and decisively, and finally for Israel, all the peoples of the earth, and the entire cosmos, in the life, death, resurrection, and coming again of Jesus, in such a way that God's purpose for Israel, all humanity, and all creation, is critically, decisively, and finally disclosed and effected in the history of Jesus Christ. . . . The apocalypse of Jesus Christ is not a religious event, but a world-making event.[153]

Within the Jesus-event, it is especially the cross and resurrection of Jesus that facilitate this apocalypse. As Charles Cousar notes, "Something earthshaking (apocalyptic) has taken place in the cross, with sweeping implications for human history."[154] Yet the cross only attains this meaning because of the resurrection.[155] As 1 Cor 15:13–14 states: "If there is no

151. See Ramsaran, "Resisting Imperial Domination," 95–100.

152. See Martyn, *Theological Issues*, 18–22; Barclay, *Mind of Saint Paul*, 208–13; Aune, *Apocalypticism, Prophecy, and Magic*, 8–10; Schoeps, *Paul*, 200; Vos, *Pauline Eschatology*, 12, 17–18, 24; Roetzel, *Paul*, 2.

153. Harink, *Paul Among the Postliberals*, 68, 89; see also 120; Beker, *Paul's Apocalyptic Gospel*, 30–34.

154. Cousar, *Introduction*, 44.

155. Badiou words this well: "What constitutes an event in Christ is exclusively the Resurrection, that *anastasis nekron* that should be translated as the rising up of the dead,

[uprising] of the dead, then [the Anointed] has not been raised; and if the Anointed has not been raised, both our [heraldic proclamation] [*kerygma*] and your [loyalty] [*pistis*] are in vain." Without the resurrection, the crucifixion is simply one among thousands of others. But allegiance to the crucified person who is heralded as a resurrected Lord changes everything. As the Pauline faction observes in Rom 1:4, it is the resurrection from the dead that reveals Jesus to be the Son of God (in power) and Lord. Therefore, Jennings notes, "Between our injustice and our being made just stands an event: the event of the resurrection of the executed."[156] It is this combination of cross-resurrection that is taken to be the turning point of the ages.[157] This is the evental truth (*aletheia*) heralded by Paulinism.[158] It is an intrusion, interruption, and revolutionary break with the view of the world proposed by the rulers who had crucified Jesus.[159]

The whole idea of the resurrection of the dead had arisen in the context of "extreme imperial repression."[160] Furthermore, within the context of a supposedly golden age of Neronian abundance and fertility, the proclamation of the resurrection of the dead was an "undoing of the imperial order of (pro)creation that has the murderous violence of conquest inscribed on the very act of giving life."[161] As such, it gives rise to a particular and provocative ethics. It has a significant impact upon the ways in which one tries to live now.[162] In the words of various scholars, it offers a "bodily resurrection," an "ascension ethic," a "liberated ethic," and "an eschatological ethic of hope that engenders a this-worldly praxis in anticipation of the coming

their uprising, which is the uprising of life" (*St. Paul*, 68).

156. Jennings, *Outlaw Justice*, 81.

157. See Martyn, *Theological Issues*, 92–94; Wright, *Paul*, 52; Roetzel, *Paul*, 5, 23; Pate, *End of the Age Has Come*, 46; Sauter, *What Dare We Hope?*, 110–12; Balthasar, *Theology of History*, 17, 139.

158. Badiou speaks of truth, for Paul, as evental (*St. Paul*, 14). For more on truth as *aletheia*, as understood by Heidegger, see volume 3 of this series.

159. See Yeo, *Chairman Mao*, 18; Horrell, *Introduction to the Study*, 77–80.

160. Carter, "Matthew Negotiates the Roman Empire," 127.

161. Kahl, *Galatians Re-Imagined*, 261. In a Paulinist effort to transcend the mutual interplay of apocalypticism and imperial ideology, Ward Blanton argues that the resurrection reveals that "neither the revolutionary nor the nonrevolutionary mean anything; what matters is new creation" (*Materialism for the Masses*, 134). He further states that this helps to free us from the dialectical opposition that works itself out in repetitions of the same in order to attain a "politics of new creation" (153). While all this sounds very nice, I'm not exactly sure what it means when it comes to actual praxis.

162. See Horrell, *Social Ethos*, 82–83; Hays, *Moral Vision*, 19.

kingdom"—and this implies, as we will see in more detail, that all of this is oriented around justice.[163] Yet this apocalyptic ethics of justice is fundamentally different than and opposed to the supposed return of Justice to the earth that was proclaimed by the ideo-theology of Rome. This is so because this resurrection ethics is intimately connected to the belief that it is *the crucified* who has been raised to new life. This, then, results in an ethics of "cooperative solidarity with human need everywhere" because "a responsible apocalyptic recognizes that, without the salvation of our 'neighbour' in the world, our final salvation can be neither asserted nor desired."[164] But, this is not simply solidarity with general human need—it is a solidarity that arises among those who also face the possibility of crucifixion, those who have been vanquished and enslaved, those who have been conquered and left for dead. It is among these people that the proclamation of the resurrection of the crucified arrives, and the arrival of this proclamation inspires their uprising (*anastasis*). Or, as the Pauline faction writes in Rom 6:5, those who live a life that resembles the death of the Anointed can now also live in the likeness of the Anointed's uprising. These themes are also paired and repeated in Phil 3:10–11, although the emphasis there falls more on sharing in sufferings akin to the Anointed's so that one may know the power of the Anointed's resurrection into a new life that is stronger than death. With the resurrection of Jesus, the old age has passed, the new has come, and those who exist in the place of no place, as dead but yet still alive, are now also participants in that resurrection.[165] As 2 Cor 5:17 says, "If anyone is in the Anointed—new creation! The old things have passed away, behold, everything has become new" (see also Gal 6:15).

It is the presence of the eschatological Spirit within the individuals and assemblies of those united in their loyalty to the crucified and resurrected Jesus that enables immediate participation in the *anastasis* life of the new age. Those who gather in the assemblies associated with the Pauline faction are possessed by this Spirit, which liberates them, marks them as members of the household of God, and transforms them into living temples. Those who have been repeatedly and violently violated by others are thus transformed into sacred spaces. Thus, the Pauline faction writes, "Hope does

163. Walsh and Keesmaat, *Colossians Remixed*, 156 (emphasis removed); Crossan and Reed, *In Search of Paul*, 133–35; Crossan, *God and Empire*, 183–86. The particulars of this ethic will be explored in volume 3 of this series.

164. Beker, *Paul's Apocalyptic Gospel*, 109.

165. Thus, as Crossan and Reed observe, resurrection becomes more a process that has been initiated than a simple, singular event (*In Search of Paul*, 171–74, 186–87).

not put us to shame, because the love of God has been poured out in our hearts through the holy Spirit" (Rom 5:5). And again: "Do you not know that you are God's temple and that God's Spirit dwells in you?" (1 Cor 3:16; see also 6:19; 7:40; Gal 4:3–6, 29; 1 Thess 4:8) And again: "Now we have been severed from the [rule of] Law, having died to that which held us captive, so as to be slaves [to him who has risen up from the dead] in newness of Spirit" (Rom 7:6; see also 7:4–6). Thus, those who now belong to the Age of Resurrection are no longer dominated by the powers of the Old Age (Sin, Flesh, Law, Death) but instead walk according to the Spirit (see Rom 8). The Spirit is a seal, first installment, and guarantee of the New Age (2 Cor 1:22; 5:5; Gal 3:14) that both guarantees the consummation of that age and inaugurates that age now. One sees this in the fruit, gifts, and work of the Spirit (1 Thess 1:5–6; Gal 3:2–5; 5:22–23; Rom 1:11; 7:4; 8:23; 11:16; 14:17; 1 Cor 1:7; 2:4, 12; 12:1–31; 14:1–5; 15:20–23; Phil 1:19). Gordon Fee is emphatic about this—it was the presence of the Spirit that made the members of the early Jesus movement "a radical alternative within their culture."[166] This is an experience of the Spirit as an empowering agent. The Spirit is "the *experienced, empowering* return of God's own *personal presence* in and among us [*sic*], who enables us to live as a radically *eschatological* people in the present world."[167] This is clearly communicated in Rom 8:11: "If the Spirit of the one who raised Jesus from the dead inhabits you, the one who raised the Anointed from the dead will also make your mortal bodies alive through the indwelling of his Spirit in you." Resurrection life is experienced as the giving of life to those left for dead now. It is they who "abound in hope by the power of the holy Spirit" (Rom 15:13). This hope, which does not disappoint or put to shame those who are inspired by it, is presented not simply in fleeing the various vices the Pauline faction mentions (e.g., 1 Cor 6:9–10; Gal 5:16–26) but rather inspires the imaginations of those who experience it so they can begin to embody a more just, liberated, and liberating way of inhabiting God's new creation. Imagination enables "the presentation of the otherwise absent."[168] Imagination is required because,

---

166. Fee, *Paul, the Spirit, and the People of God*, xiv.

167. Fee, *Paul, the Spirit and the People of God*, xv.

168. Hart, "Imagination for the Kingdom," 54. He goes on to write: "The power of the future to transform the present lies chiefly in the capacity of God's Spirit to capture our imagination and open up for us a new vision of God's promise and the present which it illuminates, thereby stimulating alternative ways of being in the world in the present, living towards the future. Imagination is thus a vital category in eschatology as in theology more generally" ("Imagination for the Kingdom," 75).

although the New Age has dawned, the Old Age persists—and it persists in powerful ways. Thus, for the Pauline faction, the apocalyptic binary between the ages differs from the clean, instantaneous break posited by the ideo-theology of Rome.[169] Three (often intertwined) misunderstandings about this overlap need to be addressed.

First, there are those who posit that the overlap between the ages is strictly experienced as an internal struggle that each individual "believer" has in relation to "sinfulness" and "righteousness."[170] In this reading, the Old and New Ages have little, if anything, to do with a change in one's environment or material circumstances and instead relate to a de-politicized moral struggle generally related to things such as sex, drinking, family duties, or whatever else. Granted, as we will see, the apocalypse of the *anastasis* of the crucified accompanied by the pouring out of the eschatological Spirit does have an impact upon the subjectivities of those who gather in the assemblies of early Jesus loyalists and, granted, such personal moral issues do matter to Paul and his coworkers, but the proclamation of the passing of the Old Age and the dawning of the New Age relates to much more than this.

Second, in a similar manner, some explain the overlap of the ages as existing strictly in a spiritual domain. The overlap is understood vertically, as one between heaven and earth, instead of horizontally, as something that has socioeconomic, political, and material implications.[171] Paulinism is thus held to adhere to an otherworldly mysticism that deliberately moves away from the domain of politics.[172] However, while the Pauline faction certainly does use spiritual language and claims to have had heavenly visions, this is spiritual language that is thoroughly apocalyptic and blatantly challenges and contradicts the imperial eschatology that is promoted throughout the empire. It is a mistake to see this as a move away from the political instead of understanding it as a form of political critique.

169. Many scholars see this as a modification of Judean apocalyptic thinking. See, for example, Pate, *End of the Age Has Come*, 30, 46; Beker, *Paul the Apostle*, 145; *Paul's Apocalyptic Gospel*, 38–41; Cousar, *Introduction to the New Testament*, 96–97; Gorman, *Reading Paul*, 58–61; Käsemann, *New Testament Questions of Today*, 124–35; Hays, *Moral Vision*, 20–21.

170. See, for example, Pate, *End of the Age Has Come*, 102–20.

171. See Vos, *Pauline Eschatology*, 36–40; Witherington, *Jesus, Paul, and the End*, 57–58.

172. See Bammel, "Romans 13," 380–81; Kee, *Christian Origins in Sociological Perspective*, 122, 152–53. See also Sauter's pushback against Pannenberg, Moltmann, and liberation theology in *What Dare We Hope?*, 149–54.

Finally, in a more Stoic manner, there are those who propose that the overlap of the ages is experienced as a "call to be inwardly free and aloof from the world."[173] This detachment shuns both quietism and radicalism. Its adherents can simply continue to do what they can to make the world a better place, all while remaining very aware that the world is passing away. This stance is far removed from the passion and intensive labor we see practiced by Paul, the ambassador of the Anointed, whose reign brought a damning judgment upon the rulers who had crucified Jesus.

Again, this does not mean the apocalypse of Jesus as the crucified and risen Anointed has no impact upon the inward life or subjectivity of Paul or others in the early assemblies of Jesus loyalists. Paul's claim that the resurrected Jesus appeared to him (1 Cor 15:8; Gal 1:12; see also Acts 9:4; 22:7; 26:14) appears to have completely reconstituted him as both a subject and a witness to the Jesus-event.[174] This transformation seems to involve a sense of "becoming whole and wholly different."[175] Paul seems to have personally experienced what he took to be a breakthrough from one age to the next, which enabled a new becoming, premised upon the death of his old self and the uprising of the Spirit of the Anointed, the Spirit of resurrection Life, within him.[176] In truly apocalyptic fashion, Paul is now woke (1 Thess 5:6). Hence, the call in 1 Cor 15:34: "Awaken justly!" And, as Larry Welborn argues, this awakening creates an unmistakably militant subject who is part of an awakened collective.[177]

As we will see in more detail in volume 3, it is this collectivity that is the true work of the Spirit and the true entity that is created in the overlap of the ages.[178] If things like justice, liberation, and resistance to death-dealing

173. Schrage, *Ethics of the New Testament*, 182–83. See also Collins, *Apocalyptic Imagination*, 267.

174. See Harink, "Introduction," 2; Badiou, *St. Paul*, 44–45. Badiou pushes this further by arguing that the Jesus-event reveals that God is neither a God of wisdom (as per the Greeks) nor of power (as per the Judeans) but rather is revealed, in the Jesus-event, as "*what happens to us*" (*St. Paul*, 48).

175. Sauter, *What Dare We Hope?*, 107.

176. See Dunn, *Theology of Paul the Apostle*, 179–81; Moltmann, *Coming of God*, 24; Welborn, *Paul's Summons to Messianic Life*, 40–41.

177. See Welborn, *Paul's Summons to Messianic Life*, 45. Thus, when commenting on Moltmann, Sauter argues that eschatology is brought to serve revolutionary engagement by altering one's consciousness and, therefore, the way in which one engages the world (*What Dare We Hope?*, 145, 133–47).

178. See Martyn, "Gospel Invades Philosophy," 31–32; *Theological Issues*, 234; Hansen, "Messianic or Apocalyptic?," 217.

rulers are to take place meaningfully, they can only do so in a communal context (and, in Paul's context, far removed from contemporary emphases upon individuals, it would only makes sense for a communal context to be the location where these events are occurring). Thus, the assemblies of Jesus loyalists are eschatological communities that are creatively, imaginatively, and with considerable struggle (as if undergoing labor pains) birthing the age of which they speak.[179] They are the "avant-garde" of new creation, "creating beachheads in this world of God's dawning new world."[180] This is far removed from any notion of apocalypticism as some kind of "compensatory fantasy" and, instead, provides a "comprehensive picture of what is wrong and why, and how life ought to be organized . . . [providing] the basis for lasting rearrangements of social relationships, for building new institutions."[181] Thus, the assemblies of Jesus loyalists proclaimed in both word and deed the Lordship of Jesus, of which they now took part as they incarnated the future in the present.[182] This is "the domain of enacted hope."[183] Hence, this apocalyptic eschatology is highly participatory—it requires active exertion, struggles, straining, groanings, and combat.[184]

All of this is inescapably political.[185] And it is political in a way that is extraordinarily unsettling for those who crucify, conquer, and either enslave the vanquished or leave them for dead. It is political in a way that dissents.[186] In Moltmann's words, it "bores like a thorn in the flesh of every present [and all those who benefit from the trajectories established within the present] and opens it for the future."[187] This form of anticipation, marked by resurrection (already) and Spirit (now), gives birth to resistance

179. See Aune, *Cultic Setting*, 12–13; Vos, *Pauline Eschatology*, 71; Elias, *Remember the Future*, 515; Gorman, *Apostle of the Crucified Lord*, 61–63.

180. Beker, *Paul the Apostle*, 155. Blanton echoes this more militant language: "For the Paulinist there remains only a lived surging of a transformative insurgency into the *paradeigmata* of a cultural setup" (*Materialism for the Masses*, 88).

181. Meeks, *First Urban Christians*, 174.

182. See Cullmann, *Christ and Time*, 73, 76; Elias, *Remember the Future*, 515.

183. See Moltmann, *Theology of Hope*, 288–91.

184. See Rehman, "To Turn the Groaning into Labor," 82; Badiou, *St. Paul*, 2; Schnackenburg, *Moral Teaching*, 195; Beker, *Paul the Apostle*, 326; *Paul's Apocalyptic Gospel*, 110; Roetzel, *Paul*, 28–30.

185. See Hansen, "Messianic or Apocalyptic?," 199, 208, 220–22; Schoeps, *Paul*, 97; Elliott, "Strategies of Resistance," 117–19.

186. See Zimmerman, "Hermeneutics of Unbelief," 248, 252.

187. Moltmann, *Theology of Hope*, 88.

to all that tries to trap the Jesus loyalists within the dynamics of the Old Age. Those marked by hope and filled with a new sense of agency are not content to let events simply unfold as they will—"they do not wait, they reach out for redemption [i.e., *apolytrosis*—emancipation, liberation from slavery]."[188] The result of this is the formulation of a seditious eschatology that mocks and counters the imperial ideology of the Augustan and Neronian Golden Ages(s).

Pauline talk of conflict with anti-God, enslaving Powers is a primary example of this. Once again, this is thoroughly apocalyptic language.[189] Sin and Flesh (Rom 7:14–8:2), Powers and Principalities (Rom 8:38), Elemental Spirits (Gal 4:3), Satan (2 Cor 2:11), along with Death itself (Rom 5:14; 8:2, 38; 1 Cor 15:26) appear as "supra-human cosmic actors" engaged in combat with God, the Anointed, and the Spirit of Life.[190] All of creation suffers because of this war (Rom 8:22). However, in true apocalyptic fashion, these Powers do not simply exist in the spiritual or heavenly realm, they are intimately connected to individuals and corporate bodies in the present. Hence, the anti-God powers are linked to "the rulers of this age, who are doomed to perish" (1 Cor 2:6), who exhibit "the wisdom of this age" (1 Cor 2:6), and who "crucified the Lord of glory" (2 Cor 2:8).[191] Indeed, it is likely that Nero is whom the Pauline faction has in mind when, in 2 Cor 4:4, they say that "the god of this age has blinded the thoughts of the disloyal ones [i.e., those with alternative allegiances], so that the light of the good news [*euanggeliou*] of the glory of the Anointed—who is the image [*eikon*] of God—may not shine forth" (my translation). Nero, like his predecessors, claimed to be the image of God (like Augustus, his appearance was likened to that of Apollo), and through the imperial ideo-theology of Rome, he actively propagated a gospel that made any belief in a crucified God appear as a depraved form of folly.[192] It is with this embodied system of belief

188. See Rehman, "To Turn the Groaning into Labor," 75–76.

189. See Harink, *Paul Among the Postliberals*, 68–69.

190. See Martyn, "Gospel Invades Philosophy," 7. Roman religion, as it engaged with other belief systems, including apocalyptic traditions, also placed astrological powers in a position of prominence. See Kee, *Beginnings of Christianity*, 470–71.

191. Howard-Brook and Gwyther, *Unveiling Empire*, 83; Ramsaran, "Resisting Imperial Domination," 94; Meeks, *Origins of Christian Morality*, 117. The Romans, too, had linked astrological powers to the Caesars. See Kee, *Beginnings of Christianity*, 471. Wright is correct to argue, then, that apocalyptic is not about the "end of the world" but rather about the end of the present world order (*New Testament and the People of God*, 298–99).

192. Larry Welborn captures this well when he argues that the Pauline proclamation

that the Pauline faction has their main conflict.[193] And it is precisely the claim that the Anointed—and him crucified—apocalypses the overthrow of these Powers and the agents and institutions that are in their service (just as all of them are ultimately in the service of Death [1 Cor 15:26]) that lies at the heart of the gospel Paul and his coworkers assemble among the nations.[194] The assemblies of Jesus loyalists thus find their existence in "the front trenches of [an] apocalyptic war."[195] But they do so fully aware that a "dramatic reversal of imperial logic" has taken place.[196] The rulers, however, are blind to this (perhaps because they are full of the wisdom of the Old Age but, perhaps more importantly, because the status quo of the Old Age is hugely profitable to them) and so their destruction is assured.[197] The in-breaking of the coming universal rule of the Anointed, which rightly orders the cosmos, of which the empire is only one small part, thus counters Roman claims to cosmic and universal rule.[198]

Furthermore, Paul and his coworkers then go on to directly counter other key themes of the realized Roman eschatology. Over against the proclamation of a golden age, they proclaim the need to be emancipated from "the present evil age" (Gal 1:4).[199] Here, the Pauline faction unveil a reality

---

of a *crucified* Anointed as a manifestation of divine power and wisdom is "the most ridiculous statement imaginable. . . . Paul employs oxymora that sound positively blasphemous" (*Paul, the Fool of Christ*, 180).

193. See Gorman, *Apostle of the Crucified Lord*, 164; Moltmann, *Experiences in Theology*, 131. N. T. Wright argues that the main conflict within Pauline eschatology was with paganism, but this statement is far too vague (*Paul*, 151). The primary "paganism" Paul and his coworkers confronted was the imperial ideology disseminated throughout the provinces from Rome, commonly referred to as the imperial cult. I will further criticize Wright's focus on paganism in volume 3 of this series.

194. On the cross as the key battle waged in an apocalyptic war between God and the powers united in the service of Death, see especially Martyn, *Theological Issues*, 282–86. Also, Yeo, *Chairman Mao*, 18. Balthasar picks up on this and argues that this struggle is "the ultimate truth of history" (*Theology of History*, 149; cf. 145–49).

195. Martyn, *Theological Issues*, 297.

196. See Elliott, *Arrogance of Nations*, 119.

197. Welborn, *Paul, the Fool of Christ*, 160–66.

198. See Hansen, "Messianic or Apocalyptic?," 209–10; Beker, *Paul's Apocalyptic Gospel*, 34–37; Moltmann, *Experiences in Theology*, 175.

199. See Kahl, *Galatians Re-Imagined*, 163–64; Carter, *Roman Empire*, 88. Crossan and Reed, along with Pate, argue that the Pauline faction declares that a new golden age has begun in the Anointed (Crossan and Reed, *In Search of Paul*, 128; Crossan, *God and Empire*, 78–82; Pate, *End of the Age Has Come*, 100). This seems an overstatement. A new age has begun, certainly, but it is not yet defined by goldenness—the vision of which we

that would be well known to inhabitants of the empire (although few would be willing to speak boldly about this): the Golden Age was only golden for a very few. For everyone else, it was defined by slavery, displacement, hard work, and premature death—all too often, death on a cross. In such an age, far from discovering a world full of virtue, justice, or piety, vices, like those listed multiple times in the Pauline letters, are all too common (and most visible in the lives of the elites).[200] An overflowing natural abundance does not result from this, although this may appear to be the case for those who have grown rich from plundering the vanquished and colonized provinces. Instead, the very earth groans and cries out like a woman in labor.[201] As Robert Jewett says, "Not jubilant deliverance but agonized groanings define nature after Augustus."[202] This is a groaning that would be familiar to the dispossessed, colonized, and oppressed members of the assemblies of Jesus loyalists. It would be part of "the daily reality of life in the Roman Empire."[203] An age like this can only be overthrown by an apocalyptic rupture—this "present age is so fully enthralled by the hostile powers that something more than its fulfillment, renewal, or renovation is required."[204]

Another place where Paul and his coworkers push back against the imperial vision of the empire is by rejecting the end of history proclaimed in the realized eschatology of Rome.[205] The ultimate doom of the rulers, powers, and authorities (Rom 11:25; 13:11–12), the completion of the *anastasis* of the dead (1 Cor 15:1–58), and the *parousia* of the Anointed (1 Thess 2:19; 3:13; 4:15; 5:23; 1 Cor 15:23) are still to come. Over against the passivity that is mandated by the closure of history, this understanding of the future results in a renewal of one's current struggle against all that operates in the service of Death.[206] As the Pauline faction argues, precisely because the night is so advanced and the day has drawn near, Jesus loyalists should "put away the works of darkness, and put on the weapons of

---

owe more to John's apocalypse than to Paulinism.

200. See Welborn, *Paul's Summons to Messianic Life*, 23–26; Jennings, *Outlaw Justice*, 37–39.

201. See Jewett, "Corruption and Redemption of Creation," 25–46.

202. Jewett, "Corruption and Redemption of Creation," 41.

203. Rehman, "To Turn the Groaning into Labor," 78; see also 77–80.

204. Furnish, *Theology and Ethics in Paul*, 130.

205. See Gorman, *Cruciformity*, 346; Pate 20–21; Wengst, *Pax Romana*, 84–86; Elliott, "Ideological Closure," 153.

206. See Elliott, *Arrogance of Nations*, 150–52; Moltmann, *Experiences in Theology*, 241.

light" (Rom 13:12 [my translation]). The militancy of this language is deliberate and confrontational. It is repeated in 2 Cor 6:7, when Paul and his co-authors urge the Corinthians to fight as the day of salvation is at hand, although, as they make clear in 2 Cor 10:3–4, the war they are fighting is an apocalyptic war. It is a call to arms against the closure of history within the eternal now of empire.[207]

Lastly, although this will be explored in considerably more detail in the next chapter and volume 3, it is worth briefly noting that human-divine primary actors are at work in both the imperial eschatology and Pauline apocalyptic eschatology. As Georgi notes, "The divinization of the Caesar is countered by the humanization of the Pauline (biblical) God."[208] This results in a polemical comparison of Caesar and Jesus that produces an embodied proclamation that is, as we will see, foolish, blasphemous, and seditious.

However, despite the intentions of the Pauline faction, two sobering remarks must be made. First, empires have always worked to "assimilate and transform ideas that oppose [them]," as they retool and reinvent themselves "in the face of resistance and counterclaims."[209] We have already seen Rome do this with elements of Judean messianism and parts of the apocalyptic tradition, especially the Sybilline Oracles. The same thing happened very quickly with the apocalyptic Pauline tradition. Part of what makes this possible, and this is the second remark, is that imitating imperial motifs— like the imposition of a divinely-inspired universal rule which claims to be more just than its predecessors—paves the way for the reintegration of adherents of this ideology into the trajectories of the status quo. Talk about the *parousia* of the Anointed in 1 Thess is a particularly obvious example of imitation intended to be subversive that can later be redeployed in a manner that affirms an oppressive status quo. Clearly, Paul and his co-authors are echoing the imperial discourse that speaks of the emperor coming or returning to a city as a savior who brings peace.[210] The prominent leaders in the city would go out to meet the emperor and then return to the city in triumph with him (which was great for the elite, but, as Garnsey and Saller note, the more general population would be prone to suffering a food shortage as a result of the redirection of food to the emperor, his court,

---

207. Again, I will have more to say on this point in volume 3.

208. Georgi, *Theocracy*, 30.

209. See Portier-Young, *Apocalypse Against Empire*, 22–23.

210. See Elias, *Remember the Future*, 261–62; Maier, *Picturing Paul in Empire*, 52–54.

and his army during imperial visitations).[211] In 1 Thess, Paul and his co-authors are presenting Jesus as the true Lord who comes triumphantly to bring peace. The members of the assemblies of Jesus loyalists are the key citizens who go out to greet him, and those who are outside of the assembly are, perhaps, those doomed to suffer hunger and want.[212] However, were the powerful ever to co-opt the early Jesus movement (and it did not take long for them to do so—the rapid growth of the movement made such an occurrence almost inevitable), such a proclamation could easily be used to support the militarism of the Christian form of imperialism that has dominated so much of the history of the Occident. Thus, as Warren Carter says, "While Rome's imperialism must be exposed, so too must Paul's."[213] I will return to this point a few times, but for now, it is worth recalling Wayne Meek's observation: "Not only can we not replicate the golden age of Christian beginnings, there was not a golden age to replicate."[214] There has ever only been struggle in the overlap of the ages.

Conclusion: Hope and Longing

Augustus, like the Caesars who came after him and the rulers who served him in "this present evil age," was a man with a past. His family's history, harkening back to the heroic founders of Rome and the gods themselves, was well-known and highly praised. He claimed the noblest lineage, being both highborn and well-born. To the Romans, this mattered a great deal, for, in Rome, a person without this kind of history was nothing. Thus, the Caesars were both the lords of history and the culmination of history. But as the culmination of history, the Caesars possessed no future beyond their efforts to transform the present into an eternal now. In light of this, deification was sometimes small comfort (as Vespasian remarked in 79 CE, when he became fatally ill: "Woe is me, I believe I am becoming a god").[215] The emperors were well historied, they possessed the present, but they had no future. Consequently, as the discourse of an eternal Golden Age spread

211. Garnsey and Saller, *Roman Empire*, 94. Thus, the argument that inscriptions that praise benefactors for rescuing a city from a famine and inscriptions that praise those who provide for an imperial visitor are related.

212. Gorman touches on this much more generally in *Cruciformity*, 334.

213. Carter, "Paul and the Roman Empire," 24.

214. Meeks, *Origins of Christian Morality*, 215.

215. See Suetonius, *Twelve Caesars*, 772.

throughout the empire (and rapidly got old in certain circles), the Cynics also became a prominent presence within the Roman elite. Cynicism, as an expression of hopelessness that the wealthy and wellborn can afford to possess, then trickles down from the aristocrats (although material goods never do and the gap between the rich and poor continually increases).

But for those who have nothing—whose very bodies often do not belong to them—cynicism is unaffordable and so hope surges upwards.[216] According to the Pauline faction, the future does not belong to the rulers of this age and their allies—it belongs to the dead (who have died in solidarity with the crucified) and to those who have been left for dead but who remain and who rupture the present in the power of the Spirit of Life. These are the stillbirths Paul mentions in 1 Cor 1:28. Literally, they are the "unborn," people with no lineage, no history, and no rank, who do not even count as being born and who are thus utterly disposable. Yet it is precisely these people whom Paul and his coworkers declare have been designated by God to shame the strong and utterly annihilate the things that are as divine justice re-forms the earth.

Hope frequently flourishes in precisely the people and places designated by others, especially outsiders and overlords, as hopeless. As Latin American migrant workers in American-occupied territories have often said, "*La esperenza muere última* [hope dies last]."[217] Paul and his coworkers said much the same. Thus, for example, Paul and his coworkers write in Romans: "We boast in our hope . . . and hope does not disappoint us" (5:2–5); "in hope we have been saved" (8:24); "rejoice in hope" (12:12); "may the God of hope fill you with all joy and peace in believing that you may abound in hope by the power of the holy Spirit" (15:13). It is this hope that inspires the unborn to act with such boldness against all that the well-born hold dear and against everything the highborn try to use to destroy them (see 2 Cor 3:12; 1:7–13; 1 Cor 15:32; Phil 1:20; 1 Thess 1:3; 5:8). This is a hope that inspires justice (Gal 5:5) and which sits alongside loyalty and love as the three abiding virtues mentioned in 1 Cor 13:13. Such hope arises out of suffering but refuses to resign itself to that suffering—it actively works to change things.[218] It does this, in part, because it believes critical changes

216. As Moltmann says, "It will certainly not be the ennui of the children of the rich which leads to the resurgence of history. It will be the real misery of the hungry masses and the no less real misery of the ruined system of the earth" (*Coming of God*, 225).

217. Terkel, *Hope Dies Last*, xv.

218. See Moltmann, *Theology of Hope*, 21; *Broad Place*, 101–3; "What Has Happened," 116; *Coming of God*, 234–35; Horsley, *Liberation of Christmas*, 151–52; Davies,

have taken place. A crucified nobody was raised to new life by God, and the Spirit of *anastasis* Life has now been poured out on all those living in the shadows of their own crosses.

Such uprisings of Life are happening everywhere, as hope is rooted in communities that are oriented around alternative practices and alternative ways of being. These communities are involved in life-and-death struggles with the pluriform institutions of the death-dealing status quo of the imperial golden age. It is the hope felt by those who rose up in Saint-Domingue in 1791, of those who held the barricades of the Paris commune in 1871, of those who marched on Washington in 1963, of those who withstood the Canadian army at Kanehsatake in 1990, those who occupied Tahrir Square and refused to leave in 2011, and those who stood up against corporate security and militarized police at Standing Rock in 2016. Time after time, it is the same—the harder Death presses down, the more vigorously Life rises up.

No wonder, then, that some who write of Paul speak of the intensity, vividness, and immediacy of his hope.[219] The intensity of this longing has led some to conclude that Paul acted on a belief that the end of the struggle, the *parousia* of the crucified and now risen Jesus, would take place in or around his lifetime. However, there is no need to extrapolate certainty from longing or assurance from desire. Those fighting for their lives—and for the lives of others whom they love—want every next battle to be the last. But this does not mean that all their planning, ethics, and actions are rooted in the conviction that the next battle actually will be the last. Like many among the dead who foolishly refuse to die and the unborn who foolishly rise up to new life, Paul and his coworkers were wiser than that.

Jewish and Pauline Studies, 219; Deissmann, *Paul*, 216–20; Käsemann, *New Testament Questions of Today*, 110; Hart, "Imagination for the Kingdom," 62–63; Brunner, *Eternal Hope*, 8–9; Wright, *Surprised by Hope*, 191; Kee, *Renewal of Hope*, ix, 30–40, 46–47, 109–14; Gorman, *Cruciformity*, 342–45.

219. See Beker, *Paul the Apostle*, 146–48; Barclay, *Mind of Saint Paul*, 218–19.

3

THE IDEO-THEOLOGY OF ROME: JUSTIFYING EMPIRE

> Roman, remember by your strength to rule
> Earth's peoples—for your arts are these:
> To pacify, to impose the rule of law,
> To spare the conquered, battle down the proud.
>
> —Virgil, *Aeneid* 1.151–54

> No doubt, there was peace after all this, but it was a peace
> stained with blood.
>
> —Tacitus, *Annals* 1.10

Introduction: Situating Empire in the Foreground

HAVING PROVIDED AN OVERVIEW of matters related to wealth and status distributions within the eastern portion of the Roman Empire in the first century CE, and having examined the eschatological visions of Paulinism and of Rome, it is time to more fully examine the ideo-theology of Rome— the combination of beliefs and practices that provided the moral, spiritual, political, and economic foundations for the widespread implementation of imperial power. Exploring the "big picture" in this way is invaluable to reading the Pauline letters today.[1] A fuller understanding of the influence of imperial Roman ideo-theology will provide us with information that is critical for establishing both what the Pauline faction was saying and what precisely they were doing in their role as the Anointed's ambassadors to the nations.

As will be shown, the ideo-theology of the Roman Empire was a pervasive and all-invading reality in Paul's time. Consequently, Warren Carter is absolutely correct to assert that we must situate the empire in the "foreground" of Pauline studies, instead of treating it as "background" material, viewed as an interesting but largely inconsequential niche market for scholars competing to make a distinctive mark in a flooded labor market. As Carter writes: "Rome's empire does not disappear or go away when it is not explicitly mentioned. It is always there. . . . [It is] the ever-present political, economic, societal, and religious framework and context for the New Testament."[2]

Therefore, in this chapter, I will begin by examining what I understand to be the four cornerstones of Rome's imperial ideology. These are: (1) the household unit; (2) cultural conceptions of honor and shame; (3) the practice of patronage; and (4) traditional Roman religiosity.[3] This will then prepare the way for a detailed examination of Rome's ideo-theology, especially as it was expressed in the imperial cult(s) that spread rapidly in the eastern half of the empire during the Julio-Claudian period. All four of the cornerstones were in place prior to the establishment of the imperial cult(s), and each of them was fundamental to the development of the

1. At the risk of sounding redundant, it is worth remembering that "Paul's letters neither begin with what we know about the world nor make any attempt to explain their ancient world settings in terms we might understand from our own contemporary experience" (Malina and Pilch, *Social-Science Commentary*, 3; see also 1–9). This is a prominent theme in Malina's other writings. See, for example, Malina, "Social Levels, Morals and Daily Life"; *New Testament World*.

2. Carter, *Roman Empire*, ix, 1. See also Carter, *John and Empire*, x, 11; "Vulnerable Power," 453; Gorman, *Apostle of the Crucified Lord*, 8.

3. Others have laid out what they perceive to be the building blocks of the empire more generally. For example, Malina points to the four social institutions of kinship, politics, economics, and religion (Malina, "Social Levels, Morals and Daily Life," 82–83, 370–71). Walsh and Keesmaat also point to four elements: centralization, socioeconomic and military control, legitimating myths, and attempts to control the public imagination through the proliferation of imperial images (Walsh and Keesmaat, *Colossians Remixed*, 58). In light of these efforts, I should emphasize that I am looking at the building blocks, not of the empire itself but the imperial ideo-theology.

imperial cult—even as they were, in turn, impacted and transformed to varying degrees by that cult.

The Cornerstones of Roman Ideo-Theology:
The Household, Honor, Patronage, Religion

The Household Unit

No timid dove, do warlike eagles breed.

—Horace, *Odes* 4.4.31–32[4]

The household operated as the basic foundation of social life around the Mediterranean in the first century CE and was one of the most significant units of Roman society.[5] The Roman household unit was composed of a *familia* that contained not only blood-relations or kin but also slaves and, especially among those with higher status, clients and freedpeople who would be present daily, even though they did not reside in the home of the patron.[6] In many ways, the household provided a microcosm of society, and the empire often extended Roman household relationships, power dynamics, and values into the realm of international politics.[7] Two especially important social elements are present here: kinship and slavery (patronage and religiosity are also related to the household but will be explored independently below). Both kinship and slavery contained important power dynamics that were critical to maintaining and spreading Roman imperialism.

---

4. Text slightly modified. These lines are from a larger section devoted to praising Augustus as the model of a father and a person devoted to his family. See Horace, *Odes* 4.4.21–32.

5. See, for example, Judge, *Social Distinctives*, 24, 118; Lassen, "Roman Family," 104; Gorman, *Apostle of the Crucified Lord*, 12–13; Horsley, *Covenant Economics*, 89.

6. See deSilva, *Honor, Patronage, Kinship, and Purity*, 173–74; Osiek, "Family Matters," 201–20.

7. The ways in which Roman family values and imperial conquest are entangled have interesting parallels to the ways in which the spread of capitalism has often gone hand-in-hand with the imposition of heteronormative patriarchy onto colonized populations.

Kinship

Kinship was the most basic marker of status within Roman society and a primary reference point for both personal and public perceptions of one's identity.[8] Status in relation to kinship was based upon one's family of origin and one's place within the family unit. The family was also the basic unit for the transmission of wealth and status.[9] In this context, genealogies, familial honor, and the pressure to live up to the reputation that one has inherited are all important.[10] This "focus on the family" created a strong pressure to adhere to a moral conservatism. Pressures to adhere to traditional family roles and to not act in an innovative manner (which would shame loved ones) were very strong. Romans prided themselves upon their family values, which were part of a strong moral tradition passed down from one generation to the next. Examples of this are easy to find in Roman literature, and I mention three here. First, in his *Georgics*, Virgil claims that "Justice left earth" during the time of the Roman civil wars precisely because the Romans had ceased to follow through on their family values, which were intimately connected to religious piety. Thus, when describing the sort of life that is experienced in a world where Justice has returned to earth, Virgil pairs "Reverence for God" with "respect for family."[11] Second, in *The Aeneid*, Virgil states that those who are tormented in the afterlife include those who hated their brothers, who beat their parents, who put no resources aside for relatives, and who committed adultery.[12] Finally, in his account of *The Twelve Caesars*, Suetonius gives extensive reports upon the ways in which each emperor treated his family members. The "good" emperors tend to properly care for their families, while the "bad" emperors

---

8. See deSilva, *Honor, Patronage, Kinship, and Purity*, 158. Also Malina, "Social Levels, Morals and Daily Life," 375. Malina goes so far as to say that kinship was *the* focal institution of Mediterranean societies, giving it precedence over all other political, economic, or religious institutions. The problem with this assertion is that scholars can be found who argue that each one of the four cornerstones I'm exploring here (the household, honor, patronage, and traditional religion) is *the* most crucial element of Graeco-Roman society. I find it difficult, in light of the evidence, to prioritize one of these elements over the others.

9. Garnsey and Saller, *Roman Empire*, 126.

10. See deSilva, *Honor, Patronage, Kinship, and Purity*, 159–63.

11. See Virgil, *Georgics* 2.467–68, 472–74.

12. See Virgil, *Aeneid* 6.814–18.

demonstrate their lack of worth by the atrocities they commit against their kin.[13]

Due to familial pressures, children were expected to adhere to the religion and values of their parents, and a refusal to do this could result in a child being disowned, bringing great shame to that child and leading to him or her experiencing social ostracism.[14] As David deSilva explains, "kin" are those who are "kind" in the sense of "being of the same sort as oneself, being like oneself."[15] In this way, kinship establishes a regulatory pattern of social norms.[16] From birth, each person is assigned a role and is expected to conform to it. Children are forever under the full authority of their parents and are forever indebted to them for the gift of life.[17] Parents, on the other hand, are responsible for educating their children with the goal of "the development of an inner pedagogue, an internalized commitment to virtue," which of course means that children were taught to internalize the ways and values of the status quo, and their place within it.[18]

Marriage and child-rearing was also part of one's duty to society, and Augustus passed legislation encouraging people to marry, remain married, and have multiple children.[19] Maintaining a sense of civic or patriotic duty around marriage was useful within the context of arranged marriages, wherein unions were created based upon politics, status, economics, and strategic alliances.[20] It was also critical for the maintenance of the aristocratic class, although the aristocracy strongly resisted the Augustan marriage reforms, which were, ultimately, abandoned.[21] Adoption became a prominent way of addressing the problems of childless marriages (or of marriages that produced less than ideal children). Through adoption, a meritocratic ideology was able to merge with a dynastic ideology and men without heirs, including bachelors, were able to adopt.[22] Adopted children

13. Suetonius, *Twelve Caesars*.

14. See deSilva, *Honor, Patronage, Kinship, and Purity*, 194.

15. deSilva, *Honor, Patronage, Kinship, and Purity*, 164; see also 164–66.

16. See Malina, "Social Levels, Morals and Daily Life," 134–35.

17. deSilva, *Honor, Patronage, Kinship, and Purity*, 185–86.

18. The quotation is from deSilva, *Honor, Patronage, Kinship, and Purity*, 190; see also 188–90.

19. See Yarbrough, *Not Like the Gentiles*, 41–46; Garnsey and Saller, *Roman Empire*, 126.

20. See deSilva, *Honor, Patronage, Kinship, and Purity*, 177–78.

21. Garnsey and Saller, *Roman Empire*, 143–45.

22. See Peppard, *Son of God*, 50–53.

were in no way considered inferior to biological children.[23] Thus, for example, through adoption (first his own and then, ultimately, through the adoption of Tiberius), Augustus was able to ascend to power and handpick an heir to pass on the charismatic nature of his office.[24] In the process, names were changed (Octavian took on the name of Caesar), the adopted person stopped acting as a *paterfamilias* in his own home (as Tiberius did when adopted by Augustus), and all the tools of imperial propaganda, from coins to public proclamations, declared and celebrated the transformation.[25] Thus, far from being merely a technical or symbolic act, adoption was said to be something that reconstituted the very core of a person's identity.[26]

Focusing on fathers and sons is not misplaced here. Roman society was patriarchal and woman were generally viewed as the possessions of men (whether their husbands or their fathers), subsequently valued for being submissive, modest, and chaste, sharing the religion and values of the man, and existing primarily within private spaces.[27] This subordination was justified because women were said to be "weak," inferior "by nature," and akin to "wild beasts," unable to control their emotions and passions.[28] In this way, relationships between Roman men and women (and Roman men and slaves, as we will see in a moment) came to represent the ways in which Romans viewed their conquests over the nations. In the sexualized imperial images of conquest, victorious Romans were portrayed as powerful males, and conquered nations were portrayed as submissive women about to be pierced or penetrated by some phallic object.[29] Indeed, the very foundation

23. Peppard, *Son of God*, 54; see also 61.

24. See Ando, *Imperial Ideology*, 34; Peppard, *Son of God*, 63

25. See Peppard, *Son of God*, 69, 75, 77.

26. One finds adoption fulfilling this function in some Indigenous nations on Turtle Island wherein adoption is that which can transform an otherwise non-Indigenous person into a truly and properly Indigenous person (a practice that is relevant, in part, because it rejects settler colonial notions of indigeneity being rooted in blood quantum and percentages related to blood purity—notions developed and deployed in order to ultimately make Indigenous peoples qua Indigenous peoples disappear altogether from Turtle Island, thereby eliminating any challenge to settler colonial sovereignty over stolen territories).

27. See deSilva, *Honor, Patronage, Kinship, and Purity*, 183–85; Crossan and Reed, *In Search of Paul*, 257–58.

28. See, for example, Tacitus, *Annals* 3.33–34; Seneca, *De clementia* 1.5; Plutarch, *Brutus* 13.

29. See Crossan and Reed, *In Search of Paul*, 257–58, 261, 264, 268; Lopez, *Apostle to the Conquered*, 26–117. A good example of this is a dream that Julius Caesar is reported

of *Romanitas* is rooted in the rape of the Sabine women.[30] The valorization of rape is a thoroughly Roman project.

This is not to suggest that Roman women did not enjoy some comparative advantages over other women. Augustus created an entirely new realm of possibility for women when he granted his wife and sister what were previously exclusively male political and religious rights, and women close to the emperors continued to gain power as the principate advanced, especially during the reigns of Claudius and Nero.[31] Further, Roman women could be named as equal heirs in wills and at least had the possibility of escaping from the authority of their father (albeit only by transferring to the authority of their husband).[32] However, some women were able to retain personal property by remaining under their fathers' authority, even while married, thereby becoming independent property owners upon the death of their fathers.[33] Wives were also able to divorce their husbands.[34] This is a notable level of independence granted to women in the Mediterranean world of the first century CE, but it was often limited or annulled by common conceptions about male power and other factors like old men marrying very young wives in order to create dependency, exploit vulnerability, and maintain a substantial imbalance of power between husbands and wives.[35]

The most important person in the household, and the most exploited point of contact between the household and Roman imperialism, was the

---

to have had before crossing the Rubicon. Caesar dreamed he raped his own mother and was told that this meant he would conquer/rape the whole earth—the universal mother (see Plutarch, *Julius Caesar* 32).

30. See Livy, *Ab urbe condita* 1.9.

31. Saller, *Personal Patronage*, 64–65.

32. See Garnsey and Saller, *Roman Empire*, 130. Although the observation that Nero murdered both his own mother and his pregnant wife puts this claim in better context.

33. Garnsey and Saller, *Roman Empire*, 130. As Garnsey and Saller also note, the principate further strengthened the possibility of the financial independence of women by banning the use of wives as sureties for the husband and by prohibiting gifts between husbands and wives—leaving some men with no legal authority over their wives . . . but also no obligation to care for them.

34. Garnsey and Saller, *Roman Empire*, 135.

35. Garnsey and Saller, *Roman Empire*, 131, 134. It is also a far cry from the level of equality and authority women were experiencing in the northern parts of Turtle Island at this time—something worth noting given that the Romans are sometimes held up as being the best of all the essentially terrible options available to women at this time in history.

father of the family—the *paterfamilias*. The father was the ruler of the household and, in a uniquely Roman manner, held an unassailable moral, legal, economic, disciplinary, and sexual dominion over all the extended members of the *familia*.[36] Roman fathers had the sole right to own property within the family unit and retained power over their children up until death.[37] Rather than understanding this as a form of despotic power, the father's role was seen as a grave duty, a moral responsibility that he was granted because of his (superior) piety.[38] Given the utility of this to powerful men, it is not surprising that socio-economic and political authorities in Rome adopted the language of fatherhood in order to justify their power. Senators in Rome are regularly referred to as "conscript fathers" and governors of the provinces also frequently understood themselves in paternalistic terms.[39] This notion of fatherhood then becomes the image that the emperors embrace and propagate when speaking of their role in relation to the Roman Republic.[40] Given that Roman tradition favored models of rule that at least had some kind of democratic semblance, and given that Rome had sworn never to be ruled by another king (after the people rose and killed the last of the Roman kings c. 510 BCE), the emperors were cautious about explicitly claiming total power over the Republic. Indeed, Augustus witnessed his predecessor and adoptive father, Julius Caesar, overreach in this regard, and he was not interested in sharing Caesar's fate. Therefore, after Julius Caesar, the emperors employed the imagery and language of the household in order to subvert republicanism and impose imperialism.[41] This is why, in the firsthand account of his life that Augustus had published after his death, the title of *Pater Patriae*—"Father of the Fatherland"—is the

36. See Lassen, "Roman Family," 104–6; Sherwin-White, *Roman Citizenship*, 158–59; deSilva, *Honor, Patronage, Kinship, and Purity*, 180–81; Garnsey and Saller, *Roman Empire*, 136.

37. See Garnsey and Saller, *Roman Empire*, 137.

38. See Barclay, "Family as the Bearer of Religion," 67–68; de Silva, *Honor, Patronage, Kinship, and Purity*, 179; Sherwin-White, *Roman Citizenship*, 158–59.

39. On governors, see Garnsey and Saller, *Roman Empire*, 31. For examples of senators being referred to as "conscript fathers," see Cicero, *In Catalinam* 4.1, 4, 9, 11, 14 (twice), 16, 18 (and throughout); *Orationes philippicae* 2.1, 5, 37, 59, 69, 76, 84, 92, 101, 108.

40. See Lassen, "Roman Family," 110–14; Walsh and Keesmaat, *Colossians Remixed*, 58–59.

41. See Judge, *Social Distinctives*, 17–24; Eder, "Augustus and the Power," 31. Eder argues that while Augustus is the father, the emphasis falls upon the corporate identity of the family.

final, climactic, and highest title that Augustus mentions receiving from the people of Rome in 2 BCE.[42] Upon receiving this honor, Augustus is said to have exclaimed: "Fathers of the Senate, I have at last achieved my highest ambition."[43] Here, Clifford Ando is astute to note that the traditional usage of *Pater Patriae*—a title granted for specific achievements like saving a city or saving the lives of many citizens—was transformed from a title to a role and a way of ruling.[44] Thus, while Augustus worked hard to transform and attain this title, several later Caesars claim it as a matter of course. For this reason, any attack upon the emperor was treated as a parricide.[45] By this means, the emperor was able to avoid being labeled a tyrant and, instead, was presented as a pious and concerned father caring for his children— whose best interests he always has in mind, even when disciplining (or crucifying) them.[46] This understanding of the *Pater Patriae* as the loving disciplinarian was central to the construction of this imperial identity. For example, during the reign of Nero, Seneca writes:

> What, then, constitutes his [Nero's] duty? It is that of good parents, who are accustomed to scold their children, sometimes gently, sometimes with threats, and at times to enforce correction even with a beating. Surely no father in his right mind disinherits his son for a first offence! . . . No one reaches the point of punishing without using up all means of a cure. This is the action to be expected not just of a father but also of an emperor, whom no mere empty flattery has prompted us to call "Father of his Country" . . . by bestowing the title "Father of his Country" we wish him to know that he has been given the power of a father, which shows the greatest toleration in looking to the welfare of his children and places his own interests behind theirs.[47]

---

42. "In my thirteenth consulship the senate, the equestrian order, and the whole people of Rome gave me the title of Father of my Country" (Augustus, *Res Gestae* 35.1). Of course, provincials, keen to cash in on possible advancement by heaping praise on Augustus, are quick to not only call him father of the fatherland but, in part because they cannot claim to be members of that fatherland, acclaim Augustus as father of the entire human race (Ando, *Imperial Ideology*, 403).

43. Suetonius, *Twelve Caesars*, 84.

44. Ando, *Imperial Ideology*, 399–400. See also Peppard, *Son of God*, 61.

45. Seneca, *De clementia* 1.9.

46. See Carter, *Roman Empire*, 32–33; *John and Empire*, 36–38; Eder, "Augustus and the Power," 28; Lohse, *New Testament Environment*, 199–200; Keresztes, *From Herod the Great*, 5–6.

47. Seneca, *De clementia* 1.14.

The concomitant point made by this understanding of the imposition of imperial violence as a last resort of a loving parent was that any who were on the receiving end of this violence were automatically assumed to be impious ingrates who fully deserved the punishments meted out to them.

Having explored these points of contact between Roman conceptions of kinship and imperialism, it is worth noting one more ambiguous—and potentially subversive—element of kinship relationships within Graeco-Roman society. While vertical, hierarchical relationships existed between men and women, parents and children, and the *paterfamilias* and all others, horizontal relationships of mutuality and solidarity were supposed to exist between siblings and members of comparable status within the extended family.[48] David deSilva argues that these horizontal relationships, especially between siblings, were to be defined by cooperation, trust, loyalty, harmony, concord, unity, mutual protection of honor, forgiveness, gentleness, and forbearance.[49] Importantly, this cooperation and solidarity was not just affirmed ideologically or conceptually but also was to be practiced materially—property, wealth, and goods were to be shared among siblings so that there was enough for everybody. It is worth keeping these things in mind when we come to the Pauline faction's understanding of the assemblies of Jesus loyalists and their preference for referring to other members as siblings.[50]

Slavery

The second major social element of the household was the relationship that existed between masters and slaves. Rome's political economy was dependent upon slave labor and slaves were ubiquitous and plentiful (during the first century, some estimate that as many as one out of every five people in Rome was a slave).[51] The primary sources of slavery were war and poverty.

48. See Malina, "Social Levels, Morals and Daily Life," 378.

49. See deSilva, *Honor, Patronage, Kinship, and Purity*, 166–73.

50. It is also worth recalling that sibling relationships among Romans, and especially among those with high power and status, often did not live up to these ideals. Thus, after Nero murdered Britannicus (the son of Claudius) in order to ensure he had no proper rivals, Tacitus observes that the people of Rome were ready to forgive him this act "when they remembered the immemorial feuds of brothers and the impossibility of a divided throne" (*Annals* 13.17).

51. See Horsley, "Introduction," 13; Kautsky, *Foundations of Christianity*, 25–34, 38, 41, 49–50; deSilva, *Honor, Patronage, Kinship, and Purity*, 190.

Foreign nationals were brought, en masse, to Roman-controlled cities after military campaigns. Julius Caesar alone is said to have brought in one million slaves during his Gallic campaigns between 58 and 51 BCE.[52] Then, with the increasing pacification of large amounts of the empire and an increasing focus upon maintaining borders instead of gaining new territories, a great deal of new slave stock came from the rapidly growing population of poor people who congregated within urban centers (many of whom were driven to cities due to the loss of their lands to wealthy landowners given the rise of *latifundia* within the imperial period). Thus, even after the end of the civil wars and the rise of Augustus, there is no evidence suggesting that the number of slaves fell significantly.[53] Even in the city, away from the tens of thousands working in farms and mines, the wealthy could possess an immense number of slaves. For example, Lucius Peanius Secundus, the prefect of Rome during the early years of Nero's reign, is reported to have had four hundred slaves in his townhouse alone.[54]

In terms of its relationship to Roman ideo-theology, slavery served three important purposes. First, it normalized the treatment of foreigners and poor people as objects. Slaves were "living tools" who had no legal standing, who could not marry, and who could only have children (i.e., "breed") with the consent of their masters.[55] They were not permitted to possess weapons.[56] Slaves were considered to be so subhuman that it was standard practice to torture them in the law courts when they testified because it was thought that otherwise they could not be relied upon to speak honestly.[57] Juvenal mocks the notion that slaves should be treated as human beings, and a character in the *Satyricon* of Petronius (Nero's "Arbiter of Excellence") vehemently asserts: "I'm a man and not a slave."[58] In fact, to the Romans, slavery was considered a manner of being dead while still living. One became a slave in a situation where one would otherwise have died,

52. Finley, *Ancient Economy*, 72.

53. Garnsey and Saller, *Roman Empire*, 72.

54. Finley, *Ancient Economy*, 72.

55. See de Silva, *Honor, Patronage, Kinship, and Purity*, 190–93; Osiek, "Family Matters," 210; Garnsey and Saller, *Roman Empire*, 116.

56. Cicero tells a story of a governor of Sicily who is impressed with the size of a dead giant boar. When he asks who killed it, the shepherd who did so comes forward expecting a reward, but when he explains that he killed the boar with a hunting spear, he is immediately crucified (*In Verrem* 2.5.7).

57. Tacitus, *Annals* 2.30.

58. Juvenal, *Satires* 6.220–24; Petronius, *Satyricon* 81.6

and in Roman law, a slave could not owe debts or be in any binding moral relation with another person because the slave was already dead. Therefore, if a Roman soldier was captured and lost his liberty (which Cicero calls "the greatest of all evils, something to be resisted not just with war, but even with death"), his family was expected to read his will and dispose of his possessions.[59] Hence, slavery was a form of violence that transformed people into people-yet-property, who were living-but-dead.[60]

This less-than-fully-human or less-than-fully-alive status that the rich imposed upon slaves also strongly influenced relationships governing those who had been freed from slavery along with their descendants (who were freeborn).[61] Petronius consistently mocks freed people in his writings, and the *Satyricon* itself is a sustained attack upon the vulgar, uneducated, and repulsive pretentiousness of freedpeople. Horace is also full of scorn for most of the members of this class (although he himself was the son of a freedman and was mocked because of this).[62] Thus, although legally freed in some (but not all) ways, freedpeople remained subhuman.[63] As Tacitus observes, they still had "slavish spirits."[64] Consequently, as the numbers, wealth, and influence of some freedpeople increased from Augustus onwards, the senate began to enforce new legal measures in order to ensure that the proper traditional hierarchies and power (im)balances were maintained. Ultimately, during the reign of Nero, and with the sort of finessed rhetorical vaguery so well-deployed by the powerful who are able to manipulate the law to serve their interests, the senators created a law that stated that the freedom of some could be revoked if they proved themselves to be "undeserving" of it.[65]

---

59. Graeber, *Debt*, 168–69. The Cicero quote is from *Orationes philippicae* 2.113.

60. Finley, *Ancient Economy*, 62–63; Graeber, *Debt*, 170–71.

61. Although when slaves were first emancipated, any children they had as slaves continued to be slaves and only children born after emancipation were considered free. See Finley, *Ancient Economy*, 77.

62. See Horace, *Epodes* 4.1–20; *Satires* 1.2.3; 1.6.2. Thus, Horace emphasizes his own virtue over against the crass wealth and status-seeking behavior of others, which grants him the attention of his patron, Maecenas (*Satires* 1.2.3).

63. See Harrill, "Paul and Slavery," 585.

64. Tacitus, *Annals* 2.12. On some of the social tensions created by this conflict, see Garnsey and Saller, *Roman Empire*, 120.

65. See Tacitus, *Annals* 13.26. Garnsey and Saller note that regulations designed to slow (but not block) the emancipation of slaves were already enacted under Augustus (Garnsey and Saller, *Roman Empire*, 200).

Second, because of this perception of the ontological status of slaves, slavery also normalized violence directed against foreigners and poor people. Masters had complete control over their slaves and were permitted to beat, torture, rape, and (at times) even crucify them. Indeed, the sexual penetration of slaves by Roman males was a practice that directly replicated imperial visions of conquest. Roman males were permitted to penetrate male slaves without being considered "effeminate" or immoral (but would be considered womanly and perversely degraded if they permitted themselves to be sexually penetrated by male slaves).[66] This is also why Roman males, under the proper conditions, were permitted to marry female slaves, whereas Roman females were forbidden from doing so. This was considered a "heinous role reversal between superior and inferior."[67] Male slaves—always referred to as "boy"—were also forced to have sex with female owners.[68] Consequently, given the violence, shame, and torture associated with slavery, Lucan asserts that true Romans will easily choose suicide over slavery. Describing one of the battles that occurred during the civil wars, he contrasts defeated Romans—who chose to kill themselves—with other nationalities who permitted themselves to be enslaved; he writes: "Even after the example of these [suicidal Roman] warriors, cowardly / races will not grasp that to escape slavery by one's own hand / is not an arduous act of valour."[69] Regularly experiencing, witnessing, being vulnerable to, and being forced to participate within brutal acts of violence was part of the daily life of the slave. And this was all considered normal and as it should be.

Third, the perception of slaves as both subhuman and as targets of violence leads to the perception of slaves as dangerous—beings or things to be feared. The Roman elite were terrified by even the slightest hint of a slave rebellion. Given their high numbers, steps were taken to ensure that the slaves would not realize how much of the population they composed

66. See Lopez, *Apostle to the Conquered*, 46–48, 50, 104–5, 108–10.

67. Osiek, "Family Matters," 210.

68. Finley, *Ancient Economy*, 82–83. Wealthy Romans who wanted to have beautiful children were also reported to take Judean slaves they found especially sexually attractive and tie those slaves naked to their beds, forcing them to participate in the sexual activity of those Romans with the hope that the beauty of the slaves would be transmitted to the children conceived then. See Frankopan, *Silk Roads*, 18.

69. Lucan, *Civil War* 4.575–77. The point being that in such a situation suicide is a non-arduous (or easy) act of valor. This also tends to be a perspective associated with Stoicism, which was the philosophy favored by Lucan and many Roman soldiers.

in cities like Rome.[70] This fear was also why all the slaves of a household would be killed if even one rebelled and murdered the master.[71] Lucan expresses the elite perspective well: "The poverty of slaves is dangerous not to themselves but to their masters."[72] Note what this says of how the elite imagine the status and well-being of those who are enslaved. Poverty is not a danger to slaves because, from the Roman perspective, everything that Rome brought to the vanquished was a great gift. Slaves and other conquered people should feel gratitude towards Rome (even if the Romans should also never be slaves). And it is ever only the masters who are placed at risk when giving this gift to others (which further demonstrates their nobility of character). However, for those who remained less grateful (further confirmation of their inferiority), the festival of *Saturnalia* was established. This was a day of role-reversals, where masters were treated as slaves and slaves were treated as masters. In this way, anger was given a release, the restless were (momentarily) appeased, obedience was rewarded, and the social order was maintained.[73]

Therefore, in all three of these ways, we see how the household practice of slavery contributed to the ideo-theology required to maintain the empire. This view of foreigners and the urban poor as subhuman, targets of violence, and as objects to be feared justified military campaigns abroad and oppression at home. It also contributed to the notion of an ontological hierarchy within humanity, spanning from the much-less-than-human crucified slave to the surely-more-than-human divine emperor.

70. Seneca observes that during the reign of Nero, some had thought of distinguishing slaves from freedpeople by means of their clothing, but they decided against this because the slaves might start to count their numbers (Seneca, *De clementia* 1.24). See also Tacitus, *Annals* 4.27, when similar fears are expressed during the reign of Tiberius.

71. See Tacitus, *Annals* 13.32; 14.44.

72. *Civil War* 3.152.

73. See Harrill, "Paul and Slavery," 594. Horace writes a piece that records a slave's mocking words to his master during *Saturnalia* (*Satires* 2.7). Others have found interesting parallels between *Saturnalia* and Pauline reflections upon the crucified Anointed (see, for example, Heen, "Role of Symbolic Inversion"). Hence, we see some of the ambiguity that can be found in conciliatory practices of the empire—that which is meant to appease without creating change may still be subverted and contribute to a deeper change, while that which is subversive is simultaneously incorporated into the smooth functioning of the status quo.

Cultural Constructions of Honor and Shame

Death before Dishonor.

—Horace, *Odes* 4.9.50

Given that references to the significance of cultural constructions of honor and shame have arisen in prior remarks about socioeconomic status and kinship, and given its pervasive influence in Graeco-Roman culture, it is necessary to further develop how this foundational construction operated. Within first-century Graeco-Roman culture, honor was a core value related to a person's identity and may be defined as "one's own sense of worth and the corroboration of that understanding by a relevant group."[74] In an honor-based context, one would be constantly aware of how one's actions would be perceived and understood by the group. On the other side of honor, shame had both positive and negative aspects. Positively, it denoted a sensitivity to one's reputation within the opinion of the group, and negatively, it meant acting in a way that contradicted the values of the group.[75] A "fool" would be anyone who attempted but failed to lay claim to a certain degree of honor. Any who acted in a way that violated honor codes—those who did not recognize the rules intended to govern one's actions, for example—would be ostracized (especially if they then went on to valorize or celebrate this way of being).[76] Thus, within Graeco-Roman society, one's conscience (*conscientia*) is that which provided a person with an awareness of one's degree of honor and that which internally counseled a person to continue to live in a manner reflective of that degree of honor.[77] This is all a part of the strong group orientation of first-century Mediterranean culture.[78] Consequently, honor and shame are closely connected to

74. Esler, "Mediterranean Context," 16. See also deSilva, *Honor, Patronage*, 25; Jewett, "Paul, Shame, and Honor," 551–57; Malina, "Social Levels, Morals and Daily Life," 29–31; Malina and Pilch, *Social-Science Commentary*, 368–71; Witherington, *Paul Quest*, 44–50.

75. See deSilva, *Honor, Patronage, Kinship, and Purity*, 25; Malina, "Social Levels, Morals and Daily Life," 49.

76. See Malina, "Social Levels, Morals and Daily Life," 32, 49–50. See, for example, the remarks Horace makes about those who have the audacity to forgive themselves instead of seeking forgiveness from the group. Such people are "foolish and impious . . . and worthy to be stigmatized" (*Satires* 1.3.2).

77. Malina, "Social Levels, Morals and Daily Life," 58.

78. See Esler, "Mediterranean Context," 16–17; deSilva, *Honor, Patronage, Kinship, and Purity*, 35–36; Malina, "Social Levels, Morals and Daily Life," 60–67; Malina and

notions of kinship. Thus, for example, Horace speaks of a fellow who demonstrated his shamelessness by departing from the ways of his family and only further demonstrated his lack of honor by refusing to kill himself after doing so![79] This is also why Horace proclaims "death before dishonor"—a sentiment echoed by others.[80]

Consequently, we can see how notions of honor and shame, much like conceptions of kinship, go hand-in-hand with moral and political conservatism. Values, roles, and one's place in the whole have been pre-assigned, and any violation or rejection of these things would result in the shaming of transgressors in order to bring them back in line. As deSilva asserts: "Honoring and shaming became the dominant means of enforcing all those values that were not actually legislated and of reinforcing those values that were not covered by written laws."[81] Or, as Bruce Malina notes, "Honor causes a society to derive what ought to be done from what in fact is done. . . . The social order as it should be is derived from the social order as it actually is."[82] Significantly, the sort of actions that were considered honorable could vary depending upon one's place in the social pyramid.[83] Consequently, the wealthy, powerful, and well-established had the freedom to engage in honorable actions (like the accumulation of some degree of property and wealth), which would be considered dishonorable for those who were poor, powerless, and uprooted.[84] Thus, this cultural construct ended up acting as a form of "soft" power that produced self-disciplining individuals who do not need to be forcefully coerced by the authorities but more easily chose to accept the way things are.[85] Roman imperialism

---

Neyrey, *Portraits of Paul*; Malina and Pilch, *Social-Science Commentary*, 343–47. Personally, I feel that the cultural distance emphasized here is sometimes overplayed. The search for "respect" and an orientation towards affirmation from a group is a strong element of contemporary culture.

79. Horace, *Odes* 3.27.49–50.

80. Horace, *Odes* 4.9.50. In Tacitus's biography of his father-in-law, Agricola, he quotes Agricola as saying that an honorable death is better than a life of shame (*Agricola* 33). Others who echo this sentiment continue up until the present day, and the saying "death before dishonor" remains common within the military culture of US imperialism.

81. deSilva, *Honor, Patronage, Kinship, and Purity*, 36.

82. Malina, "Social Levels, Morals and Daily Life," 46.

83. See Meeks, *Moral World*, 38.

84. See Malina, "Social Levels, Morals and Daily Life," 91–98.

85. Foucault's classic study, *Discipline and Punish*, explores these forms of violent and non-violent expressions of power.

employed this cultural construction in order to perpetuate the status quo of the empire and in order to have people internalize the values of that status quo.

However, there is also an agonistic element to honor and shame. Yes, one's family of origin and one's political and economic location were strong factors in determining one's level of honor, but honor could also be gained by demonstrating virtue and could be won and lost in competitions between individuals.[86] In many ways, the honor of masters and conquerors was premised upon stripping the vanquished and enslaved of their honor.[87] Beyond that, there were also competing perspectives about what was considered honorable among the various kinship groups and factions that existed under the dominion of Rome. This agonistic element was further exacerbated by the cultural belief in a "limited good," wherein one person's accumulation of anything—including honor—was believed to come at the expense of others.[88] Thus, constructions of honor and shame were not simply about one's understanding of one's self within a certain group but also were about the understanding of the relation that one's group had to other groups and, especially, to the dominant group. Consequently, subordinate or oppressed groups would often do things like developing their own "courts of reputation," undermining the importance of approval from outsiders and even labeling persecution from outsiders as a source of honor.[89] For this reason, the Romans needed to exercise some caution in their conquests. Given that they understood themselves in a competition for honor with others, they would both conquer others and humiliate those whom they defeated.[90] However, they would also want vanquished nations and individuals to become incorporated into the empire and would therefore want them, particularly the local elites, to accept Roman constructions of honor and shame. To this end, it was important that the vanquished internalized the Roman system of honor so that they would act in an appropriately disciplined manner. As Seneca observes, "A man lives with more

---

86. See deSilva, *Honor, Patronage, Kinship, and Purity*, 26, 29; Jewett, "Paul, Shame, and Honor," 551–53; Malina, "Social Levels, Morals and Daily Life," 32–36.

87. See Graeber, *Debt*, 170.

88. See Esler, "Mediterranean Context," 18; Malina, "Social Levels, Morals and Daily Life," 89–90.

89. See deSilva, *Honor, Patronage, Kinship, and Purity*, 36–42.

90. See Horsley, *Jesus and Empire*, 30–31.

circumspection if he has something left to lose. No one shows regard for a reputation he has lost."[91] Malina explains this well:

> If people are alienated, the effort to shame them is irrelevant and may only be a badge of honor. Thus to be crucified by conquering Romans who likewise crucified [for example] many of one's fellow Israelites would not be shameful to fellow ethnics. But to be handed over by one's fellow Israelites for crucifixion by out-group Roman authorities would be public shame, indeed.[92]

Therefore, the spread of the imperial cult among local elites (a point explored momentarily) was a primary means by which the Roman constructions of honor and shame, which were inextricably connected with the conservation of the status quo of empire, were imposed upon foreign populations. Local elites had a lot to benefit from accepting Roman hierarchies and values. However, by simultaneously trying to hold onto values indigenous to their territories, they were able to shame deviants (in ways the Romans could not), in order to try and prevent those deviants from developing into local heroes. In these ways, they made themselves valuable allies to Rome.

The Practice of Patronage

> I [Augustus] found Rome built of sun-dried bricks; I leave her clothed in marble.
>
> —Suetonius, "Augustus" 29.1

Turning to patronage, it is once again worth emphasizing the central role this practice played in structuring and normalizing power imbalances in relationships between diverse parties.[93] This ideologically-loaded practice was found in all elements of society and marked relationships in everything from trades, to religion-based collegia, to the household, to the associations of freedmen and women, to public festivals, to civic relationships

91. Seneca, *De clementia* 1.22.

92. Malina, "Social Levels, Morals and Daily Life," 46.

93. On the centrality of patronage and benefaction and its diffusion throughout the empire, see Dunn, *Beginning from Jerusalem*, 551; Chow, "Patronage in Roman Corinth," 104–25; Crossan and Reed, *In Search of Paul*, 297; Elliott, *Arrogance of Nations*, 28–29; Malina and Pilch, *Social-Science Commentary*, 382–85; Horsley, "Introduction," 14–15.

between powerful individuals and cities, to individuals within ethnic or national groups, to international relationships between Rome and conquered nations.[94]

Patronage was the practice of asymmetrical, vertical relationships of dependence and exchange between patrons and clients, wherein patrons would assist clients in meeting material or legal needs and clients would be bonded to patrons, committed to enhancing the honor and status of their patrons.[95] Patronage was another practice of "soft" power. It was fundamental to the maintenance of a violent and exploitative imperial system, but it did not operate through forceful impositions. Rather, it was dependent upon voluntary and (to a limited extent) mutually beneficial relationships that sustained the status quo and entrenched people within steep and sharply demarcated pyramids of power, wealth, status, and moral value.[96] To borrow the language of Foucault, patronage produced a self-disciplining populace—people who willingly resigned themselves to their poverty and low status because they were still able to gain some benefits by playing by the rules of the game (and by ostracizing those who refused to do so). That said, the powerful were ultimately well aware that this system served their interests most of all. Hence, they used language that tried to mask this. This is why patrons almost always avoided the terms *patronus* and *cliens* (patron and clients), and, while clients may honor their patrons as patrons in epigraphic and other media, the patrons preferred the language of *amicitiae* (friendship) in order to demonstrate their sensitivity to the feelings of their clients and avoid implications of social inferiority or degradation.[97] The language of friendship implied a mutual *pistis* (loyalty) and masked the practice of power.[98] To get a sense for the powerful bond that

94. Chow, "Patronage in Roman Corinth," 117–24; Crossan and Reed, *In Search of Paul*, 300, 306; Malina, "Social Levels, Morals and Daily Life," 374. Here, one thinks of Foucault's notion of the capillary distribution of power throughout society (*Power/Knowledge*, 3).

95. See Chow, "Patronage in Roman Corinth," 105; Lampe, "Paul, Patrons, and Clients," 288; Friesen, "Paul and Economics," 46–47; Agosto, "Patronage and Commendation," 104; deSilva, *Honor, Patronage, Kinship, and Purity*, 97; Saller, *Personal Patronage*, 1, 128.

96. See Elliott, *Arrogance of Nations*, 28–39; Horsley, *Jesus and Empire*, 22–24; "Patronage, Priesthoods, and Power," 88–89; Meeks, *Origins of Christian Morality*, 40.

97. See Saller, *Personal Patronage*, 8–11. In a comparable move, consider how many bosses in workplaces don't like to be called "The Boss" but instead prefer a more amicable form of address.

98. See Lampe, "Paul, Patrons, and Clients," 493; deSilva, *Honor, Patronage, Kinship*

friendship was supposed to create, one can turn to Horace. In his *Satires*, he urges friends to forgive one another and emphasizes his point by arguing that, while it may be heinous to crucify a slave for a petty offence, it is far worse to dislike a friend for a small error![99] Friendship language more deeply entrenched the power imbalance within the practice of patronage, for, in Roman society, a person who acted against a friend was considered the worst kind of person. As Juvenal asserts: "A man who attacks strangers is called a criminal, a man who attacks friends, a monster."[100] Or, as Seneca writes on a related point: "Homicides, tyrants, traitors there always will be; but worse than all these is the crime of ingratitude."[101] Thus, any who challenged the patronage system or abandoned or betrayed their patrons were automatically considered to be monstrous, not worth consideration, and condemned. As Sallust says, "To the Roman people it seemed better, already from the beginning of their empire, to seek friends rather than slaves since they thought it safer to rule by consent than by force."[102] In this way, patronage prevented other more horizontal, less hierarchical systems of organization from emerging and prevented something like "class consciousness" or "solidarity" from developing among people experiencing dispossession and oppression.[103] Patronage was fundamental to the maintenance of Roman sovereignty, not just by the elite at Rome but also by Roman governors in the vanquished provinces. It was, as Richard Saller argues, "patronage and the patronal order" that "provide[d] stability in societies with enormous centrifugal pressures . . . pulling them apart."[104] Of course, admission into political and liturgical positions that carried influence and power was, itself, controlled by the patronage system—a system generally dominated by

---

and, Purity, 99; Agosto, "Patronage and Commendation," 105–7. Although, as Garnsey and Saller note, Roman practices of friendship were usually marked by superior and inferior friends, and actual equality among friends was difficult to maintain and fraught with tensions (*Roman Empire*, 149, 156).

99. Horace, *Satires* 1.3.3–4. This is also a useful reminder of the low value placed upon the lives of slaves in comparison to the value placed upon those who were considered to be properly human beings.

100. Juvenal, *Satyricon* 115.

101. Seneca quoted in Garnsey and Saller, *Roman Empire*, 148. See also Saller, *Personal Patronage*, 14.

102. Sallust quoted in Ando, *Imperial Ideology*, 144–45.

103. See Howard-Brook and Gwyther, *Unveiling Empire*, 97–98; Lampe, "Paul, Patrons, and Clients," 492; Horsley, "Patronage, Priesthoods, and Power," 90–91.

104. Saller, *Personal Patronage*, 38; see also 32, 141, 168–69; Finley, *Ancient Economy*, 151–53.

Romans but increasingly open to provincials who found both the army and the pursuit of education to be particularly reliable routes to social advancement through the building of patronage networks.[105]

The understanding of patronage as a technique used by rulers to maintain and advance their rule may be observed in the "hidden transcripts" of the powerful—within texts that were not intended to be read by or to the illiterate masses.[106] To provide just one example, we can turn to Lucan's account of the Roman civil wars. In this text, Julius Caesar accuses Pompey of manipulating the cost of corn in order to produce a famine and then, through his monopoly on corn, become a patron to those in need, thereby becoming their ruler.[107] Of course, as Suetonius notes, Caesar himself manipulated the patronage system—liberally providing many people with loans on little or no interest—thereby becoming "the one reliable source of help to all who were in legal difficulties, debt, or living beyond their means," leading many to be amazed by his liberality but also leaving them wondering what "the sequel" might be to this.[108] What becomes clear is that to become a patron of others is to rule over them.

With the rise of the principate, patronage became increasingly connected to the Caesars.[109] Even before his conflict with Pompey, Julius Caesar paved the way for this process by supporting local and provincial elites, engaging in "magnificent public works" in Rome (and all the main cities in Asia), and hosting public meals, shows, games, and gladiatorial contests.[110] In fact, his rise to power was premised upon exercising patronage liberally, even though this drove him into a considerable amount of debt. Supporting the prior quotation from Suetonius, Plutarch observes: "[Caesar's] enemies judging that this favor of the common people would soon quail, when he could no longer hold out that charge and expense, suffered him to run on,

105. See Garnsey and Saller, *Roman Empire*, 20, 32–33, 130, 135–36, 151–54, 176–87.

106. See Elliott, *Arrogance of Nations*, 30–33.

107. See Lucan, *Civil War* 3.56–58. See also Downs, "Is God Paul's Patron?," 137–41. Lampe also notes how during the Republic, one's political power was linked to the number of one's clients, but this decreased in political significance during the imperial period due to the Caesarian monopoly upon patronage ("Paul, Patrons, and Clients," 490–91).

108. Suetonius, *Twelve Caesars*, 22. "The sequel" was Caesar's ascension to imperial power.

109. See Elliott, *Arrogance of Nations*, 28–29; Horsley, *Jesus and Empire*, 24; "Patronage, Priesthoods, and Power," 91–94; Garnsey and Saller, "Patronal Power Relations," 96–103; Meeks, *First Urban Christians*, 12.

110. Suetonius, *Twelve Caesars*, 22, 27, 30; Plutarch, *Julius Caesar* 4–5, 48, 57.

till by little and little he was grown to be of great power," so that the Senate and the nobles came to fear him because he could "make the people do what he thought good."[111] Julius Caesar also continually acted as a generous patron to his soldiers, before and after the wars with Pompey and Cato, thereby ensuring that the military remained on his side.[112] Then, after winning wars with his rivals, he continued to act as the patron of the people of Rome, even giving to them generously in his will.[113]

From Julius Caesar onwards, the emperor became the greatest public benefactor, offering everything from relief from oppression, to pardon for crimes, to universal peace and stability.[114] The clients of the emperor expanded to include everyone from his (masses of) freedmen, to the urban Roman *plebs*, to the army and navy, to local provincial elites, and, ultimately, to all who fell under the rule of Rome.[115] As usual, Augustus was the most influential in this regard. After the assassination of his adoptive father, he realized the value of employing patronage as a strategy to gain power and immediately began his long-term strategy of giving generously to the people and to the soldiers.[116] All in all, Augustus claims to have given over two billion sesterces from his private wealth to a mixture of the plebs, soldiers, and the general treasury (including grain rations to more than one hundred thousand people at any one time).[117] As the highest patron, he also claimed control over the distribution of senatorial ornaments and priesthoods, grew the equatorial class into imperial administrators, appointed procurators and the four great prefectures (the vigils, the annona, Egypt, and the Praetorian Guard), guided manumissions, and granted citizenships.[118] He engaged in multiple building projects to better cities throughout the

111. Plutarch, *Julius Caesar* 4, 7.

112. See Plutarch, *Julius Caesar* 17, 55.

113. See Plutarch, *Julius Caesar* 55, 68; *Brutus* 20.

114. deSilva, *Honor, Patronage, Kinship, and Purity*, 101.

115. See Lampe, "Paul, Patrons, and Clients," 493–94.

116. See Plutarch, *Brutus* 22; Tacitus, *Annals* 1.2; Eder, "Augustus and the Power," 23.

117. Augustus, *Res Gestae* 15.1–18.1. It is hard to get one's head around the magnitude of this number. By way of contrast, the largest estate held in the republic prior to Augustus was that of Pompey, who claimed to possess, in total, two hundred and eighty million sesterces—a sum far smaller than the benefactions Augustus mentions in his eulogy! In his will, Augustus also leaves over forty-three million sesterces to the people of Rome, one thousand sesterces to *every* praetorian soldier, and three hundred sesterces to *every* legionary who was a Roman citizen (see Tacitus, *Annals* 1.8).

118. See Saller, *Personal Patronage*, 32–36, 45, 50–53.

empire, he hosted public festivities and games that were unprecedented in their number and in their extravagance, he offered support to various towns and cities-states that were struggling (and founded a number of colonies), and was the patron of kings throughout the empire, while also offering gifts to people from all classes, doing so "not to win popularity but to improve public health."[119] Of course, this last quote should be taken with a grain of salt for, as Augustus states in a letter to Tiberius: "That is how I like it: my generosity will gain me immortal glory, you may be sure!" Augustus certainly did gain immortal glory and the "mutually beneficial" patronal relationship he established with Rome left the ever-flattering Horace wondering if the people were more solicitous for the emperor's welfare, or if the emperor was more concerned with the welfare of the people.[120] To further consolidate his monopoly on an ever-elevating honor, Augustus made sure to end all cults devoted to other human benefactors during his reign.[121] In this way, Augustus became the greatest of all patrons (a patron to whom the entire world owed an unrepayable debt), but he did not achieve a total monopoly on patronage—senators maintained reduced patronage networks and also agreed to an arrangement wherein they functioned as brokers of imperial patronage.[122]

Other emperors did not always live up to the example set by Augustus. According to Suetonius, Tiberius was noted for his miserliness, building no magnificent public works and hosting no public shows, and Claudius also fell short of expectations.[123] Tacitus tempers this view somewhat and notes both how Tiberius engaged in various distributions of money to those in Rome (including giving one million sesterces to the populace after a fire devastated part of the city) and how Claudius built an aqueduct into Rome to benefit the people.[124] Suetonius praises Caligula for doing both of these things in abundance.[125] Nero also showed early signs of living up to the Augustan example. Upon entering his political career, he immediately began to give gifts to the soldiers and the populace of Rome, and after

119. Suetonius, *Twelve Caesars*, 75; see also 67–68, 76–77, 79, 85.

120. Horace, *Epistles* 1.16.3.

121. See Elliott, "Apostle Paul's Self-Presentation," 70.

122. See Garnsey and Saller, *Roman Empire*, 149–50; Saller, *Personal Patronage*, 73–77.

123. Suetonius, *Twelve Caesars*, 133–34, 194–95.

124. Tacitus, *Annals* 2.42, 48; 6.45; 11.13.

125. Suetonius, *Twelve Caesars*, 159–60.

Claudius died (probably poisoned at the behest of Nero's mother), he immediately ensured his assent to power by giving gifts to the soldiers.[126] He also established gymnasia at Rome, to be used by knights and senators, and made an annual present to the state of sixty million sesterces.[127] Nero's actions were also not limited to Rome. Upon attending the Isthmian Games in Corinth, he freed the entire province and gave money and citizenships to the judges.[128] Actions like these prompted Seneca to say to Nero: "You are the recipient of thanks; no human being has ever been so loved by another as you are by the people of Rome, its considerable and permanent blessing."[129] Thus, by Paul's day, the practice of patronage, targeting both provincial elites and the broader Roman public, had become centered upon the imperial household. The imperial cult was a natural response to this.[130] As deSilva observes: "The extreme form of response to benefactions from rulers was the offering of worship—those who gave gifts usually besought from the gods were judged to be worthy of the honors offered the gods."[131]

It is useful to further explore how this ideological practice of patronage worked itself out among the parties involved. The first thing to observe in more detail is the specific roles played by patrons and clients. Given that access to goods was limited within the Graeco-Roman world, personal channels became the means of facilitating a mutually beneficial exchange process.[132] Within this process, there were three primary roles: the patron, the client, and possibly the broker (who may facilitate a relationships between a patron and a client).[133] The patron, who could be called everything from *dominus* (lord) to *rex* (king) would give business assistance, legal advice, represent clients in court, host dinners and sporting events, provide money and loans, and increase the prestige of the clients.[134] In return, the

126. Tacitus, *Annals* 12.41, 69.

127. Tacitus, *Annals* 14.47; 15.18.

128. Suetonius, *Twelve Caesars*, 223.

129. Seneca, *De clementia* 2.6.

130. See Gordon, "Veil of Power," 126–37; Agosto, "Patronage and Commendation," 104; Horsley, "Introduction," 16–17.

131. deSilva, *Honor, Patronage, Kinship, and Purity*, 101–2.

132. deSilva, *Honor, Patronage, Kinship, and Purity*, 96.

133. I will focus upon patrons and clients. For more on brokers, see deSilva, *Honor, Patronage, Kinship, and Purity*, 97; Esler, "Mediterranean Context," 18. See also an example of Horace acting as a broker to imperial power in a letter he writes to Augustus (*Epistles* 1.9.229).

134. See Lampe, "Paul, Patrons, and Clients," 491; Downs, "Is God Paul's Patron?,"

clients would participate in morning salutations to the patron, accompany the patron on daily business, vote and canvass for the patron, increase the fame of the patron, and exhibit loyalty and dependability to the patron, often to the exclusion of all others.[135] Thus, in order to sustain this, two mindsets were required: the patron was supposed to give without a thought of return, and the recipient was never to forget his or her debt to the giver.[136] The giver could imagine that he or she was acting from pure and virtuous motives (altruistically wishing only for the good of others), while the receiver would forever be indebted to the giver and would be branded as a social ingrate of the worst kind if this attitude of gratitude ever flagged.[137] Indeed, if a client ever failed in this regard, he or she would be seen as a "Nothing," a person who would lose all social status. Thus, we begin to realize how the "soft" power of patronage functioned as a *morally* persuasive force.[138] Furthermore, once a client became involved in this relationship, it became very difficult to opt out or claim that one's debts had been cleared, as every return of favor was met by further favors and, always, the favors granted by the more powerful were considered to be greater than the returns of the less powerful.[139] This, then, is the Roman social context in which "grace" comes to the fore. "Grace" refers to three things: the willingness of the patron to grant petitions, the gift that is granted, and the gratitude exhibited by the recipient: "Grace must be met with grace; favor must always give birth to favor; gift must always be met with gratitude."[140]

Here it is interesting to note that Plutarch places the practice of patronage at the etymological root of the patrician title given to the Roman elite. He writes that Romulus, upon founding Rome, decided to call the elite

---

135; Agosto, "Patronage and Commendation," 105.

135. See Downs, "Is God Paul's Patron?," 135; Agosto, "Patronage and Commendation," 105; deSilva, *Honor, Patronage, Kinship, and Purity*, 113–16. Horace also touches upon these roles and their mutual benefits and requirements in his writings, although he usually focuses upon how these things impact clients (see *Odes* 4.8.20–29; *Satires* 2.1.1; *Epistles* 1.17.2, 3).

136. See deSilva, *Honor, Patronage, Kinship, and Purity*, 117–18.

137. See deSilva, *Honor, Patronage, Kinship, and Purity*, 106–11.

138. See MacMullen, *Changes in the Roman Empire*, 193–96. As Lampe notes, clients were linked to their patrons economically, socially, and morally ("Paul, Patrons, and Clients," 491).

139. See Saller, *Personal Patronage*, 15–17; Graeber, *Debt*, 119–20.

140. deSilva, *Honor, Patronage, Kinship, and Purity*, 105; cf. 104–6. See also Saller, *Personal Patronage*, 21.

"patricians" because "[Romulus] thought the chiefest men should have a fatherly care of the meanest sort."[141] So, from the very founding of Rome, the practice of patronage is established in order to maintain the status quo and the power divide between patrons and clients. Family language is incorporated. Plutarch argues that patronage was used to teach the populace "that they should not fear the authority of the greater, nor envy at their honors . . . but rather in all their causes should use their favor and goodwill, by taking them as their fathers."[142] In this way, Plutarch goes on to say, Romulus was able to breed "marvelous great love and goodwill" between the elite few and the indebted many, making them beholden to one another "by many mutual courtesies and pleasures."[143]

However, it is important to remember that Graeco-Roman patronage was never intended to be exercised as charity towards the most needy members of society.[144] Instead, it targeted people from close to the same level of society who had undergone some sort of misfortune.[145] It tended to benefit those who were close to the status of the patrons and not those who were far removed from positions of wealth and power. This is made clear in a decree made by Tiberius when a bankrupt fellow applied to him for financial assistance:

> If all poor men begin to come here and to beg money for their children, individuals will never be satisfied, and the State will be bankrupt . . . industry will languish and idleness be encouraged, if a man has nothing to fear, nothing to hope from himself, and

---

141. Plutarch, *Romulus* 13.

142. Plutarch, *Romulus* 13.

143. Plutarch, *Romulus* 13. Plutarch then goes on to describe the various duties of patrons and clients, which have already been mentioned above.

144. Charity to the truly poor is expressed more simply as doing something like tossing "a few coins to the needy" (Seneca, *De clementia* 2.6). But the suggestion of Hesiod seems to prevail: "Give to one who gives, but do not give to one who does not give" (quoted in Finley, *Ancient Economy*, 39; see also 38–39).

145. See Countryman, *Rich Christians in the Church*, 105; Malina, "Social Levels, Morals and Daily Life," 94–95. Regarding the criteria for commendation that existed when a patron wanted to recommend a client to another powerful person, see Agosto, "Patronage and Commendation," 107–8. Because of the power dynamics involved, "aristocrats sometimes rejected gifts from those whose equality or superiority they refused to concede" (Saller, *Personal Patronage*, 127). As the old Roman saying goes: "Not everything, not every time, not from everyone" (quoted in Saller, *Personal Patronage*, 165).

every one, in utter recklessness, will expect relief from others, thus becoming useless to himself and a burden to me.[146]

One only assisted the poor when it became absolutely critical to one's well-being or security to do so—and, if possible, one did this at the expense of others.[147] In relation to this selective practice of patronage (between the deserving and undeserving poor), the language of friendship that was employed in the patronage system is actually not quite so hyperbolic. Given the risk involved in business ventures and the tumult of the times, giving gifts to other wealthy friends could be an insurance measure against possible future misfortune.[148] The elite needed to maintain a united front against a common threat—the poor and exploited masses. Naturally, then, these masses were not taken into consideration except as the practice of patronage "trickled down," not so much to the benefit of all people but more as relationships between people at all levels of society became colonized by abusive hierarchical dynamics. Thus, people in lower classes also mimicked those in higher classes and created their own mini-empires (in their neighborhood, in their tenement building—but the histories of the powerful generally pay no attention to kingdoms such as these).[149] The only significant exception to this discriminatory practice of patronage was the funding of public works, which would benefit an entire city through the creation of temples, aqueducts, fountains, baths, roads, and so on. However, the result of this would be the creation of an entire populace indebted to the patron(s) who provided these things.[150]

Therefore, we see how the exercise of patronage is a means of sustaining the status quo of empire and maintaining traditional hierarchies while also promoting the emperor to the position of supreme patron. Within these highly moral hierarchical relationships of dependency, the system of patronage ensured that any who refused to accept the way things are were branded as immoral and subhuman. This also created divisions among the oppressed as individual people were driven to participate within

146. Tacitus, *Annals* 2.38. In this way, Tiberius sets the standard for every model employee in contemporary government-based income assistance programs.

147. See Finley, *Ancient Economy*, 171. See also Garnsey and Saller's discussion of how cities managed food crises (*Roman Empire*, 100–101).

148. See Saller, *Personal Patronage*, 25, 122.

149. Saller, *Personal Patronage*, vii.

150. See deSilva, *Honor, Patronage, Kinship, and Purity*, 100–101; Winter, *Seek the Welfare of the City*, 26.

the patronage system so that they could advance themselves and attain a slightly better situation than the one in which they started or to which they had fallen.

Traditional Roman Religiosity

It is sufficient for me, if I can preserve the morality traditional from my forefathers.

—Horace, *Satires* 1.4.3

The final element worth observing, before turning to a more detailed examination of the imperial cult(s), is the strong presence of traditional religion and values within Roman culture. In many ways, this system mirrors the contemporary expressions of traditional religiosity and "family values" found within the political religion of conservative Christianity.

Modernity, academia, and capitalism predispose us to imagine "politics," "culture," and "religion" as distinctly separate domains of life, but politics, culture, and religion were fully integrated within Roman society. Thus, it must be emphasized that religion in Roman and Greek societies was not something believed and practiced in a realm separate from the socio-economic, cultural, and political aspects of one's daily life. Religion permeated every domain. Here, it is worth quoting Esler's exploration of this subject:

> There was political religion and domestic religion, but not "religion" per se. Political religion employed the roles, values and aims of politics in religious ideologies and rites. It was characterized by functionaries combining cultic and political functions and tending towards powerful deities who provided well-being and prosperity or, if provoked, the opposite. . . . Domestic religion, on the other hand, used the roles, values and aims of the household in religious expression. Its functionaries, to the extent that it had them, were family members, and it focused on the deities as the source of familial solidarity and commitment, and well being for family members.[151]

To this, one should add the presence of civic religions and cults based upon certain locations and linked to civic pride—for example, the predominance

151. Esler, "Mediterranean Context," 15.

of the Artemis cult in Ephesus. Esler believes that political religion tended to be linked to the "Great Tradition" of the powerful, and domestic religion tended to be connected to the "Little Tradition" of the lowly.[152] If this is true, then one of the strengths of the imperial cult was the way in which it incorporated domestic religion into the interests of political religion. As Eder notes: "The Roman Republic in its heyday was based upon the consensus of the powerful boiled down to a system of traditional concepts and principles that could be adapted time and again to changing realities . . . only the power of tradition enabled Augustus to transform a republic safely into a principate."[153] This will be explored momentarily. Here, I wish to emphasize the comprehensive scope of religion in the Roman Empire and its integration into all areas of daily life. Understanding this integration helps to demonstrate why those who refused to participate within established systems were criminally and politically charged as *atheists*.

The Roman system itself was multicultural and religiously syncretistic, providing the opportunity for a plurality of religions to partner with the Roman ideology.[154] Rather than forcefully excluding or annihilating all religious beliefs and practices—an exercise of power that would have met with a greater degree of resistance throughout the empire—the Romans sought to incorporate and control foreign cults. Thus, all cults needed official sanction from the Roman political authorities. As Cicero asserts: "No one shall have gods to himself, either new gods or alien gods, unless recognized by the State."[155] But many cults were permitted as long as the devotees were happy to accept the rule of Roman law and the ultimate authority of Roman power.[156] Thus, Roman religious pluralism had its limits. Any religions that were reported to be especially debauched and immoral were condemned and eradicated, and those most violently condemned were religions that rejected or subverted Rome's law, order, and god-given right to rule (and

152. Esler, "Mediterranean Context," 15.

153. Eder, "Augustus and the Power of Tradition," 15, 32.

154. This mirrors the ways in which multiculturalism and religious pluralism is employed in our context to serve the interests of global capitalism and contemporary forms of colonialism. See, for example, Coulthard, *Red Skins, White Masks*.

155. Cicero quoted in Tellbe, *Paul between Synagogue and State*, 26.

156. See Tellbe, *Paul between Synagogue and State*, 26, 30–31; Keresztes, *From Herod the Great*, 49; Crossan and Reed, *In Search of Paul*, 250; Kautsky, *Foundations of Christianity*, 139; MacMullen, *Paganism in the Roman Empire*, 2; Hardin, *Galatians and the Imperial Cult*, 40–41.

that dared to encourage others to do the same).[157] It is important to keep this religious pluralism within clearly defined limits in mind given the persecutions experienced by the early Jesus loyalists.

In terms of the content of traditional Roman religiosity, one finds an emphasis upon many of the virtues valued within any imperialistic system: honesty, bravery, self-sacrifice, honoring one's parents, raising one's children to be well-behaved and properly educated, being faithful to one's spouse, obeying the duly appointed authorities, respecting the traditions and values one has inherited, being self-sufficient, living simply, accepting one's place in society, refusing to exploit one's neighbor in order to get ahead, and so on.[158] Here, the power of tradition, of the *mores maiorum*, is significant. Essentially, at least from Augustus onwards, *religio* simply meant scrupulously aligning one's thoughts and actions with what was conventionally designated as prudent.[159] This *religio* is much more focused upon practices than beliefs (although, of course, the beliefs are entangled with the practices).[160] Here, piety means the "faithful observation of one's [traditional] duty."[161] Thus, the impious person not only wrongs the gods but also wrongs his or her ancestors, as each consecutive generation was expected to carry on the values and beliefs of the former generation.[162] One gets a sense of this in Roman descriptions of the piety of such notable figures as Aeneas, Cato, and Gnaius Pompey. Throughout the *Aeneid*, Virgil observes that Aeneas is constantly praised for his pious devotion to the gods and the traditions of his ancestors.[163] Thus, he is described as "first in reverence for the gods."[164] In the same way, Lucan states that the piety of Cato is exhibited in the

157. See Crossan and Reed, *In Search of Paul*, 255; Tenney, *New Testament Times*, 116; MacMullen, *Paganism in the Roman Empire*, 2; Meeks, *In Search of the Early Christians*, 124; Tellbe, *Paul between Synagogue and State*, 27.

158. See, for example, Zanker, *Power of Images*, 156.

159. Thus, Edwin Judge quotes Verrius Flaccus, who wrote under Augustus, as saying the following: "People are called 'religious' when they show discrimination in performing and passing over divine matters according to the practice of the city, and do not involve themselves in superstition" ("Did the Churches," 503). This then helps to make sense of Koester's observation that Roman divinities tended to be more abstract powers who only became personal through Estrucan and Greek influences (*History, Culture, and Religion*, 347–48).

160. See Hurtado, *Destroyer of the Gods*, 42–43.

161. Koester, *History, Culture, and Religion*, 348; Kahl, *Galatians Re-Imagined*, 184.

162. See MacMullen, *Paganism in the Roman Empire*, 2–3.

163. Virgil, *Aeneid* 1.519–22; 3.110–24, 393–97.

164. Virgil, *Aeneid* 11.394.

observations that he is the guardian of the law, that he is moderate, devoted to his country, born not for himself but for the world, a good husband, a keeper of justice and strict morality, serving others, championing freedom, and loving legality and the fatherland.[165] Similarly, Lucan demonstrates the piety of Pompey by the ways in which he wields power without infringing on the liberty of others, in his refusal of "excessive" wealth, and because of the benefits he brought to Rome.[166]

In distinction to this focus upon *religio* as veneration of tradition, Romans looked down upon *superstitio*—belief in some sort of personal contact with divinities or any sort of religious experience that challenged or existed outside of traditional morality.[167] Thus, Seneca writes that "religion does honor to the gods, while superstition profanes them."[168] The wealthy and powerful members of Roman society tended to scorn the superstitions that were more influential among the uneducated, lowly, and poor, and especially mocked any belief that suggested that the gods acted within the domain of history.[169] Thus, for example, Horace mocks the Judeans for believing in miracles because such a superstitious view requires a god to intervene within history.[170] This scorn does not only reflect elite "enlightenment"—it is also politically expedient because those who believe that gods act in history are more inclined to also act in a revolutionary manner to change history.

Thus, we see that traditional Roman religiosity was an important exercise of "soft" power and one that contributed to the spread of the imperial status quo. As MacMullen bluntly states, "Religion served to strengthen the existing social order."[171] Religion was either employed to keep the masses down or to stimulate a form of religious belief and practice that revered the

165. Lucan, *Civil War* 2.286–325; 9.27–30.

166. Lucan, *Civil War* 9.190–207.

167. As Judge observes, much of what we call "religion" today, would be deemed "superstition" by the Romans, just as much of what they call "religion" we would classify as "traditionalism" or "conservatism." See Judge, "Did the Churches," 503.

168. Seneca, *De clementia* 2.5.

169. See MacMullen, *Paganism in the Roman Empire*, 70.

170. See Horace, *Satires* 1.5.9.

171. MacMullen, *Paganism in the Roman Empire*, 57.

powerful.[172] As Crossan and Reed conclude: "Roman religion was of the state, for the state, and therefore controlled by the state."[173]

Traditional ancient Mediterranean religious concepts of purity and pollution only further contributed to this. As David deSilva observes: "Purity codes are a way of talking about what is proper for a certain place and a certain time. . . . [Purity] is fundamentally concerned with the ordering of the world and making sense of one's everyday experiences in light of that order."[174] Thus, any anomalies that violated purity codes were disciplined, reduced, controlled, marked for avoidance, seen as a public hazard, or (when all else failed) ritualized and reincorporated into the dominant code.[175] Here, as elsewhere, religious beliefs operated as an exercise of socio-economic and political power. As such, they made those who were oppressed internalize the status quo of oppression and provided the oppressors with a monopoly not only on wealth and power but also on morality.

With the rise of the emperors and the imperial cult(s), all traditional Roman religiosity and purity codes continued to function in these ways, but the focus shifted from reverence of the traditional gods to the emperors as the mediators or objects of that reverence. New imperial power dynamics required new religious dynamics and observances if they were to be integrated into Roman identity.[176] Because, after all, the Romans did not define themselves as a race but understood their degree of "Romanness" to be related to their "participation in political and religious rituals that were variously open to or required of people of different legal ranks."[177] It is for this reason that, without any exaggeration or hyperbole, Tertullian, a few centuries later, can conclude that the imperial cult is the religion of the Romans.[178]

---

172. MacMullen, *Paganism in the Roman Empire*, 57–59.

173. Crossan and Reed, *In Search of Paul*, 250.

174. deSilva, *Honor, Patronage, Kinship, and Purity*, 243, 246. Thus, Malina talks about purity exhibiting "degrees of exclusivity" and setting limits or drawing boundary lines, within a "general cultural map of social time and space" (Malina, "Social Levels, Morals and Daily Life,"163–64).

175. See Malina, "Social Levels, Morals and Daily Life," 165–69; deSilva, *Honor, Patronage, Kinship, and Purity*, 249–52. Of course, within the Jesus movement, we see a significant challenge to these purity codes. Joel Green's commentary on Luke does an especially good job of highlighting this (*Gospel of Luke*).

176. See Garnsey and Saller, *Roman Empire*, 163; Ando, *Imperial Ideology*, 408.

177. Ando, *Imperial Ideology*, 339.

178. Tertullian quoted in Ando, *Imperial Ideology*, 394.

Sources for the Study of the Roman Imperial Cult

Art and architecture are mirrors of a society. They reflect the state
of its values, especially in times of crisis and transition.

—Paul Zanker, *Power of Images in the Age
of Augustus*, v

Having explored the four cornerstones of the ideo-theology of Rome—the
household unit, cultural conceptions of honor and shame, the practice of
patronage, and traditional Roman religiosity—we are now equipped to turn
to a more detailed study of the Roman imperial cult(s), beginning with an
examination of source material. In this examination, we will see the ways
in which this form of imperialism, like traditional religiosity, inundated
all areas of life and played a crucial role throughout the eastern part of the
empire.[179]

The primary evidence of the influence of the imperial cult throughout
the empire is non-literary. This is not surprising given that literacy was not
widespread. Instead, we discover an abundance of evidence in images, art,
architecture, and events or festivals—all of which were the means by which
the theopolitical vision of Rome was communicated.[180]

From Augustus onwards, one perceives a thorough "aestheticization
of politics" that sought to determine how people "thought of, perceived,
and imagined their rulers and forms of government."[181] This aesthetic was
employed in order to "portray how the world *should* be perceived and make
this message normative."[182] Roman imperialism sought to counter other
claims and other social imaginaries by engaging in a campaign of "myth-
management" that combined art with politics in order to both illustrate

179. It is common to observe that Roman imperialism spread primarily in the East
through the imperial cult and primarily in the West through urbanization or through the
process of "civilizing" the vanquished. This is true to some extent, although it should be
noted that these elements were generally intertwined and Tacitus observes that the very
first temple to Augustus was established in the West (see Price, *Rituals and Power*, 91–98;
Sherwin-White, *Roman Citizenship*, 397–98; Zanker, *Power of Images*, 297). That said,
the focus of this Pauline study will remain upon the East.

180. The classic sources here are Price and Zanker. Kahl does a fine job of following
in their footsteps and developing their insights in relation to Galatia.

181. Beacham, "Emperor as Impresario," 162–63 (emphasis removed).

182. Kahl, *Galatians Re-Imagined*, 28.

and constitute the imperial ideology.[183] Artistic freedom was limited and controlled (for example, Augustus claimed a monopoly on all the imagery related to triumph), and any changes in pictorial imagery had to be initiated by the imperial court.[184] In this way, a new visual language was created, which supported new (imperial) dynamics of power and created a new (imperial) mythology about Rome, the emperors, the gods, vanquished nations, and those outside the boundaries of the empire.[185] This new aesthetics then began to impact all areas of public and private life—from the shaping of public civic spaces, to the designs of temples, to private art like wall paintings or vases—creating an environment wherein one could not help but be impacted by the imperial ideology, regardless of whether or not one was conscious of the art and its impact.[186] John Dominic Crossan summarizes this well: "Think of Roman imperial theology as an immensely successful advertising campaign that inundated everyone, everywhere, from all sides and at all times"; or, as he writes earlier with Jonathan Reed, "See the image, get the message, buy the product. Roman imperial ideology worked well as a magnificent advertisement for what many people wanted to believe."[187] Thus, everything from coins, to statues, to tomb monuments, to landscape paintings, to public notices (read aloud at designated times to permit the illiterate masses to understand) were crafted in such a way as to present a powerful and positive message about the emperor and the imperial status quo.[188] From Augustus onwards, the emperors distributed official

183. See Beacham, "Emperor as Impresario," 151–58; Price, *Rituals and Power*, 170–206.

184. See Zanker, *Power of Images*, 110–14, 338; Elliott, "Apostle Paul's Self-Presentation," 71. Other emperors followed this in various ways. Thus, for example, during the reign of Caligula, permission was needed from the emperor in order to be able to erect any statue or bust of a living person. See Suetonius, *Twelve Caesars*, 167.

185. See Zanker, *Power of Images*, v, 4.

186. See Zanker, *Power of Images*, 265–74, 282, 312.

187. Crossan, *God and Empire*, 15–16; "Roman Imperial Theology," 60; Crossan and Reed, *In Search of Paul*, 288; cf. 136, 142–43.

188. On coins see, for example, Zanker, *Power of Images*, 37, 299; Hardin, *Galatians and the Imperial Cult*, 30; Ando, *Imperial Ideology*, 230. All three authors note that, prior to Augustus, it was unheard of to place a living person upon a coin. For more on the ubiquity of coins and their use in spreading the imperial ideology, see Ando, *Imperial Ideology*, 215; Maier, *Picturing Paul in Empire*, 10, 52, 95–97, 110–11; Winter, *Divine Honours for the Caesars*, 11–13, 250. See also Zanker's discussions of statues (*Power of Images*, 211–12, 239–55, 263), tomb monuments (291–95), and landscapes (285–91). On public notices, see Ando, *Imperial Ideology*, 101–3.

portraits to be used and copied throughout the empire, and the portraits functioned as a stand-in for the emperor's presence—they (the portraits) witnessed oaths, received cultic acts, and sealed diplomatic arrangements, while also allowing people (from governors, to money-changers, to merchants, to homeowners, to entire cities during festivals) to publicly and prominently proclaim their loyalty.[189] Oaths sworn in front of the imperial portraits were especially important. An annual oath of loyalty was required from conquered cities, and oaths sworn before and to the emperor (and to uphold the deeds of the divine Augustus after his *apotheosis*) were also required at other significant moments in the lives of individual citizens.[190] The sacredness of the images before which these oaths were sworn and the other works of art associated with the imperial ideology was so significant that during the Julio-Claudian reign, the charge of treason (*maiestas*) was applied to any who infringed upon the dignity of the imperial image—as Ando observes, people could be charged for striking a slave near a statue of Augustus, changing clothes near an imperial statue, or taking a coin or ring with an imperial image into a bathroom or a brothel.[191]

Another strong and related source revealing the ubiquity and significance of the Roman imperial cult(s) is found in the architecture that developed with Augustus and continued with his successors.[192] The multiple building projects of the Caesars (which received significant funding from important allies like Herod Agrippa) created a new environment that was presented as a restoration of the past glory of Rome and of the Golden Age in order to ensure that contemporary manifestations of imperialism remained concretely rooted within Roman traditionalism.[193]

We see this ideological architectural project especially powerfully expressed in the abundance of temples devoted to the imperial cult that

189. See Ando, *Imperial Ideology*, 231–37, 251, 368–69; Maier, *Picturing Paul in Empire*, 1.

190. See Ando, *Imperial Ideology*, 359–61. Ando goes on to argue that: "The format of the imperial oaths . . . suggested that the emperor possessed powers beyond those of mortal men. The inclusion of the emperor himself or his *genius* or *numen* among the divinities sanctioning an oath clearly attributed to him, or to the divine potentiality within him, omniscience in knowing if that oath should be broken and omnipotence in his power to punish the perjurer" (*Imperial Ideology*, 389–90).

191. Ando, *Imperial Ideology*, 221. Ando also notes that, after Nero died, coins showing his image were regularly defaced or shunned (*Imperial Ideology*, 223, 227).

192. See Price, *Rituals and Power*, 133–69; Crossan and Reed, *In Search of Paul*, x; Zanker, *Power of Images*, 82–85; Horsley, *Religion and Empire*, 98.

193. See Zanker, *Power of Images*, 135–47, 192.

rapidly spread throughout the empire in the first century CE. Not only were new temples built but also old temples—which housed local deities or were sites of pilgrimages and centers of worship for other major deities—were transformed, and members of the imperial family were included therein.[194] The temples themselves were associated with the most powerful municipal and imperial citizens, as they were built and sustained by the elite allies of Rome.[195] They were central hubs of imperial propaganda. As such, they were critical to incorporating local elites into webs of imperial patronage while also becoming central nodes for the distribution of the imperial ideo-theology to the masses. For example, fragments of the *Res Gestae* have been found near temples of Augustus in Apollonia, Pergamon, and Pisidian Antioch as well as at the Temple of Augustus and Roma in Ancyra.[196] However, as I have already noted, the temples also functioned as central hubs of social life—they were used as theaters for public entertainment, they housed parks, museums, and galleries, they hosted concerts, lectures, and public meals, as well as functioning as banks, marketplaces, state treasuries, financial headquarters, and central spaces for commerce.[197] Given that these temples were centers "of an entire world of meaning" related to Roman imperialism, they could not help but exercise "a powerful though silent influence" upon the entire population of their respective cities as they fulfilled these roles.[198] Not only this, but the presence of the imperial cult was not limited to these (very large and central) spaces; hubs of worship

194. Albeit generally in a subordinated manner. See Price, *Rituals and Power*, 146–62. Winter notes that, in Asia Minor alone, archaeologists have discovered at least ten temples and sanctuaries built and dedicated to the imperial cult within the first half of the first century CE, another seven built in the second half of the first century, and fifteen built in the first half of the second century (*Divine Honours for the Caesars*, 59). As one example, Maier mentions a "huge" temple at Aphrodisias built to honor Augustus and his successors where Nero was also enthroned as the cosmic ruler over defeated nations represented as women (*Picturing Paul in Empire*, 78, 87–88).

195. See MacMullen, *Paganism in the Roman Empire*, 24.

196. See Maier, *Picturing Paul in Empire*, 86–87.

197. See MacMullen, *Paganism in the Roman Empire*, 18–21, 26–27, 35–36, 40; Howard-Brook and Gwyther, *Unveiling Empire*, 103–4; Winter, *Divine Honours for the Caesars*, 11. Of course, the imperial cult was not only related to public places, but was also practiced in private homes. Thus, Petronius records a common toast given at private dinner parties: "God save Augustus, the Father of his People" (*Satyricon* 72). Peppard mentions how the worship of Augustus became prevalent in homes in Rome itself and, even during Augustus's own lifetime, the compital altars placed at significant intersections had been appropriated by the Lares Augusti (*Son of God*, 65–66).

198. Crossan and Reed, *In Search of Paul*, 188; Tenney, *New Testament Times*, 110.

honoring the emperors could also be found along main avenues, on routes of city festivals, in city gates, close to theaters, in porticos, and in gymnasia.[199] All of this was already widespread and well-established in the eastern provinces of the empire in the first century CE, where the imperial cult(s) could both stand alone or become integrated into almost all other cults to a degree acceptable to both the Romans and the locals.[200] Thus, for example, already in 5 CE we find inscriptions in Sardis offering prayers to Augustus, we read of requests to set up a temple devoted to Gaius along with a temple to Augustus, and coins were minted with imperial family members on them portrayed as gods.[201]

Finally, it is worth recalling the powerful influence of public festivals, holidays, and games. The imperial cult(s) reorganized the public calendar (creating one common calendar throughout the empire) and came to dominate and regulate the shared rhythms of life.[202] Entire cities would participate within imperial holidays (for example, celebrating the birthday of Augustus or a triumph of one of the Caesars), and by this means an entirely new sense of community was created.[203] The pattern of civic life was restructured and focused upon the emperor "as the divine source of life and savior of society."[204] All members of a city would participate in these festivals—from the very wealthy to the very poor—in both their public and private lives.[205]

I have already explored some of these festivities while examining the realized eschatology of Rome. Here, it is worth looking at the ideological function of gladiatorial shows and games. All of the major Roman games (the *Ludi Romani, Ludi Plebes, Ludi Cereales, Ludi Megalenses,* and *Ludi Florales*) were closely linked to Roman religiosity and were usually hosted by priests.[206] Furthermore, Augustus, as we already observed, funded the new Golden Age by celebrating the *Ludi Saeculares*—the Games of the New

---

199. See Maier, *Picturing Paul in Empire*, 2.

200. See Winter, *Divine Honours for the Caesars*, 2; Peppard, *Son of God*, 25, 32, 38.

201. See Winter, *Divine Honours for the Caesars*, 50–51.

202. See Walsh and Keesmaat, *Colossians Remixed*, 61–63; Horsley, *Religion and Empire*, 100–101.

203. See Price, *Rituals and Power*, 101–32; MacMullen, *Paganism in the Roman Empire*, 40; Zanker, *Power of Images*, 299.

204. Horsley, *Religion and Empire*, 99.

205. See Price, *Rituals and Power*, 107–13, 117–21.

206. Jeffers, *Greco-Roman World*, 32.

Age—in 18 BCE, thereby thanking the gods for universal peace, purifying the citizens for participation in that peace, and exercising a great deal of patronage that permitted people to celebrate at the expense of the state.[207]

However, beyond this point of contact with the imperial cult, the games were also used to sharpen the loyalty of the people and to teach suitable lessons about patronage, wealth, popularity, power, piety, and triumph.[208] Brigitte Kahl explores this in considerable detail.[209] She observes how the games provided the people with the image of a melting pot, wherein all were present to participate together in their desire for the blood of "the Other," while also providing a space for the unequal practice of benefaction and the reaffirmation of the proper order of society (both through seating plans and the imposition of death upon those in the arena).[210] Thus, the games demonstrate triumph over nature (with, for example, the creation of artificial lakes) while also segregating and punishing criminals, liminals, and enemies.[211] Kahl also demonstrates the ideo-theological connection between the cross and the arena. In the arena

> what needs to be shown is not just the execution of a criminal but the elimination of a rebellious, transgressive other and the restoration of the proper order of the world. . . . It shows that Golgotha is not an insular Jewish or New Testament topos that was first understood by Paul in its universal theological implications for all the nations/Gentiles of the world. Rather, it already had a salvific and global connotation within the overall framework of Roman imperial world order, world law, and world religion. Crucifixion represented an inter-national event, ubiquitous among the vanquished nations under Roman rule, both at Rome and in the

207. Jewett, *Romans*, 47.

208. See Beacham, "Emperor as Impresario," 161; Zanker, *Power of Images*, 147–53.

209. See Kahl, *Galatians Re-Imagined*, 148–64.

210. Kahl, *Galatians Re-Imagined*, 149–56. One sees this social order firmly inscribed into the "melting pot" of the arena by order of Julius Caesar and then even more emphatically by Augustus, who gave the closest seats to the senators, then to the knights, then ambassadors and other allies, and who also separated soldiers from senators, married people from single people, and young people (with their tutors) from older people. See Suetonius, *Twelve Caesars*, 27, 77. Nero later modifies this to make more room for the growing number of knights (Tacitus, *Annals* 15.32). That others were sensitive to this seating plan is reflected in the writings of Juvenal: "The hardest thing to bear/ In poverty is the fact that it makes us ridiculous. / 'Out of those front seats,' we're told. 'You ought to be / Ashamed of yourselves—your incomes are far too small, and / The law's the law'" (Juvenal, *Satires* 2.153–57).

211. Kahl, *Galatians Re-Imagined*, 152–54.

provinces, inside and outside the arena, and was as universal as the Roman Empire itself.[212]

The deaths of those in the arena, much like the crucifixions of transgressors elsewhere, demonstrated Roman rule and re-inscribed the proper order of things into the world and the consciousness of any viewer. Furthermore, by viewing and celebrating the deaths in the arena (with gladiators always dressed as foreign fighters), audience members were able to participate in Roman triumphs, re-enacting imperial victories, and reconfirming the power of the Caesars.[213]

Consequently, by Paul's day, the imperial cult had come to dominate all public urban space and communal gatherings. Urbanization was linked to the Romanization of the provinces, and that Romanization process went hand-in-hand with the spread of the imperial cult.[214] This urbanization process was developed through the creation of colonies and cities composed of disbanded soldiers, through the adornment of public space with buildings, temples, statues, baths, and fountains, and through the creation of aqueducts, roads, and ports.[215] Through urbanization, Rome was able to breakdown pre-existing, sometimes more egalitarian or mutualistic tribal ways of organizing life together and were able to centralize power (which was also necessary for the facilitation of taxation and the production and distribution of resources throughout the empire).[216] In this way, the topography of prominent cities throughout the empire and the most central, public, and visible spaces in those cities were overwhelmed with images of

212. Kahl, *Galatians Re-Imagined*, 158–59.

213. See Hurtado, *Destroyer of the Gods*, 148–49; Maier, *Picturing Paul in Empire*, 76; Winter, *Divine Honours for the Caesars*, 24–25.

214. See Wengst, *Pax Romana*, 40–46; Zanker, *Power of Images*, 298; Dunn, *Beginning from Jerusalem*, 550–51. Of course, the spread of imperial control by means of urbanization was not unique to Rome. The spread of the Greek empire under Phillip II and especially under Alexander was also closely linked to the development of Greek cities within conquered territories. See Meeks, *First Urban Christians*, 11–16, 28–29; Frankopan, *Silk Roads*, 6–8.

215. See Crossan and Reed, *In Search of Paul*, 183–90.

216. See Kahl, *Galatians Re-Imagined*, 188–91. Tacitus comments on some of these more democratic tribal modes of governance in his account of the tribes of Germany. He writes: "About minor matters the chiefs deliberate, about the more important the whole tribe . . . the king or chief, according to age, birth, distinction in war, or eloquence, is heard, more because he has influence to persuade than because he has power to command. If his sentiments displease them, they reject them" (*Germ.* 11).

the Caesars and the presence of the imperial cult.[217] Neil Elliott is entirely correct to refer to this reorientation of public space as "aggressive, pervasive, and systematic."[218] It was a deliberate propaganda campaign waged by Rome to ensure that conquered peoples internalized the Roman vision of the world and understood their places within that world. Here, it is worth quoting Tacitus at length, for he exhibits a moment of surprising transparency. In the passage quoted, Tacitus describes the actions of Agricola in Britain, but the description accurately describes the urbanization project that was aggressively pursued throughout the empire:

> For, to accustom to rest and repose through the charms of luxury a population scattered and barbarous and therefore inclined to war, Agricola gave private encouragement and public aid to the building of temples, courts of justice and dwelling-houses, praising the energetic, and reproving the indolent. Thus, an honorable rivalry took the place of compulsion. He likewise provided a liberal education for the sons of the chiefs, and showed a preference for the natural powers of the Britons over the industry of the Gauls that they who lately disdained the tongue of Rome now coveted its eloquence. Hence, too, a liking sprang up for our style of dress, and the "toga" became fashionable. Step by step they were led to things which dispose to vice, the lounge, the bath, the elegant banquet. All this in their ignorance, they called civilization, when it was but a part of their servitude.[219]

Consequently, we may be confident that during the age of the Caesars, the development of art, images, architecture, social centers, holidays and festivals, and city layouts all helped create a certain (conscious or unconscious) way of understanding the world and one's place in it. In the first-century Roman Empire, this was powerfully aided by the spread of Roman imperial cult(s), which valorized the wealthy few and normalized the world

217. See Carter, *Roman Empire*, 47; Zanker, *Power of Images*, 328; Hardin, *Galatians and the Imperial Cult*, 30; Price, *Rituals and Power*, 136–46. It is also worth noting that in addition to this sustained propaganda campaign, entire civic populations were made to take oaths of loyalty to the imperial family. See Hardin, *Galatians and the Imperial Cult*, 45–46.

218. Elliott, "Apostle Paul's Self-Presentation," 69. As Garnsey and Saller observe, "Rome's main export to the empire was the cult of the emperors" (*Roman Empire*, 164).

219. Tacitus, *Agricola* 21. The overlap between these tactics and those employed by contemporary colonial powers—like those that function in present-day Canada in the ongoing relationship between the Canadian political and business elites and sovereign Indigenous peoples on Turtle Island—is quite striking.

in which they—not unlike the great philanthropocapitalists of today—are viewed as justified, rightful lords and beneficent saviors of the world.

The Roman Imperial Cult

The Eastern Background to the Imperial Cult

It is now time to look in more detail at the Roman imperial cult itself. Before looking at its function during the New Testament period, as well as its dominant themes, one further piece of background material should be provided—the way in which the eastern part of the empire was particularly suited to the spread of this cult.

Within the Hellenistic tradition, which spread throughout the empire established by Alexander, there already existed cults dedicated to kings, rulers, or heroic individuals.[220] Much like the inspiration for the Roman imperial cult, the Greek variant of this practice emerged from Greek philosophy in the fifth century BCE, when crises related to the Greek cities gave birth to the belief that "only a divinely gifted individual would be able to re-establish peace, order, and prosperity."[221] Consequently, already during his lifetime, Alexander was revered as a god in some Greek cities (and he was also considered the son of Ammon Re by some in Egypt), and this was further encouraged by the Diadochi who divided the empire after Alexander's death (two of the Diadochi were also welcomed as "Savior Gods" by the Athenians).[222] Therefore, in the centuries leading up to Roman imperialism, Greek ruler cults became common in the East and were either encouraged or made mandatory—in part due to their political expediency and in part due to the ways in which they permitted cities to come to terms with new types of power.[223]

220. See Judge, *Social Distinctives of the Christians*, 16, 34; Lietzmann, *Beginnings of the Christian Church*, 163; Peppard, *Son of God*, 25. Although, of course, as Roetzel observes, connections between gods and kings go back to the dawn of recorded history (*World That Shaped*, 72–75).

221. See Koester, *History, Culture, and Religion*, 36. Thus, Koester observes that divine honors were earlier ascribed to the Spartan general Lysander, and to Phillip II of Macedonia.

222. Koester, *History, Culture, and Religion*, 36–37; Lietzmann, *Beginnings of the Christian Church*, 163; Lohse, *New Testament Environment*, 216–18.

223. See Price, *Rituals and Power*, 23–40; Lietzmann, *Beginnings of the Christian Church*, 164.

With the rise of Augustus, these themes were adopted and the practice of ruler-worship was appropriated across the Roman Empire.[224] Here, the worship of Augustus (and other members of the imperial family, including subsequent emperors) is more consciously modeled upon divine cults and less upon cults dedicated to human heroes.[225] In order to consolidate power in this way, Augustus puts an end to the rise of any cults dedicated to heroic individual citizens. Such cults had been on the rise in the first century BCE, but their presence became politically undesirable as the emperor—along with designated members of his family—became divine.[226] In this way, Hellenistic views of a savior-ruler as the epiphany of a god were combined with Roman worship of transcendent power as it operated through a particular individual.[227]

The Imperial Cult During the New Testament Period

It is important to stress the presence and power of the imperial cult(s) in the New Testament period because prior scholarship has often assumed that the imperial cult did not really gain prominence until after the first century CE. Yet the accumulation of evidence already mentioned shows how quickly the imperial cult(s) spread from Augustus onwards. In Paul's day, all the major cities in the East contained temples dedicated to this religion.[228] In fact, during the first century CE, it was the imperial cult, and not the movement that coalesced around Jesus, that was the fastest growing religion throughout the empire.[229]

In many ways, the imperial cult, from Augustus onwards, became the "glue" that held the empire together.[230] Public life, as we have seen, became

224. See Judge, *Social Distinctives of the Christians*, 17; Lohse, *New Testament Environment*, 218–19.

225. See Price, *Rituals and Power*, 32–36.

226. Price, *Rituals and Power*, 47–51.

227. See Koester, *History, Culture, and Religion*, 350–51.

228. See Gorman, *Apostle of the Crucified Lord*, 16–17.

229. See Hardin, *Galatians and the Imperial Cult*, 23; Wright, *Paul*, 64; Tellbe, *Paul between Synagogue and State*, 32; Price, *Rituals and Power*, 78–100. Sherwin-White observes that this spread happened, in part, because it was easier to assimilate the emperors into the pantheon of the gods than more abstract entities like the senate, the (Roman) people, or Roma herself, although cults also were dedicated to these entities early on during the principate (*Roman Citizenship*, 406).

230. Crossan, "Roman Imperial Theology," 59; Howard-Brook and Gwyther,

centered upon it, and it created a "public cognitive system" that centralized the emperors, making them indispensable to the well-being of all.[231]
Michael Gorman states it well:

> Devotion to the emperor . . . was a multifaceted affair that perme-
> ated the culture. It was a form of religious and nationalistic, or
> theopolitical, allegiance, both to deified humans (the emperors)
> and the political entity (the Roman Empire). In many respects,
> therefore, it was one of the most fundamental cohesive elements in
> the empire, helping to hold its diverse constituencies together.[232]

The imperial cult(s) created a sense of cohesion that transcended what we
might now call class lines.[233] It also transcended all other divisions—between male and female, slave and free, citizens and non-citizens, victors
and vanquished—all were now one in Caesar's body.

As the ideo-theological "glue" holding the empire together, the imperial cult in the East became a crucial means by which both the conquerors and the conquered made sense of their new situation and a means to
negotiate new power structures. Through the cult(s), new power relations
were accepted, normalized, and made to work in the interests of both Rome
and the provincial elites; it continued the process of "flexible adaptation"
demonstrated by people groups living in the East first under the Greek
empire and then again under Rome.[234] Essentially, a gift-exchange system
was created between subjects and rulers, and although this was *politically*
beneficial (for example, the imperial cult gave some of its devotees direct
access to the emperor), the *religious* element should not be neglected—the
imperial cult was politically beneficial because of its intrinsic religious significance.[235] With that in mind, one may observe various ways in which the
imperial cult(s) benefited the local elites. To begin with, as Tacitus notes

---

Unveiling Empire, 101–3; Garnsey and Saller, *Roman Empire*, 202.

231. See Price, *Rituals and Power*, 7–9.

232. Gorman, *Apostle of the Crucified Lord*, 15.

233. See Pickett, "Conflicts at Corinth," 118; Horsley, "Introduction," 17.

234. See Price, *Rituals and Power*, 1, 40–77.

235. See Price, *Rituals and Power*, 65–73; Zanker, *Power of Images*, 302; Harries,
"Armies, Emperors and Bureaucrats," 35; Sherwin-White, *Roman Citizenship*, 403; Jeffers, *Greco-Roman World*, 100–102; Howard-Brook and Gwyther, *Unveiling Empire*,
91–94. Of course, as Price emphasizes in his ground-breaking book, it is anachronistic
to speak here of "politics" and "religion" as if they are two separate things—a nuance that
is sometimes lacking in earlier works (see, for example, Lohse, *New Testament Environment*, 220–21).

in his *Annals*, the greatness of Rome was a guarantee of protection against other foreign powers who had aimed to overthrow those elites.[236] Thus, Roman generals could (and did) remind the local leaders that peace is "equally for the interest of both."[237] Tacitus also quotes a German ally as saying that "steadfast loyalty" to Rome not only provided him with a Roman citizenship but also was in the interest of his own country, for he "held that Romans and Germans have the same interests . . . that peace is better than war."[238] In another text, Tacitus observes that Agricola, in Britain, did what Rome had done everywhere else in the empire: "Maintaining the ancient and long-recognized practice of the Roman people, which seeks to secure among the instruments of dominion even kings themselves."[239]

However, it is worth emphasizing that this acceptance of new power dynamics was an acceptance rooted primarily among the local elites. Local elites were willing to accept the loss of some autonomy, power, and revenue by accepting Roman rule because they were also able to retain a great deal of those things by working with Rome. They were accepting not so much their own subjugation as the subjugation of their peoples. In this way, the local elites collaborated with Rome against the masses.[240] This is why rulers and leading citizens throughout the empire were the most prominent members, sponsors, and priests of the imperial cult.[241] This is not to say that there was no benefit found for the common people in the adoption of the imperial cult(s). In fact, given the ways in which the eastern provinces were plundered during the Roman civil wars, Tacitus observes that the provinces did not dislike the rise of imperialism because it helped limit the rapacity of local magistrates who constantly plundered the provinces in order to finance rivalries at Rome.[242]

This elite-base of the imperial cult(s) also helps to explain its rapid and natural spread throughout the eastern part of the empire during the first century CE. Rulers and prominent citizens in different cities and provinces

236. See Tacitus, *Annals* 4.5.

237. Tacitus, *Annals* 15.13.

238. Tacitus, *Annals* 1.58.

239. Tacitus, *Agricola,* 14.

240. See Wengst, *Pax Romana*, 24–26; Zanker, *Power of Images*, 320–23.

241. See Zanker, *Power of Images*, 118–23, 332; Dunn, *Beginning from Jerusalem*, 551; Kahl, *Galatians Re-Imagined*, 186.

242. See Tacitus, *Annals* 1.2. However, this benefit is more realistically comparable to feeling relieved that one has found a master who will only beat and rape his slaves instead of being bound to a master who beats, rapes, and then tortures his slaves to death.

were actively competing for the favor of Rome and the patronage of the emperor.[243] Any members of the elite who refused to participate in this system would come under enormous pressure as their refusal would not only compromise themselves but also the status of the entire city in which they lived.[244] Not only did elite individuals compete with one another in specific cities (a competition encouraged by the Romans themselves) but also cities and collections of cities would compete to try and outdo one another in giving honor to the emperors.[245] Participating within and contributing to the imperial cults were primary ways of going about this.[246]

This also explains the prominence of devotion to the imperial cult among freedpeople. The cult offered people who had gained an increase in status a means of continuing in that (admittedly quite limited) upward trajectory while also giving them a chance to demonstrate their commitment and loyalty to the empire (and shielding them from the potential loss of their new and fragile status).[247] From Augustus onwards, freed slaves (and their descendants) were deliberately courted by means of the imperial cult(s), especially as imperial elements modified the cult of the *Lares* in Rome and among the *augustales* throughout the empire. Indeed, Zanker notes that membership in the college of the *augustales* was "the greatest goal a freedman could attain."[248]

It is also worth observing that this attachment to local elites and others with relatively higher status (like freedpeople) was an important tactic employed to divide the interests of conquered peoples. Here, Rome walked a fine line between becoming the primary beneficiary of each local power group while also continuing to ensure that each group was

243. See Price, *Rituals and Power*, 62–65, 126–32; Sherwin-White, *Roman Citizenship*, 402–3; Zanker, *Power of Images*, 303, 316; Hardin, *Galatians and the Imperial Cult*, 42–43; Tacitus, *Annals* 4.55–56.

244. See Price, *Rituals and Power*, 64. Hardin also notes how in some cities those who refused to participate in a civic procession related to the imperial cult could be fined 2,000 drachmas (*Galatians and the Imperial Cult*, 43–44).

245. See Ando, *Imperial Ideology*, 58–59, 132–34; Garnsey and Saller, *Roman Empire*, 39.

246. See Ando, *Imperial Ideology*, 214; Maier, *Picturing Paul in Empire*, 10; Peppard, *Son of God*, 39; Winter, *Divine Honours for the Caesars*, 58–59.

247. See Price, *Rituals and Power*, 113–14; Zanker, *Power of Images*, 129–35; Jeffers, *Greco-Roman World*, 233. Other offices not initially accessibly to emancipated slaves, like magistracies and membership on city councils, became accessible to their freeborn children (see Garnsey and Saller, *Roman Empire*, 45).

248. Zanker, *Power of Images*, 319. See also Garnsey and Saller, *Roman Empire*, 121.

properly disciplined and divided (or at least in competition with) other power groups. Thus, Tacitus observes, while fear is necessary in order to retain the provinces (for those like the Gauls, Germans, and Britons had fought Rome longer than they had been her allies, and if fear ceased then they would begin to more actively and openly express hatred of Rome), he also notes the importance of segregating the conquered: "May the tribes, I pray, ever retain if not their love for us, at least hatred for each other; for while the destinies of empire hurry us on, fortune can give no greater boon than discord among our foes."[249] This is a particularly important point to keep in mind when we arrive at our examination of the trans-national project in which the Pauline faction was engaged among the vanquished, and which found particularly poignant (and dangerous) expression in their collection for the poor in Jerusalem.

Finally, it is also worth emphasizing the prominence of the imperial cult in Palestine in the early first century CE. In 37 BCE, after three years of war and with the assistance of Roman legions, Herod the Great conquered Jerusalem and ended the Hasmonean Dynasty (this occurred after the assassination of Julius Caesar but prior to Augustus's consolidation of power). The Roman senate permitted Herod to adopt the title "king," and although he sided with Antony until Augustus (then Octavian) triumphed, Herod was able to convince Augustus of his utility and loyalty, and he became a favored client of the emperor.[250] Herod also became close friends with Marcus Vipsanius Agrippa, one of the central figures responsible for the rise and rule of Augustus (Agrippa also married Augustus's daughter and Herod Agrippa, who ruled Palestine when the Jesus movement was born, derived his name from this Marcus Vipsanius Agrippa). Due to these connections, along with his tendency to use ruthless force, his willingness to deploy foreign mercenaries against his own people (a standard tactic used within partnerships between Romans and local rulers), and his campaign to increase surveillance and control over the countryside through the building of fortresses (at Masada and Herodium) and military colonies (at Gaba and Bathyra), Herod was able to rule until his death in 4 BCE. During his reign, he initiated a campaign of urbanization, Romanization, and the spread of the imperial cult in Palestine that was "virtually unprecedented"

---

249. The reference to fear comes from Tacitus, *Agricola* 32. The quotation about discord is in *Germ.* 33.

250. See Horsley, *Religion and Empire*, 76; *Covenant Economics*, 83.

in the Roman Empire at that time.[251] Herod rebuilt the seaport of Caesarea for the city of Sebaste (both places were named after Caesar Augustus), and both projects were modeled off of Roman ideals about Hellenistic cities. Both centers were developed in order to facilitate trade and the shipping of tributes to Rome, and massive statues of both Caesar and the goddess Roma were built there.[252] A temple dedicated to the worship of Augustus and Roma was also built at Caesarea.[253] Herod also rebuilt the temple in Jerusalem in a Hellenistic style, offering daily sacrifices to the well-being of the emperor, and, notoriously, erected a Roman eagle, a symbol of his loyalty to Rome, above the temple gate.[254] He further pushed a Roman urbanization project in Jerusalem through other building projects, such as the Hippodrome he built for the staging of races and games.[255] These building projects as well as the staggering tributes Herod sent back to Caesar took a high toll upon the Judeans (many of whom had already been decimated over several generations of conflict and loss to foreign invaders), but they did secure for the Judeans, in a declaration from Augustus, the legal right to practice their own religious traditions and the legal permission to collect a temple tax from Judeans living in the diaspora.[256]

This close connection to the imperial center of power was maintained, to a lesser degree, by Herod's heirs. Claudius reaffirmed Augustus's declaration granting the Judeans their special religious, political, and economic exemptions due to his close friendship with Herod Agrippa I, who assisted Claudius in his rise to power and who, in return, was granted kingship in Judea.[257] Similarly, Herod Antipas (whom the Romans made tetrarch of Galilee and Perea, deciding it best to divide Herod's territories due to ongoing revolts and general unrest, especially after Herod's death) continued this process of urbanization, Romanization, and spreading of the imperial cult. The projects aided both the collection of taxes and the suppression of

---

251. Horsley, *Liberation of Christmas*, 42, 44–47; *Covenant Economics*, 83; *Jesus and the Powers*, 35; Sanders, *Paul*, 64.

252. See Horsley, *Jesus and the Powers*, 35; *Covenant Economics*, 84.

253. Winter, *Divine Honours for the Caesars*, 76–77.

254. Horsley, *Jesus and the Powers*, 32, 34–35; Winter, *Divine Honours for the Caesars*, 96–98.

255. See Horsley, *Covenant Economics*, 84.

256. Winter, *Divine Honours for the Caesars*, 99.

257. See Sanders, *Paul*, 85; Winter, *Divine Honours for the Caesars*, 101–5.

rebellions.[258] Initially, Antipas rebuilt the Galilean city of Sephoris (badly damaged or destroyed in a rebellion after Herod the Great died), renamed it Autocratis, the Imperial City (or, alternatively translated, "Belonging to the Emperor"), and made it a mainly Greek-speaking city (with prominent mosaics dedicated to both Helios and Dionysius) with its own Roman theater, palace, and bath houses.[259] Autocratis was only a few miles from Nazareth, and it is possible that if Joseph was an itinerant worker and carpenter and if Jesus learned Joseph's trade, they may have participated in the building boom that was taking place there at that time. However, between 18 and 20 CE, Antipas decided to build an entirely new, more magnificent, and more Roman city as his capital. He destroyed several villages on the shore of the sea of Galilee, just south of Magdala, and built the city of Tiberias (named after the ruling emperor, Tiberius).[260] As a result, the Sea of Galilee was also briefly renamed the Sea of Tiberius. Tiberias was designed to be a city within Galilee without Judean inhabitants. Antipas moved non-Judean inhabitants of the land there although, from a Judean perspective, the whole city was perpetually unclean because it was built on top of an ancient cemetery.[261] In this way, Antipas continued to demonstrate his devotion to the imperial family while showing the least respect possible for the beliefs of those indigenous to Palestine. Roman governors, when they became involved, only further encouraged this. Thus, for example, Pilate added a shrine dedicated to Tiberius to the temple in Caesarea where Augustus was already being worshiped.[262] Consequently, one should not think of the imperial cult as something possibly "out there" in other areas of the empire (where the Pauline faction may or may not have encountered it). It was all-pervasive, and it already had a central presence not only in Greek cities but also in Galilee at the time of Jesus.

258. Horsley, *Covenant Economics*, 87.

259. See Horsley, *Liberation of Christmas*, 78; Horsley and Silberman, *Message and the Kingdom*, 24.

260. See Horsley, *Covenant Economics*, 87; *Liberation of Christmas*, 77–78.

261. See Horsley and Silberman, *Message and the Kingdom*, 36–37.

262. See Winter, *Divine Honours for the Caesars*, 170–75.

Central Themes of the Imperial Cult
During the New Testament Period

What are the central themes of the imperial cult? Various scholars have attempted to summarize these in overlapping ways. For example, Wes Howard-Brook and Anthony Gwyther argue that the five foundational elements of the ideo-theology of Rome are empire, peace, victory, faith, and eternity.[263] Crossan and Borg see central imperial themes as structured in a movement from religion to war, to victory, to peace—or, more succinctly stated, "peace through victory."[264] Mikhail Tellbe focuses more upon the religio-political language of *Victoria, Concordia, Clementia, Pax, Fortuna, Felicitas,* and *Libertas.*[265] Virgil also proposes a succinct summary: "Remember, Roman, to rule the nations with your dominion—these will be your arts—to crown peace with rule of law, to spare the defeated, and to conquer the proud."[266] All of these are useful guides, but a detailed analysis of the several and often overlapping themes of this ideo-theology is beneficial before we draw any summary conclusions.

Predestination to Universal Rule

To begin with, the Romans believed that their rule over the nations was predestined and ordained by the gods—especially by Jupiter, the father of the gods, who displays a special investment in the Romans, partially at the behest of Venus (who, after all, is the mother of the Roman people given that she is said to have birthed Aeneas, who is said to have fathered the Romans after successfully fleeing Troy). Rome is predestined to rule all space for all time; for, just as it was the fate of the Greeks to bring culture to the world, so it is the fate of the Romans to bring the well-ordered rule of law.[267] By means of this belief, Rome attempted to convince conquered populations that her rule was divinely sanctioned and, therefore, that it was in the best interest of the vanquished—thereby making resistance both futile and

263. Howard-Brook and Gwyther, *Unveiling Empire,* 223–35.

264. Crossan and Borg, *First Paul,* 105–6.

265. Tellbe, *Paul between Synagogue and State,* 31.

266. Quoted in Ando, *Imperial Ideology,* 49.

267. See Brunt, "*Laus Imperii,*" 25–28; Carter, *Roman Empire,* 7, 83–85; *John and Empire,* 57–58; Jeffers, *Greco-Roman World,* 295; Zanker, *Power of Images,* 207; Crossan, *God and Empire,* 16–18; Gorman, *Apostle of the Crucified Lord,* 17–18; Peppard, *Son of God,* 70–71; Wengst, *Pax Romana,* 14–15.

impious.[268] Tacitus provides an excellent example of this belief in the words of warning a Roman general is reported to have said to an opposing force: "People must submit to the rule of their betters" because the very gods of the (soon to be defeated) rebels had willed that what was to be given or taken from the peoples of the earth lay solely in the hands of the Romans.[269]

This belief is also powerfully expressed in Virgil's *Aeneid* (written during the reign of Augustus), which in many ways functions in the Roman imperial ideology in the same way that the Judean Scriptures function in Pauline theology. The *Aeneid* is the justifying, founding narrative of Roman imperialism. Thus, within the *Aeneid*, several prominent characters and gods bear witness to Rome's predestination to universal rule. Venus states: "Surely from these Romans are to come . . . To rule the sea and all the lands about it, / According to [Jupiter's] promise . . . Your own children, whom you make heirs of heaven . . . Let those you favor / Conquer."[270] Similarly, Jupiter states:

> No need to be afraid, [Venus]. / Your children's destiny has not changed. / As promised you shall see Lavinium's walls / And take up, then, amid the stars of heaven / Great-souled Aeneas . . . for [the Romans] I set no limits, world or time / But make the gift of empire without end . . . Lords of the world, the toga-bearing Romans . . . The Trojan Caesar comes to circumscribe / Empire with Ocean, fame with heaven's stars. / Julius his name, from Iulus [the son of Aeneas] handed down: / All tranquil shall you take him heavenward / In time, laden with plunder from the East, / And he with you shall be invoked in prayer. / Wars at an end, harsh centuries then will soften, / Ancient Fides and Vesta, Quirinus/ With Brother Remus, will be lawgivers, / And grim with iron frames, the Gates of War/ Will then be shut.[271]

Apollo also bears witness: "[Rome] will rule the world's shores down the years, / Through generations of [Aeneas's] children's children."[272] Therefore,

---

268. See Carter, "Vulnerable Power," 462–63; Brunt, "*Laus Imperii*," 29.

269. Tacitus, *Annals* 13.56. Tacitus expresses a similar sentiment, more vaguely elsewhere: "Everything favours the conqueror, everything is adverse to the vanquished" (*Agricola* 33).

270. Virgil, *Aeneid* 1.319, 320–21, 339; 10.57–58.

271. Virgil, *Aeneid* 1.347–51, 374–75, 385–95.

272. Virgil, *Aeneid* 7.134–35.

Virgil states that Rome will govern the earth for "as far on his rounds / The Sun looks down on Ocean, East or West."[273]

The Gospel of Roman Peace, Salvation, and Liberty

The next prominent thematic cluster within the ideo-theology of Rome is the gospel of Roman peace and salvation. Within the context of Roman propaganda, the term *euangelion* was used as a political term, referring to the ways in which Augustus and his heirs accomplished and maintained the salvation and peace of the world.[274] In this context, the establishment of peace was inextricably aligned with Rome's military prowess and ability to triumph over all others.[275] This was especially true after the decimation and scandal wrought by the Roman civil wars. In the wake of those wars, the Romans came to believe that only a supreme military commander would be able to ensure peace.[276] Thus, as Kahl observes, pre-existing Roman reverence for victory is translated into the moral discourse of salvation.[277] This combination of themes finds a concise embodiment in the Roman representations of Mars, who is portrayed as both a mighty warrior and as the guardian of peace.[278] However, these themes also came to be embodied within the emperors.

Initially, it was Julius Caesar who attempted to end the civil wars and create peace by consolidating power. Thus, Plutarch says: "The Romans inclining to Caesar's prosperity, and taking the bit in the mouth, supposing that to be ruled by one man alone, it would be a good means for them to take breath a little, after so many troubles and miseries as they had abidden in these civil wars, they chose him perpetual dictator."[279] However, Caesar misjudged the timing of this move and the tactics necessary to accomplish

---

273. Virgil, *Aeneid* 7.130–31. Similar sentiments about the illustrious predestination of both Rome and the Roman emperors are expressed in the writings of Horace, although Horace sometimes sees fate (rather than the gods) as that which ordained Rome rule. See, for example, *Odes* 1.12.46–61; 1.35.9–16; 2.13.17–20; 4.4.73–76.

274. See Georgi, *Theocracy*, 83–85; Jennings, *Outlaw Justice*, 18.

275. See Crossan and Reed, *In Search of Paul*, 70–72, 100; Wengst, *Pax Romana*, 8–11.

276. See Lohse, *New Testament Environment*, 198–99.

277. See Kahl, *Galatians Re-Imagined*, 118.

278. See Zanker, *Power of Images*, 200–201.

279. Plutarch, *Julius Caesar* 57.

it. He overreached and was assassinated. His peace was considered a fleeting and false one.

Consequently, after first triumphing over those who assassinated Julius Caesar and then triumphing over his peers (as well as over foreign enemies), Augustus was hailed as the longed-for, peace-bringing savior. Augustus became the savior of the world, the prince of peace, who had redeemed (i.e., emancipated) Rome from her bondage to a world defined by the loss, violence, and scarcity that were said to be the results of their sins, so that the proper order of the cosmos (and the nations) could be restored.[280] This Augustan peace was then celebrated widely, represented in everything from coins, to arches, to the Altar of Augustan Peace established by the senate in Rome.[281] Augustus declared that peace ruled throughout the entire world by closing the gates of the temple of Janus three times during his reign—an act that had only been accomplished twice before since the founding of Rome.[282] The poetry of the time also reflects this theme. Horace, for example, regularly praises Augustus as the savior and guardian of peace for all peoples.[283] The Roman longing for this salvation and its accomplishment in the person of Augustus was also well captured in Virgil's *Georgics*. He writes:

> O Gods of our Fathers, native Gods, Romulus, Vesta
>
> Who mothers our Tucan Tiber and the Roman Palatine.
>
> At least allow our young prince [Augustus] to rescue this shipwrecked era!
>
> Long enough now have we
>
> paid in our blood . . .
>
> Long now has the court of heaven begrudged you to us, Caesar . . .
>
> For Right and Wrong are confused here, there's so much war in the world.
>
> Evil has many faces, the plough so little,
>
> Honor, the labourers are taken, the fields untended,
>
> And the curving sickle is beaten into the sword that yields not.
>
> There the East is in arms . . .

280. Crossan, *God and Empire*, 28; Crossan and Reed, *In Search of Paul*, 102, 135; Kautsky, *Foundations of Christianity*, 97.

281. See Koester, *History, Culture, and Religion*, 295; Augustus, *Res Gestae* 12.2; Tacitus, *Annals* 1.1.

282. See Keresztes, *From Herod the Great*, 6; Augustus, *Res Gestae* 13.1; Suetonius, *Twelve Caesars*, 63.

283. See, for example, Horace, *Odes* 1.2.1–52; 1.35.29–30; 4.2.41–44; 4.5.1–2; Horace, *Epistles* 2.1.15.

> Neighbour cities, breaking their treaties, attack each other:
> The wicked War-god runs amok throughout the world.[284]

Here, we get a glimpse of the great relief felt by the Roman people when the civil wars ended, and we gain a sense of why others devastated by the wars were susceptible to the ideo-theology of the empire.

Peace, apart from ending bloodshed, brought freedom. Thus, Augustus claims to have "successfully championed the liberty of the republic when it was oppressed by the tyranny of a faction."[285] But freedom needed to be protected—by the emperors in Rome and by Roman imperial forces throughout the empire.[286] Peace is secured and it must remain secure. The ability to keep peace and maintain security (both at home and at the boundaries of the empire) go hand-in-hand.[287] This is then the message given to the local elites in territories conquered by the Romans: "Let the evidence ... teach you not to prefer rebellion with ruin to obedience with security."[288]

This image of the emperor as the savior who brings a liberating peace is not limited to Augustus. It is deliberately adopted by all of his heirs. Some were more successful at utilizing it than others. Claudius, for example, is referred to as the "savior of all mankind."[289] But Caligula is said to have complained about the peace and prosperity of his own reign because he felt that they would lead to him being "wholly forgotten," so "he often prayed for a great military catastrophe, or a famine, plague, fire, or at least an earthquake."[290] While the Pauline faction was active, Nero was venerated as "savior of the world" and as one who would restore peace and prosperity.[291] Like Augustus, Nero closed the gates of Janus to signal that "all war was at an end."[292] Thus, during his early optimism about Nero, Seneca declares

---

284. Virgil, *Georgics* 1.498–511.

285. Augustus, *Res Gestae* 1.1. Of course, as Wengst notes, this was a freedom enjoyed only by Rome and her allies (*Pax Romana*, 22–24).

286. See Judge, *Social Distinctive of the Christians*, 12–13.

287. See Wengst, *Pax Romana*, 8, 17–21.

288. Tacitus quoted in Ando, *Imperial Ideology*, 66. Ando describes the logic of this as follows: "If the stability of Rome determined the health and wealth of her subjects, they ought not to rebel, if only for their own sake."

289. Winter, *Divine Honours, for the Caesars*, 71–72.

290. Suetonius, *Twelve Caesars*, 166.

291. See Deissmann, *Light from the Ancient East*, 364.

292. Suetonius, *Twelve Caesars*, 217.

that the peace of all is linked to the well-being of Nero.[293] Not only that, but Seneca asserts that Nero's rule is defined by "a deep and swelling sense of peace, and justice set above all injustice."[294]

Because of this, any who opposed Rome were understood to be enemies of peace. Thus, in a textbook example of political doublespeak, Tacitus describes those who revolt as those "who dreaded peace with us."[295] However, more generally, revolutionaries were considered immoral, subhuman degenerates. As Nero observes in a play penned by Seneca:

> Now in its pride the monstrous mob, ungrateful, and corrupted by the good gifts of these beneficent times, cannot abide our gentle rule; hates peace, and ever discontented, now defiant, now reckless, rushes onward to its doom. It must be tamed by suffering, must be held at all times under an oppressive yoke; no other way will teach it to beware.[296]

War, Victory, and Justice

Victory is also significant within Rome's theopolitical vision. It was only after the rise of Augustus that Victory began to be venerated as a god (especially by soldiers).[297] The numerous victories of Augustus (or his generals, whose victories would be credited to Augustus) were used as the foundation for some claims made regarding his exceptional status. Victory became especially associated with Augustus, and Augustus himself officially made Victory a deity deserving special honors from the senate.[298] By closing the gates of Janus more than any of his predecessors, Augustus is claiming to be the most victorious Roman in history.[299] This alone elevates Augustus into a novel and unheard-of intimacy with the gods.[300] Several subsequent emperors continue to claim victories (even more so through their generals), but they also deepen the ideo-theology of Augustan Victory with Gaius,

293. Seneca, *De clementia* 1.4.

294. Seneca, *De clementia* 1.1.

295. Although he also notes that some who "cast off peace" did so not because of this lack of character but because of Roman rapacity; Tacitus, *Annals* 12.33; 4.72, respectively.

296. Seneca, *Octavia* 837–45 (line breaks removed).

297. See Ando, *Imperial Ideology*, 278–79.

298. See Ando, *Imperial Ideology*, 30, 279–81, 300–301.

299. Ando, *Imperial Ideology*, 283.

300. Ando, *Imperial Ideology*, 284–86.

Claudius, and Nero, all minting coins bearing the legend "VICTORIA AUGUSTI."[301]

However, Victory was also related to salvation. The Romans believed that their victory over all others was the means by which divine Justice was spread throughout the world and, itself, was granted to the Romans because of their especially pious and just way of living. So Virgil writes: "Know that our Latins come of Saturn's race, that we are just—not by constraint or laws, but by our choice and habit of our ancient god."[302] Or, as Horace writes: "You rule, Roman, because you hold yourself inferior to the gods; from them all things begin; to them ascribe every outcome."[303] In this way, Roman wars become what Crossan and Reed refer to as a "militaristic evangelism."[304] Many of those vanquished by Rome—particularly those situated among the local elite, willing to ally with Rome, but even those who suffered the most from the defeat—would find it difficult to refute the claim that Roman victory was proof that the Romans were favored by the gods.[305]

Victory was also related to honor and the glorification of the Caesars in their many triumphs. References throughout the Roman literature—from Virgil to Suetonius, to Tacitus, to Horace—are too many to mention here. Sometimes within the Roman literature, one gets a glimpse of this as a simple affirmation of technical military superiority (related more to one's weapons and technology than one's morals). Thus, in his *Eclogues*, Virgil writes: "Poems stand no more chance, when the claims of soldiers are involved, than do the prophetic doves if an eagle swoops upon them."[306] The stark brutality of conquest is also sometimes portrayed. For example, Suetonius states that Julius Caesar—during his ascent to power—had a

301. Ando, *Imperial Ideology*, 290–92. Subsequently, after Nero's fall, there is a frenzied rush of competitors wanting to show themselves as the most victorious in order to become the emperor (Ando, *Imperial Ideology*, 293–94).

302. Virgil, *Aeneid* 7.268–71. I have altered the text—the line breaks and capitalization—to read as prose instead of as poetry. This is also why Juvenal sees justice as the sister of traditional Roman morality (*Satires* 6.20–21).

303. Horace, *Odes* 3.6.5–6, quoted in Ando, *Imperial Ideology*, 283.

304. See Crossan and Reed, *In Search of Paul*, 57. Brunt also notes the ways in which Roman racism factored into this. The Romans perceived of themselves as masters governing over slaves, which then justified the imperialistic and exploitative way in which they ruled over the empire. See Brunt, "*Laus Imperii*," 31–35.

305. See Ando, *Imperial Ideology*, 337.

306. Virgil, *Eclogues* 9.11–13 (text modified from poetry to prose).

dream that he was raping his mother, but this dream was interpreted in a positive light, taken as a reference to the conquest of all the world (given that the world is the universal mother and given that rape was a standard tool used by Roman fathers and masters to assert their *postestas* and *autoritas*).[307]

However, despite such candid moments, the Romans prefer to portray themselves as going to war reluctantly—compelled to do so because of the impiety or bad faith of others. Thus, Petronius ascribes the following words to Julius Caesar: "Mars summons me to war / an unwilling warrior . . . Yet my case is already won."[308] Similarly, Virgil ascribes a similar motive to Aeneas, who is compelled to go to war because others "insist on war" and "break treaties."[309]

Therefore, the Romans believed it was their destiny to bring justice as a gift to the world—even if this "justice" was something that favored the elites and damned the less privileged to servitude, suffering, dispossession, and death.[310] Thus, Virgil describes Augustus's triumphs in this way: "Great Caesar fired his lightnings and conquered by deep Euphrates and gave justice to docile peoples, winning his way to the Immortals."[311] Similarly, Augustus describes his own conquests in this language:

> I extended the territory of all those provinces of the Roman people on whose lands borders lay not subject to our government. I *brought peace* to the Gallic and Spanish provinces as well as to Germany. . . . I secured the pacification of the Alps . . . yet *without waging an unjust war* on any people.[312]

---

307. Suetonius, *Twelve Caesars*, 13.

308. Petronius, *Satyricon* 136. The gloating of the victor also comes through in Cicero's *In Verrem* 2.5.66: "There is nothing sweeter than victory, and there is no more definite proof of victory than seeing the people you have many times been afraid of being led in chains to their execution."

309. Virgil, *Aeneid* 8.733–34. See also Aeneas's speech in 11.148–59. Thus, Aeneas is renowned for being a king who is more just than any other (1.739).

310. See Carter, *John and Empire*, 292–93; Elliott, *Arrogance of Nations*, 59; Brunt, "*Laus Imperii*," 25.

311. Virgil, *Georgics* 4.559–62 (text modified from poetry to prose). Augustus is here being likened to Jupiter and Jupiter's initial conquest over the forces of chaos is now being repeated in Augustus's conquest of the known world.

312. Augustus, *Res Gestae* 26.1–31 (emphasis added). Suetonius also refers to imperial conquests as "pacifying" troublesome tribes (see, for example, *Twelve Caesars*, 62) and confirms the picture of Augustus as a conscientious and assiduous administrator of justice (*Twelve Caesars*, 70–71). What is notably missing from the literature of the

Thus, we see war described as "bringing peace" and conquest described as "pacification," all of which is accomplished in a "just" manner.[313] This is the type of justice that Horace accurately describes as "Justice, strong as death!"[314] Here the just are the triumphant, whose very triumph affirms their moral greatness and piety. Any who are defeated and suffering are equally confirmed as unjust, impious, and immoral. It is these people who must fear the just laws of the empire—even after conquest—for, as the Romans emphasized, it is never a question of *if* vengeance and repayment will be enacted against the law-breakers but only of *when*.[315] "Justice" is that which is used to sustain the status quo of empire (thus, in a more candid moment, Tacitus observes that "justice" is simply whatever those with power determine it to be).[316] In this context, the "good man," according to Horace, is one who "observes the decrees of the senate, the laws and rules of justice" and who also ensures the safety of private property.[317] Furthermore, the "good man" embodied by the Caesars must sometimes

Augustan era is any mention of the past defeats Augustus experienced. For example, at the battle of Philippi, Brutus routed the troops of Caesar, captured his camp, and Augustus (then Octavian) barely escaped with his life—Philippi was only won because of Antony's success; Caesar was too sick to take an active part in commanding his wing and returned to Rome after the battle with the expectation that he was dying from his illness (see Plutarch, *Antony*, 22–23; *Brutus*, 41–42). Also notably absent from the ideology of victory that surrounded Augustus and his heirs are the words ascribed to Brutus shortly before his death: "They [Antony and Octavian] being naughty and unjust men, have slain good men, to usurp tyrannical power not pertaining to them" (*Brutus*, 52). Note also the words Seneca writes of the victories of Augustus during the civil war: "Then how much Roman blood was Rome to see / Poured out from her so often wounded body! / How many lives did your divine Augustus, / Whose virtues won his way to heaven, destroy!" (*Octavia* 512–15).

313. One cannot help but be reminded of similar remarks made by recent presidents of the United States. Thus, as noted above, George W. Bush can say: "I just want you to know that, when we talk about war, we're really talking about peace." Similarly, Barack Obama can talk about the end of the "combat mission" in Iraq while leaving thousands of troops actively present in Iraq as "Advise and Assist" Brigades—as if this somehow fulfills his campaign promise to end the war in Iraq!

314. Horace, *Odes* 2.17.16.

315. See Horace, *Odes* 3.3.30–32; *Epodes* 5.88.

316. Thus, while observing the wars for power that occurred between German tribes, he writes: "Where the strong hand decides, moderation and justice are terms applied only to the more powerful; and so the Cherusci, ever reputed good and just, are now called cowards and fools" (Tacitus, *Germ.* 36).

317. Horace, *Epistles* 1.16.3. This connection of "justice" to the defense of private property is also a strong theme in our culture.

even exhibit a form of justice that contradicts the fundamental democratic values of the republic. As Horace also observes: "The man that's just and resolute of mood / No craze of people's perverse vote can shake."[318] Thus, it is justice that requires the imposition of the imperial state of exception which trumps not only the values of foreigners but also, at times, the central values of Rome.

Piety

All of these things—predestination, universal rule, peace, salvation, war, victory, and justice—were connected to Roman piety. The Romans believed that they were ordained to rule because they were the most pious people on earth.[319] Romulus, after his *apotheosis*, is reported to have prophesied that the Romans would rule the earth because of their faithful devotion to the gods.[320] This is true even of the worship of members of the pantheon of the gods who were originally enemies of the Roman people. For example, Jove, the wife of Jupiter, was originally an enemy of Aeneas due to her enmity with Venus. But the Romans win her favor. As Virgil claims, Rome will "out do men and gods in its devotion, you shall see—and no nation on earth will honor and worship [Jove] so faithfully."[321] The great Roman predecessors to the Caesars—men like Aeneas and Romulus—were all noted for their piety.[322] Because of this, Rome was elected to rule, was victorious in her conquests, understood justice better than all others, and was ordained to bring universal peace and salvation. No other people were as faithfully devoted to the gods. The peace and security brought by Rome (the *pax*

318. Horace, *Odes* 3.3.1–2.

319. See Koester, *History, Culture, and Religion*, 348; Wengst, *Pax Romana*, 46–51; Crossan and Reed, *In Search of Paul*, 58; Maier, *Picturing Paul in Empire*, 9.

320. Plutarch, *Romulus* 28.

321. Virgil, *Aeneid* 12.1137–40 (text modified from poetry to prose).

322. On Romulus and his purported descent from Mars, see, for example, Plutarch, *Romulus* 4, 7. Plutarch has a great way of observing the stories that have accumulated around historical personages but of also offering more skeptical alternatives. Thus, with Romulus and Remus he mentions the story of how a virgin became pregnant with the children of Mars—the god of war—but he also mentions that this virgin may actually have been raped by her uncle. Similarly, with the famous story of the twins sucking from a she-wolf, Plutarch notes that the Latin word for female wolves—*lupas*—is the same word that was used for women who were promiscuous and he notes that the wife of the servant, who was charged to dispose of the infants, was one such woman and that this couple may have actually raised the children.

Romana) was seen as the same thing as the peace and security brought by the gods (the *pax deorum*).[323] As Cicero writes:

> On our side fights decency, on theirs depravity; on ours modesty, on theirs perversion; on ours honesty, on theirs deceit; on ours duty, on theirs crime; on ours steadfastness, on theirs hysteria; on ours honor, on theirs disgrace; on ours self-restraint, on theirs self-indulgence; on ours justice, self-control, courage, prudence, and all the virtues, fighting against injustice, extravagance, sloth, recklessness, and all the vices; finally, wealth is fighting against poverty, good principles against bad, reason against madness, and well-grounded confidence against absolute despair.[324]

The Roman civil wars that preceded the rise of Augustus were, therefore, understood by the Romans to be a consequence of the collapse of Roman piety and morality.[325] This caused a moral and theological crisis for the Roman people. Lucan well expresses the horror the Romans felt about the impious devastation wrought by the civil wars, which he describes as "legality conferred on crime" or "a mighty people attacking its own guts with victorious sword-hand," and he says were caused by "universal guilt" and absolute "madness."[326] The surrender of morals to the love of wealth is mentioned as a particularly prominent cause of the strife.[327] Horace concurs, arguing that the number of Roman graves proves the impiety of the civil war.[328] As they experienced the civil wars, Romans wondered how cosmic order could be renewed, how humans could be held accountable for their actions while also being redeemed (i.e., emancipated), and who might be able to accomplish this.[329]

Consequently, as he came to be acclaimed as the triumphant savior and bringer of peace, Augustus was also hailed as the agent who would redeem Rome and restore piety. As Horace writes:

---

323. Tellbe, *Paul between Synagogue and State*, 31, 34–35. See also Crossan and Borg, *First Paul*, 98; Maier, *Picturing Paul in Empire*, 72–73.

324. Cicero, *In Catilinam* 2.25.

325. See Zanker, *Power of Images*, 156.

326. Lucan, *Civil War* 1.1–14; see also 1.666–69; 2.286. Lucan describes the ways in which these wars not only effected people but also disordered the cosmos and disrupted natural processes (*Civil War* 5.630–36; 6.461–91; 7.617–20).

327. Lucan, *Civil War* 1.158–82.

328. Horace, *Odes* 2.1.30. See also Horace, *Epodes* 7.1–20.

329. See Kee, *Beginnings of Christianity*, 477. Kee notes that the Judeans were also asking these questions while they suffering under Roman rule.

Thy father's crimes shalt thou, the guiltless child [Augustus], repay,
O Roman, until thou restore the fanes and shrines now toppling
o'er, and statues smoke-defiled.

Only while thou before the gods bend low, can'st thou be strong.
Seek first and last their aid, whate'er the task. Ignored, they've laid
on Italy many a woe.[330]

Augustus worked especially hard to connect himself to piety and morality.[331] While his final rival, Mark Antony, came to associate himself with
Dionysus—a god associated with foreigners and festive debaucheries—Augustus associated himself closely with Apollo—a god known for his virtue,
discipline, morality, and moderation.[332] The piety Augustus adopted and
sought to inspire others to adopt was expressed in three prominent ways.[333]
First, Augustus engaged in a sustained campaign to rebuild temples, restore
priesthoods, and bring ancient rituals back into practice. While doing so,
he also ensured that only members of the imperial family were permitted
to build temples in Rome.[334] Thus, in the *Res Gestae*, he speaks of restoring
all the temples that were in disrepair in Rome, building more than twenty
new temples, and returning the spoils taken from temples that Antony had
looted throughout Asia.[335] Second, Augustus used the law and legal reforms

330. Horace, *Odes* 3.6.1–8.

331. See Beacham, "Emperor as Impresario," 162; Lietzmann, *Beginnings of the Christian Church*, 155; Zanker, *Power of Images*, 102–10.

332. Antony's family line was reputed to have descended from Hercules, and he deliberately modeled himself, in dress and action, after Hercules. Only later, after moving to
Asia and becoming entwined with Cleopatra, did he actively portray himself as Bacchus
and her as Venus (Plutarch, *Antony* 4, 24, 26,53, 60). Plutarch also heavily documents the
reports of Antony's debaucheries and even blames his activities in this regard—as a close
ally of Julius Caesar—for being one of the primary reasons why Caesar was overthrown
(Plutarch, *Antony* 6, 9, 21, 24, 25. See Beacham, "Emperor as Impresario," 157–58; Jewett, *Romans*, 48; Zanker, *Power of Images*, 44–65, 86). Zanker also notes how Augustus
dropped the direct comparison of himself to Apollo directly after the civil war ended, lest
others thought he was overreaching and decided to do to him what had been done to his
adoptive father (*Power of Images*, 90–91).

333. Tenney notes that uniting Rome under the umbrella of traditional Roman religion was a useful way of creating solidarity in a state that had been divided (*New Testament Times*, 108).

334. See Crossan and Reed, *In Search of Paul*, 83.

335. Augustus, *Res Gestae*, 19.1–21.3; 24.1–2. See also Suetonius, *Twelve Caesars*,
55. On the restoration of ancient religious rites—or, to use the words of Augustus, the
"exemplary practices of our ancestors"—see Augustus, *Res Gestae* 8.5. See also Suetonius,

in order to encourage a return to traditional morality.[336] Again, in the *Res Gestae*, he observes how the senate appointed him to be "supervisor of laws and morals without colleague and with supreme power" (elsewhere, Augustus states that he "would not accept any office inconsistent with the custom of our ancestors," but this demonstrates otherwise).[337] Thus, Suetonius notes: "The existing laws Augustus revised, and the new ones that he enacted, dealt among other matters, with extravagance, adultery, unchastity, bribery, and the encouragement of marriage in the Senatorial and Equestrian Orders."[338] Here, we see the overlapping of piety with imperial legal power and family values.[339] Third, Augustus also sought to establish himself, personally, as the shining example of piety. Both his restoration of traditional buildings and rituals as well as his legal moral reforms were a part of this, but he also came to hold all of the most prestigious religious offices. As the *princeps*—the first among equals—Augustus was a member of the four most important colleges of priests in Rome and he also became the *pontifex maximus*.[340] Thus, Augustus states: "I have been *princeps senates* for forty years. I am *pontifex maximus, augur, quindecimvir sacris faciundis, septemvir epulonum, frater arvalis, sodalist Titius, fetialis*."[341] The *princeps* was the first member of the senate called upon to share his opinion, the *pontifex maximus* presided over all the state cults in general, the *augures* interpreted signs from the gods, the *quindecimviri* supervised the foreign

---

Twelve Caesars, 69. Suetonius also notes that Claudius sought to continue the revival of ancient religious rituals (*Twelve Caesars*, 196).

336. See Crossan and Reed, *In Search of Paul*, 95; Eder, "Augustus and the Power," 14, 28; Zanker, *Power of Images*, 157. I have already noted the laws Augustus passed in relation to the family unit.

337. Augustus, *Res Gestae* 6.1.

338. Suetonius, *Twelve Caesars*, 71. Tiberius continues to follow the legal moral reforms established by Augustus and re-installs traditional punishments against married women caught behaving improperly (see Suetonius, *Twelve Caesars*, 128–29). Although Suetonius also notes that Tiberius breached the traditional family values and acted impiously (*Twelve Caesars*, 134–36, 144). Most of the later Caesars fail to live up to the standard of family values set by Augustus (on Caligula, see Suetonius, *Twelve Caesars*, 161–63; on Claudius, 200; on Nero, 227, 230).

339. Despite his dedication to this task, Tacitus notes that the changes Augustus desired in this regard mostly did not occur, and the family-oriented laws, while initially further developed by Tiberius, were dropped by later emperors and the senate (see *Annals* 2.99; 3.24–25, 28, 54).

340. See Zanker, *Power of Images*, 126–27, 159.

341. Augustus, *Res Gestae* 7.2–3.

cults that had been adopted in Rome, the *septemviri epulonum* held public banquets in honor of the gods, the *festiales* were concerned with making treaties and declaring war, and Augustus is unique in belonging to all of these colleges (the most eminent Romans in the republic seldom held offices in more than one of these priesthoods).

No wonder, then, that Augustus was widely recognized for his piety. In the sculptures of him distributed throughout the empire, he is commonly portrayed wearing his toga as a hood over his head, a Roman mark of piety. Furthermore, even the name "Augustus" was a sacred title granted to him by the senate (he was born with the name Gaius Octavius Thurinus). In a statement that is not entirely honest, Augustus asserts that he "transferred the republic from [his] power to the dominion of the senate and the people of Rome," and for this he was named Augustus, had the door posts of his house wreathed with bay leaves (a sign of victory) and mounted with a civic crown (for conspicuous bravery, usually saving the lives of others who are in danger), and had an inscribed golden shield publicly displayed in his honor, testifying to his "courage, clemency, justice, and piety."[342] The name Augustus carries multiple religious nuances. It refers to precious or sacred things, it also refers to splendor and influence, and it is connected to augury. This name also connects Augustus to Romulus, the founder of Rome, who was known for his piety (in fact, when the senate was debating as to what honorific name they might give to Octavian Caesar, they also considered calling him Romulus, but it was decided that Augustus was a greater honor).[343] Thus, by means of this multifaceted approach, Augustus was able to connect imperial power to the utmost devotion to the gods. The emperor became not only the most powerful man on earth but also the most pious. Consequently, any who challenged the emperors would be considered supreme examples of impiety.

Mercy

Connected to the themes of just war and pious devotion to the gods is the theme of mercy or clemency exhibited by Rome—especially by the emperors—towards others, notably the vanquished. Extending mercy to the

342. Augustus, *Res Gestae* 34.1–2.

343. See Suetonius, *Twelve Caesars*, 55. However, the connection between Augustus and Romulus was also pursued within the imperial Roman ideo-theology. See Scheid, "Augustus and Roman Religion," 184–86.

conquered was a way of expanding the glory of one's victory while also laying claim to moral high ground.[344] Already, even before the rise of the principate, we see this tactic being practiced by the likes of Julius Caesar and Brutus. As Caesar is reported to have said: "The Xanthians despised my goodwill, have made their country a grave of despair: and the Patareians that put themselves into my protection, have lost no jot of their liberty."[345] Augustus, following in the footsteps of his adoptive father, states the following: "As victor I spared the lives of all citizens who asked for mercy. When foreign peoples could safely be pardoned I preferred to preserve rather than exterminate them."[346] Suetonius affirms this:

> Augustus never wantonly invaded any country, and felt no tempta-
> tion to increase the boundaries of Empire or enhance his military
> glory; indeed, he made certain barbarian chieftains swear in the
> Temple of Avenging Mars that they would faithfully keep the peace
> for which they sued. . . . Even when tribes rebelled frequently or
> showed particularly ill-faith, Augustus's most severe punishment
> was to sell as slaves the prisoners he took, ordering them to be kept
> at some distance from their own country and not to be freed until
> thirty years had elapsed. Such was his reputation for courage and
> clemency that the very Indians and Scythians . . . voluntarily sent
> ambassadors to Rome, pleading for his friendship and that of his
> people. . . . There are numerous positive proofs of Augustus's clem-
> ency and considerate behavior. To supply a full list of the political
> enemies whom he pardoned and allowed to hold high government
> office would be tedious.[347]

Tiberius continues the trajectory established by Augustus while further deepening the imperial monopoly on clemency. He abolished a tradition as old as Rome herself, when he decided that imperial judgments were weight-ier than the forms of sanctuary that were previously granted to fugitives at

344. See Elliott, *Arrogance of Nations*, 87–91.

345. Plutarch, *Brutus*, 2. On Julius Caesar, see, for example, Plutarch, *Julius Caesar*, 15, 26.

346. Augustus, *Res Gestae* 3.1–2.

347. Suetonius, *Twelve Caesars*, 62–63, 81. Here Augustus is following the moral example set by his adoptive father, Julius Caesar. During the civil wars, Suetonius claims that Caesar was known for his "wonderful restraint and clemency"; whereas "Pompey declared that all who were not actively with him were against him and would be treated as public enemies, Caesar announced that all who were not actively against him were with him" (Suetonius, *Twelve Caesars*, 41). Interestingly, both of these claims are attrib-uted to Jesus at different times (cf. Matt 12:30; Luke 11:23; Mark 9:40).

temples and holy places throughout the empire.[348] In this and other actions, as Tacitus notes, Tiberius continues the practice of meting out "dreadful punishment" to those who persist in resistance but showing mercy to those who surrender.[349] Claudius, too, follows in this trajectory, and when speaking to a defeated enemy, he observes that this person deserves "an extreme and exemplary penalty" but decides to show mercy, for "it had been the principle of [Claudius's] ancestors to show as much forbearance to a suppliant as they showed persistence against a foe."[350] Therefore, during the reign of Nero, a foreign ally of Rome is reported to observe that "we shall find that subjection to Rome is lighter for those who surrender than for the conquered."[351] Consequently, Horace (during the reign of Augustus) may sing the praise of Rome by claiming she is first in war but, when war is done, also the first to spare the conquered.[352] Petronius (during the reign of Nero) makes a similar observation: "Trample on the cravens; Pride makes its own law. . . . And the victor is merciful when the fight is ended."[353]

The corollary to this point is that mercy is only for the deserving and is not to be dispensed to all. As Cicero says, "Foreign enemies either are crushed and turned into subjects or are admitted and consider themselves bound by ties of gratitude."[354] Tacitus observes that it is "the stubbornness of inferiors which lessens the clemency of our ruler," meaning that any who persist in resisting Rome are less moral, noble, and pious and therefore deserving of punishment.[355] Similarly, in a treatise written for Nero, Seneca argues it is important not to practice mercy without first considering all other factors:

> Pardon should not be exercised in an unthinking way; for once the
> distinction between bad men and good is removed, what follows

348. See Suetonius, *Twelve Caesars*, 130. On the dating of the tradition back to the founding of Rome—which was originally populated by fugitives from other nations—see Plutarch, *Romulus* 9. The early triumphs of Romulus over the Sabines, which assured Rome's ongoing existence when she was first founded, are also connected to the piety of Romulus. On more than one occasion, victory is connected to Romulus's devotion to Jupiter. See Plutarch, *Romulus* 16–17.

349. Tacitus, *Annals* 2.10.

350. Tacitus, *Annals* 12.20.

351. Tacitus, *Annals* 15.1.

352. Horace, *Carmen Saeculare* 51–52.

353. Petronius, *Satyricon* 38.

354. Cicero, *In Catilinam* 4.22.

355. Tacitus, *Annals* 16.28.

is confusion and the outbreak of vice; accordingly a wise restraint
should be shown, such as is capable of distinguishing between cur-
able characters and ones past hope. The mercy we exercise ought
not to be indiscriminate and for all and sundry but it should not
be withheld completely; for pardoning all involves no less cruelty
than pardoning none.[356]

Apart from the moral high ground claimed in the language of those
who exercise clemency, mercy was a strategy selectively employed to
benefit the empire, for, as Tacitus observes: "Little is gained by conquest
if followed by oppression."[357] The Romans had learned that overly violent
and rapacious practices, when not tempered by other dynamics, only bred
further resistance and rebellion, creating desperate people willing to lose
everything and die in their fight against Rome.[358] Showing mercy had both
economic and political benefits. Economically, empires depend upon finan-
cially exploiting conquered territories. Clemency is a useful tool because, as
Peter Brunt observes, the dead pay no taxes.[359] Politically, showing mercy
permitted Augustus to forge an international network indebted to the Roman imperial family. Furthermore, he was savvy enough to intertwine various conflicted parties within this network. Thus, Suetonius observes:

> [Augustus] nearly always restored the kingdoms which he had
> conquered to their defeated dynasties, rarely combining them
> with others, and followed a policy of linking together his royal al-
> lies by mutual ties of friendship or intermarriage, which he was
> never slow to propose. Nor did he treat them otherwise than as
> imperial functionaries, showing them all consideration and find-
> ing guardians for those who were not yet old enough to rule, until
> they came of age—and for those who suffered from mental illness,
> until they recovered. He also brought up many of their children
> with his own, and gave them the same education.[360]

Within Roman imperialism, this was to be the one and only international
network that operated in an economic and political manner. It is worth
emphasizing this now for as we will see in volume 3, Paul and his coworkers were developing an alternative economic and political network that

356. Seneca, *De clementia* 1.2.
357. Tacitus, *Agricola* 19.
358. See Seneca, *De clementia* 1.12, 16–17, 23.
359. Brunt, "*Laus Imperii*," 29.
360. Suetonius, *Twelve Caesars*, 79–80.

transcended established political and ethnic boundaries. Such a transnational entity would be seen as a threat to the imperial system established by Augustus.

Finally, it is also worth observing that by the time of Nero, the emperor was considered the best and most natural person suited to the practice of mercy (although the roots of this belief go back at least as far as Julius Caesar: the Roman people built a Temple of Clemency dedicated to him).[361] Seneca writes to Nero that the practice of mercy is essentially an exercise of justice that is greater than the letter of the law, and so those who practice it become akin to the gods.[362] Therefore, he observes that "of all men mercy becomes none so well as a king or an emperor."[363] He goes on to say that saving a life is "the special privilege of the loftiest rank, which never has greater claim on admiration than when it has the good fortune to have the same power as the gods. . . . Accordingly, let an emperor appropriate to himself the spirit of the gods."[364] Furthermore, in his specific remarks to Nero, Seneca observes that Augustus was famous, and was made divine (in part), because of the mercy he demonstrated to others—but Nero is called even greater than Augustus in this practice because he had not (at this point) spilled the blood of his countrymen.[365] To be called greater than Augustus, as we shall see, is to be called the greatest of the gods.

The Rule of Law

The practice of mercy is connected to the broader Roman emphasis upon the rule of law. Roman law was structured in order to benefit the most powerful members of society—it was a tool employed to maintain the (imbalanced) order and trajectory of the status quo. The common people were generally excluded from legal protection and dealt with on a case-by-case basis by local magistrates (usually in order to receive some form of corporal punishment).[366] Therefore, those whom Rome fights and conquers are portrayed as lawless barbarians, whereas Rome is portrayed as actively

---

361. Plutarch, *Julius Caesar* 57.

362. Seneca, *De clementia* 1.26; 2.3–7.

363. Seneca, *De clementia* 1.3.

364. Seneca, *De clementia* 1.5.

365. Seneca, *De clementia* 1.10–11.

366. Jeffers, *Greco-Roman World*, 154–57.

spreading lawfulness and civilization throughout the known world.[367] The law was supreme (i.e., it was elevated and treated with the same sacred reverence with which the rule of law is treated today). To illustrate this, during the principate, the image of the dying Galatian or Gaul became widespread and communicated an important message: "The lawless were being lawfully punished."[368] Consequently, the empire was considered "an order of law."[369] Therefore, outside of justifying conquest, Seneca explains that the law exists in order to punish for three reasons: in order to improve the character of the one punished, in order to teach a lesson to others, and, in the last resort, in order to remove an evil person from the midst of the people.[370]

However, during the principate, the emperor became he who was greater than the law. As we saw with Seneca's reflections upon the practice of mercy or clemency, it was the emperor who was permitted to create a state of exception and practice a form of justice that went beyond the law. However, despite the vocal optimism of those who benefited most from imperial rule, this state of exception did not always produce anything close to justice. Far from it, as Tacitus says, during Nero's reign, the law was manipulated by the powerful in order to "defeat justice on some legal pretext."[371] Of course, elevating the emperor above the law is a natural outcome of the lawless trajectory that produced Roman imperialism in the first place. Thus, for example, Julius Caesar is recorded as saying that the "time of war" and the "time of law" are two separate things and that laws only apply when wars are done.[372] Similarly, Augustus gains power by illegal means after he drives Antony from Italy, and the friendship of his kinship unit elevates their friends and allies above the law.[373] Tiberius, following after Augustus, also elevated himself and his family above the law.[374] Furthermore, in order to justify his exceptional power, Tiberius is recorded as stating that it is

---

367. See Kahl, *Galatians Re-Imagined*, 42–74.

368. See Kahl, *Galatians Re-Imagined*, 80.

369. See Koester, *History, Culture, and Religion*, 312.

370. Seneca, *De clementia* 1.22.

371. Tacitus, *Annals* 14.41. This is the universal function of the law and not a situation unique to the reign of Nero.

372. Plutarch, *Julius Caesar* 35.

373. Plutarch, *Brutus* 27; Tacitus, *Annals* 2.34. These reflections are far more critical than those offered by contemporaries of Augustus (for example, Horace, *Epistles* 2.1.1).

374. Tacitus, *Annals* 2.51.

better "to subvert the constitution than to remove its guardians."[375] Thus, we see that the emperors always claimed to serve justice, law, and order, while actually furthering their own agendas and consolidating their power.

The Cult of Roma

Finally, before examining the actual emperors and their *apotheoses*, it is worth mentioning the way in which the worship of Rome herself was an important part of spreading the imperial cult(s), especially during the initial stages of that spread. The worship of Roma was an older practice, dating back as early as the second century BCE in the East.[376] It was present in Laodicea and Hierapolis by the late second century BCE.[377] It was an especially useful cult after the civil wars. At that time, the eastern portion of the empire was pressing towards the divinization of the emperors, but Augustus was hesitant to fully embrace this relationship due to Roman suspicions of hegemonic power and the fate that befell his adoptive father. After Augustus, Tiberius, given his much less glorious ascent to power, was even more hesitant to accept any form of worship. Generally, this imperial hesitation regarding the acceptance of divine honors was most strongly expressed in Italy and in Rome; so, instead of focusing upon the persons of the Caesars, provincials were encouraged to worship Rome herself as divine in order to help rationalize their subordination.[378] In this regard, Suetonius notes how Augustus would not permit the provinces to grant him any divine honors "unless his name was coupled with that of Rome."[379] It was hoped that the vanquished nations would internalize the same sense of patriotism and Roman exceptionalism that the Romans had. As Horace famously wrote: *dolce et decorum est pro patria mori*—it is good and fine to die for one's fatherland—and Rome sought to inculcate this same attitude among her more and less reluctant allies.[380] Thus, the worship of Roma represents the

---

375. Tacitus, *Annals* 4.30.

376. See Hurtado, *Destroyer of the Gods*, 80. Cults venerating the Roman senate were also developed in Greek cities in Asia during the early empire. See Ando, *Imperial Ideology*, 168.

377. See Maier, *Picturing Paul in Empire*, 80–81.

378. See Crossan and Reed, *In Search of Paul*, 59–60.

379. See Suetonius, *Twelve Caesars*, 81.

380. See Horace, *Odes* 3.2.13.

veneration of both the city and the empire as a whole.[381] This worship was also accepted by the Romans themselves, although, even at Rome from an early stage, it was sometimes paired with the veneration of Augustus.

Creating a sense of Roman patriotism that was centered upon his own person was one of the fundamental achievements of Augustus.[382] Initially, he did this by inserting his own person into the loyalty oaths sworn to the Roman state and by pairing himself with the goddess Roma both in her temples and on coins.[383] However, even at Rome during his lifetime, veneration gave way at times to the rhetoric of worship—the worship of both Rome and Augustus paired together—as one observes, for example, in Virgil's *Eclogues*.[384] Augustus also tried to encourage the provincial worship of the Roman people or the Roman senate in addition to the worship of Rome, but these more corporate identities did not catch on nearly as well and quickly gave way to the veneration of the emperors and other imperial family members.

The Divine Caesars

The formal divinization of the Caesars within an empire-wide system began with Julius Caesar. Other prominent Romans like Aeneas and Romulus—the "few whom a benign Jupiter has loved or whom a fiery heroism has borne to heaven, Sons of gods"—were already treated as gods, but the sustained campaign to make emperor worship a central element of the functioning of a universal empire did not begin until the Caesars.[385] Hints of what is to come are found in some of the narratives related to Gnaeus Pompeius Magnus (Pompey). Thus, for example, during the civil wars, when Pompey refuses to plunder Greece, Cicero observes: "The result is that everyone in those places now regards Gnaeus Pompeius not as having

---

381. See Lietzmann, *Beginnings of the Christian Church*, 165.

382. See Eder, "Augustus and the Power," 29–30.

383. Ando, *Imperial Ideology*, 394.

384. Virgil, *Eclogues* 1.6–9, 42–43.

385. The quotation is from Virgil, *Aeneid* 6.190–93 (altered from poetry to prose). For more on the divinity of Romulus, see Plutarch, *Romulus* 23, 25, 27, 28–29. Interestingly, Plutarch remains skeptical about the divinity of any person and states that these are simply stories that people create in order to be gods and *equal to gods in power* (Plutarch, *Romulus* 28).

been sent out from Rome, but as having come down from heaven."[386] Other motifs associated with the divinized Caesars are associated with Pompey. For example, valor and victory in battle, paired with mercy to the defeated and fairness in his dispensing of justice at home, are all markers of Pompey's efforts to bring a universal peace.[387] However, the theme of divinity is muted and undeveloped (contributing factors here are surely the victory of Caesar over Pompey and Pompey's inauspicious end). These themes only truly move to the fore with Julius Caesar. However, while considering the divine Caesars, it is worth remembering that, for the Romans, divinity had more to do with status and power than it had to do with essence or nature.[388] In particular, it was the superhuman actions of the Caesars—creating world peace, triumphing over all enemies, and becoming patrons and benefactors of all people—that marked them as divine.[389]

JULIUS CAESAR

During his lifetime, Julius Caesar had already been set apart for divinity. He actively promoted the public recollection of the divine lineage of the Julians, who traced themselves back to Venus via Aeneas.[390] One finds inscriptions in the eastern part of the empire recognizing this and calling Julius Caesar "the God made manifest, offspring of Ares and Aphrodite, and common saviour of human life."[391] He also accepted divine honors, placed his own image among images of the gods, founded a *collegium* (the Lupercals) devoted to his divinity, and renamed the month of July after himself.[392] Such honors were granted, in large part, because of Caesar's victories, paired with his acts of clemency. Cicero comments on this:

> For such exceptional kindness, such unprecedented and unheard of clemency, such extraordinary moderation in someone who has attained absolute power over everything, and such astonishing and, one might almost say, superhuman wisdom—these are things

386. Cicero, *De imperio Cn. Pompei* 41.

387. See Cicero, *De imperio Cn. Pompei* 42; *Orationes philippicae* 2.65; *In Catalinam* 2.11.

388. See Peppard, *Son of God*, 31, 39.

389. Ando, *Imperial Ideology*, 390; Saller, *Personal Patronage*, 70–71.

390. See Suetonius, *Twelve Caesars*, 13; Kautsky, *Foundations of Christianity*, 98.

391. See Deissmann, *Light from the Ancient East*, 344.

392. Suetonius, *Twelve Caesars*, 42–43.

> I cannot possibly pass over in silence. . . . To show moderation
> towards the conquered, to take up a fallen enemy pre-eminent
> in birth, character, and virtue, and not merely raise him up, but
> actually enhance his former standing—that is the act of someone
> whom I would not rank with the greatest of men, but would judge
> akin to a god.[393]

However, Suetonius concludes that Julius Caesar overstepped his bounds by accepting divine honors and, in some ways, deserved to be assassinated since Caesar's desire to be worshiped led to a perverse desire for dictatorial power and became a tool for stripping the republic of its freedom.[394]

However, after Caesar's assassination, Augustus and his initial allies (such as Mark Antony, who Augustus later defeated at Actium) engaged in a sustained propaganda campaign in order to ensure that Julius Caesar would be included among the gods. Thus, on the night before he dies, Caesar is reported to have dreamed that he was "soaring above the clouds, and then shaking hands with Jupiter," and immediately after his death, Antony released a decree "voting Caesar all divine and human honors."[395] Then, after Augustus consolidated power, he hosted games in honor of the *apotheosis* of his (adoptive) father and a comet appeared on the evening of the opening day of those games. This comet was "held to be Caesar's soul, elevated to Heaven" and it became a common reference point to the divinity of Caesar in both literature and art.[396] Subsequently, temples devoted to the worship of Julius Caesar appear in Ephesus and Nicaea in 29 BCE, and his cult only continues to increase for the duration of the reign of the Julio-Claudian line.[397]

---

393. Cicero, *Pro Marcello* 1, 8. That said, in his Second Philippic, Cicero speaks much more critically of Caesar's clemency, which he argues was a means of dragging a free country into servitude (*Orationes philippicae* 2.116). He also celebrates the assassination of Caesar (2.32), celebrates the destruction of Caesar's tomb (3.107), and mocks any devotion to Caesar as divine (2.110–11).

394. Suetonius, *Twelve Caesars*, 42–43.

395. Suetonius, *Twelve Caesars*, 46, 48. See also Plutarch, *Julius Caesar* 67.

396. Suetonius, *Twelve Caesars*, 49. For an example of literary allusion to this event, see Virgil, *Eclogues* 9.47–49. Other Roman authors, after Augustus, also describe Julius Caesar as divine in various ways. For example, when describing Caesar's conquests, Petronius depicts Caesar like Hercules, striding with his head held high, or Jupiter, hurling lightning bolts at doomed giants (*Satyricon* 15.119.314–21).

397. For this dating of the appearance of the temples, see Hardin, *Galatians and the Imperial Cult*, 26.

AUGUSTUS

The most elevated person within the imperial cult and the person most responsible for developing and encouraging its spread was Augustus. Like his adoptive father, Augustus was keen to emphasize his divine descent. After he ensured that Julius Caesar was officially recognized as divine in 14 BCE, he adopted the title *divi filius*—Son of God—and he had this title minted on coins, along with images of Venus and Aeneas.[398] Horace refers to Augustus as the "last great son" of Venus and Anchises, the parents of Aeneas.[399] Similarly, referring to the future arrival of Augustus, Virgil quotes Apollo as saying these words to Iulus, the son of Aeneas: "By striving so men reach the stars, dear son of gods, and sire of gods to come."[400] Because of this, all subsequent Julio-Claudian emperors were also called "a son of a god."[401]

However, given that the Augustan ideology was forged in a somewhat ad hoc manner during a time of conflict and war, the story was also circulated that Apollo was Augustus's actual birth father. Suetonius tells us that the mother of Augustus was reported to have conceived after falling asleep and being "entered" by a serpent at the Temple of Apollo.[402] Furthermore, from an early age, Augustus displayed a special reverence for Apollo. During the final stage of the civil wars, as we have already seen, he depicted himself as the image of Apollo (over against representations of Antony and Cleopatra as Dionysus/Osiris and Aphrodite/Isis).[403] Virgil captures this ideo-theological conflict in a manner that clearly favors Augustus while demonizing Antony and Cleopatra in his portrayal of the battle of Actium in the *Aeneid*:

> With ships maneuverings, sea glowing gold,
> Augustus Caesar leading into battle
> Italians, with both senators and people,
> Household gods and great gods: there he stood
> High on the stern, and from his blessed brow

398. See Zanker, *Power of Images*, 35–36; Crossan and Reed, *In Search of Paul*, 136–37.

399. Horace, *Carmen saeculare* 49.

400. Virgil, *Aeneid* 9.893–94 (text modified from poetry to prose). Apollo goes on to say that these gods to come will justly bring an end to all wars, a clear reference to another prominent motif in the Augustan ideology, as we have already seen (*Aeneid* 9.895–96).

401. Winter, *Divine Honours for the Caesars*, 67. See also Peppard, *Son of God*, 28.

402. Suetonius, *Twelve Caesars*, 101–2; Crossan and Reed, *In Search of Paul*, 163–64.

403. See Zanker, *Power of Images*, 44–53.

Twin flames gushed upward, while his crest revealed
His father's star . . .

Twin snakes of death behind, while monster forms
Of gods of every race, and the dog-god
Anubis barking, held their weapons up
Against our Neptune, Venus, and Minerva.
Mars, engraved in steel, raged in the fight
As from high air the dire Furies came
With Discord, taking joy in the torn robe,
And on her heels the bloody scourge, Bellona.

Overlooking it all, Actian Apollo
Began to pull his bow.[404]

However, after he defeated Antony, Augustus quickly pulled back from this portrayal of himself as Apollo incarnate, lest he (like Julius Caesar) be seen by the senate as overstepping the power granted to him.

The perspicacity shown by Augustus did not lead to a cessation of activities and acclamations that treated him as divine—both in the provinces (as has been more widely recognized) and in Rome (as has been less widely recognized). Thus, Suetonius notes that, already during his lifetime, Romans treated the birthplace of Augustus as that of a god, stories circulated of Augustus possessing miraculous power over nature and animals from an early age, and several provinces erected altars and temples to him.[405] Already in 19 BCE the senate created the *Augustalia*, the annual celebration of the safe return of Augustus to Rome, "as if the god of the day was Augustus, and not *Fortuna Redux* [the goddess of safe return]."[406] In 12 BCE, the month of Sextilis has its name changed to the month of Augustus. In 14 CE, the Augustal Games were inaugurated and the *Augustales* was then composed of twenty-one leading men of the state, including Tiberius, Drusus, Claudius, and Germanicus.[407] In 15 CE, a province in Spain submitted a request and received permission to build the first temple dedicated solely

404. Virgil, *Aeneid* 8.915–21, 945–54.

405. Suetonius, *Twelve Caesars*, 54, 85, 102. On Augustus's power over nature, see also Horace, *Carmen Saeculare* 53–56, 81–85.

406. Scheid, "Augustus and Roman Religion," 190. Scheid also notes that games were celebrated on the birthday of Augustus from at least 20 BCE onward.

407. Tacitus, *Annals* 1.54.

to the worship of Augustus, thereby setting the precedent for the other provinces.[408]

In his own account of his life, Augustus notes how his name was included in the hymn of the Salii by decree of the senate.[409] This was a hymn performed to ensure Rome's safety and including Augustus within it placed him on par with the gods and tied the safety of Rome to his personal well-being. As his power continued to grow, provincial elites referred to Augustus as "god of gods" or in terms like these: "The Emperor, Caesar, son of a god, the god Augustus, of every land and sea the overseer."[410] But Romans were also not afraid to employ this kind of rhetoric. Horace refers to Augustus as "a present god" upon whom the Romans "confer mature honors, and rear altars where your name is to be sworn by."[411] Similarly, Virgil writes the following of Augustus:

> Whatever place in the courts of the Immortals is soon to hold you—whether an overseer of cities and warden of earth you'll be, Caesar, so that the great world honor you as promoter of harvest and puissant lord of the seasons. . . . Or whether you come as god of the boundless sea, and sailors worship your power alone, and the ends of the earth pay tribute, and Tethys gives all her waves to get you for son-in-law: or whether you make a new sign in the Zodiac. . . . Advance, and even now grow used to our invocations.[412]

Thus, in both the provinces and in Rome at various times, Augustus is said to exhibit "divine grace," enforce "divine commandments," and is called everything from "Son of God," to "Lord," "Redeemer," "Liberator," "Savior of the World," "God Incarnate," and "The God Who is to be Worshipped."[413]

408. Tacitus, *Annals* 1.78. Although, as already stated, temples dedicated to the worship of Augustus and Roma together, or the incorporation of the worship of Augustus into temples dedicated to other gods, was already fairly widespread by this point.

409. Augustus, *Res Gestae* 10.1–2.

410. Deissmann, *Light from the Ancient East*, 344, 347.

411. Horace, *Odes* 3.5.2; *Epistles* 2.1.2.

412. Virgil, *Georgics* 1.24–32, 42. Virgil alludes to the foregone conclusion that Augustus will undergo a formal and official *apotheosis*—deification—after his death. Horace also anticipates this when, during the lifetime of Augustus, he states that Augustus will be placed amidst the stars and in Jupiter's council (Horace, *Odes* 3.25.5–6). Not surprisingly, then, an ex-praetor at the funeral of Augustus swears to witnessing the spirit of Augustus soaring upwards to heaven (Suetonius, *Twelve Caesars*, 107). Consequently, writing during the reign of Nero, Seneca portrays Augustus as divine and acting as the most influential voice in the council of the gods. See Seneca, *Apocolocyntosis*.

413. See Deissmann, *Light from the Ancient East*, 347–48; Crossan, *God and Empire*,

The title "Augustus," granted to Octavian by the senate in 27 BCE, was itself a way of granting divine honors to the emperor. Previously, this title had only been applied to the traditional deities or to previously deified Romans like Romulus.[414] The title "Augustus" was an "archaic sacral title," referring to "One who deserves reverence."[415] More broadly, it referred to that which is "stately," "dignified," or "holy" and was connected with the verb *augere* (to increase), which also overlaps with the role of the Roman augurs, who were charged with discerning the will of the gods.[416] (Thus, by choosing to refer to Octavian as "Augustus" throughout, I have been deliberately employing a title that carries sacred and divine overtones—as opposed to following certain scholarly practices of referring to this personage as Octavius when referring to events that occurred from 63–44 BCE, as Octavian from 44–27 BCE, and as Augustus from 27 BCE onwards.)

Finally, given the extent of the veneration of Augustus that was accomplished during his lifetime, both in the provinces and in Rome, the conclusion that Augustus actually became *the greatest* of the recognized gods becomes increasingly compelling. One gathers hints of this in the Roman literature, when Augustus is compared not to Apollo but to Jupiter, the father of the gods. Jupiter, too, is called "savior" for saving Rome.[417] Thus, Ovid turns Augustus into Jupiter incarnate.[418] Similarly, Suetonius states that the (human) birth father of Augustus reportedly had a dream prior to the birth of his son, wherein Augustus "appeared in superhuman majesty, armed with the thunderbolt, scepter, and regal ornaments of Jupiter Greatest and Best, crowned with a solar diadem, and riding in a belaurelled chariot drawn by twelve dazzling white horses."[419] Horace also asserts, "Nothing

---

28; Crossan and Borg, *First Paul*, 100–104. That said, Augustus had titles he preferred less than others. For example, Suetonius tells us that Augustus "always felt horrified and insulted when called 'My Lord,' a form of address used by slaves to their owners . . . he would not even let his adopted children, or grandchildren, use the obsequious word" (*Twelve Caesars*, 81).

414. See Lohse, *New Testament Environment*, 199; MacMullen, *Paganism in the Roman Empire*, 103; Eder, "Augustus and the Power of Tradition," 24.

415. Koester, *History, Culture, and Religion*, 293–94, 353.

416. See Zanker, *Power of Images*, 98–99. This also ties back to the connection to Romulus as he was famous for his *augurium* (Eder, "Augustus and the Power of Tradition," 24).

417. Cicero, *In Catilinam* 3.22.

418. See Crossan, *God and Empire*, 19–20; Keresztes, *From Herod the Great*, 5–6.

419. Suetonius, *Twelve Caesars*, 102.

equal to you [Augustus] has hitherto risen, or will hereafter rise."[420] Zanker notes how art in the Hellenistic world often rendered Augustus in the guise of Jupiter.[421] Thus, as his power grows and consolidates, Augustus moved from being counted among the gods to being the greatest of the gods. In this regard, Kahl argues that Augustus's acts of piety—all the religious reforms, building projects, and restorations of priesthoods—actually turn him into the patron of the gods themselves, thereby turning him into the supreme deity.[422] Thus, she argues that Augustus crafted an imperial religion that inserted traditional religions into the framework of what was (functionally) imperial monotheism centered on the emperor.[423] Tacitus expresses a similar sentiment when he writes: "No honor was left for the gods, when Augustus chose to be himself worshipped with temples and statues, like those of the deities, and with flamens and priests."[424]

TIBERIUS, CALIGULA, AND CLAUDIUS

We shall cover the next three successors of Augustus in rapid succession. The first two, Tiberius and Caligula, were never deified (Claudius was), but this does not mean that the imperial cult did not grow and spread during their reigns.[425]

Tiberius ruled from 14–37 CE. Following in the (rather large) footsteps of Augustus, he was appropriately cautious about trying to live up to the example set by his predecessor. Although he was deemed a "son of a god," he did not permit any divine honors to be granted to himself, although the senate and the people of Rome certainly tried to grant these to him.[426] In part, this was because Tiberius could not lay claim to the Julian lineage (he was a Claudian), so he focused more upon the virtues of victory, piety,

---

420. Horace, *Epistles* 2.1.2.

421. Zanker, *Power of Images*, 130–34.

422. Kahl, *Galatians Re-Imagined*, 141, 146.

423. Kahl, *Galatians Re-Imagined*, 139.

424. Tacticus, *Annals* 1.10.

425. It is also important to note that while Tiberius and Caligula were not officially deified in Rome, they were treated as deities in the eastern provinces. See Koester, *History, Culture, and Religion*, 353.

426. Tacitus, *Annals* 1.11; 2.87; 4.37–38; 5.2. See also Koester, *History, Culture, and Religion*, 297; Deissmann, *Light from the Ancient East*, 346.

and clemency.[427] Thus, Suetonius observes that Tiberius "vetoed all bills for the dedication of temples and priests to his divinity, and reserved the right to sanction even the setting up of his statues and busts—which might not be placed among the images of the gods, but used only to decorate private homes."[428] Tiberius also declined months named after him or his mother and declined the title *pater patriae*, only accepting the title "Augustus" when it was used in letters to foreign monarchs. However, Tiberius was not always consistent in these refusals. In Palestine, as we have already seen, Tiberius was venerated at Caesarea and in the city of Tiberias. Veneration of Tiberius was also joined to the worship of Livia, the senate, Roma, the divine Julius, and the divine Augustus. Furthermore, on at least two occasions (in 14 CE and 37 CE), the Achaeans laid out plans for divine honors to be granted to Tiberius.[429] Furthermore, Tiberius continued to increase the veneration of Augustus while also deifying other members of the family of Augustus, thereby continuing to ensure the centrality and the spread of the imperial cult(s).[430] He established a temple to the Julian family and erected statues to the divine Augustus.[431] He also entered Germanicus into the cult as a divine member.[432] Outside of Rome, he permitted cities in both Asia and Spain to erect temples dedicated to himself, his mother, and the senate, and ensured that those temples received proper care.[433] He actively encouraged competition among Asian cities, and embassies from cities such as Hypaepa, Tralles, Laodicaea, Magnesia, Halicarnassus, Pergamum, Ephesus, Melitus, Sardis, and Smyrna all came to Rome to compete for the honor of raising temples dedicated to emperor worship.[434] He also punished the city of Cyzicus, even imprisoning some Roman citizens there, because it failed to complete a temple to Augustus.[435] Additionally, Tiberius created a "law of treason" that was used to condemn, punish, dispossess, or

427. Zanker, *Power of Images*, 227–30. For example, continuing the Augustan model of piety, Tiberius continues to create new temples and restore old ones. See Tacitus, *Annals* 2.49.

428. Suetonius, *Twelve Caesars*, 125.

429. See Winter, *Divine Honours for the Caesars*, 84, 92, 167.

430. Hardin, *Galatians and the Imperial Cult*, 39.

431. Tacitus, *Annals* 2.41.

432. Tacitus, *Annals* 2.54, 59, 72, 83.

433. Tacitus, *Annals* 4.15, 36–37.

434. Tacitus, *Annals* 4.55–56.

435. Winter, *Divine Honours for the Caesars*, 91.

kill any who ridiculed or spoke irreverently of the divine Augustus or did harm to any image of Augustus (or an image of Tiberius).[436] Lastly, he permitted statues and temples of the emperor to be used as places of sanctuary throughout the empire, just as people used to do "with the old gods."[437]

Caligula, who ruled from 37–41 CE, was not officially divinized (although the eastern provinces clamoured to acclaim him a god when he came to power) because his rule was disastrous, in part, because he was "seriously convinced of his divinity," and so he was killed by his own imperial guard.[438] During his brief reign, he extended the imperial palace into the temples of the gods and would mix with the statues of the gods, often conversing with the statue of Capitoline Jupiter, himself being addressed as the "Latian Jupiter," while creating a shrine to himself as a god with sacrifices, images, and priests from the most prominent citizens of Rome.[439] After his death, a belief arose that he had not really died but would return to punish or reward those who were loyal or disloyal to him. This is an interesting point of comparison to claims made about the *anastasis* of Jesus because it shows that stories of the emperor being raised from the dead (or, at least, coming back from what seemed to be death in order to judge the wicked and the just) were already in circulation prior to the story of *Nero Redivivus*. Thus, Suetonius notes, due to the terror Caligula inspired, "everyone was extremely reluctant to believe that he had really been assassinated, and suspected that the story was invented by himself to discover what people thought of him."[440]

Claudius ruled from 41–54 CE. As with his predecessors, he was treated as divine by the eastern provinces during his lifetime, but unlike Tiberius and Caligula, he was only officially deified in Rome after his death—receiving a funeral that was equal in scale to that of Augustus.[441] This despite the fact that, in many ways, he fell short of the example set

---

436. Tacitus, *Annals* 2.50; 3.66, 70.

437. Tacitus, *Annals* 3.36. Although, as noted above, he later does away with this privilege at any and all temples.

438. Koester, *History, Culture, and Religion*, 298; Winter, *Divine Honours for the Caesars*, 167, 182–83.

439. See Suetonius, *Twelve Caesars*, 161.

440. Suetonius, *Twelve Caesars*, 179.

441. See Price, *Rituals and Power*, 75; Tacitus, *Annals* 12.69; Winter, *Divine Honours for the Caesars*, 66. Suetonius notes his post-death *apotheosis* while also noting that Nero neglected and later cancelled this deification (*Twelve Caesars*, 208). This attitude is well reflected in Seneca's *Apocolocyntosis*.

by Augustus.[442] During his life, he was circumspect about receiving divine honors, but he was sometimes addressed as "our god Caesar."[443] However, this circumspection should be taken with a grain of salt—for example, in the letter Claudius sends to the Alexandrians in order to refuse divine honors they wished to grant to him, Claudius is referred to as "our god Caesar" by the prefect of Egypt.[444] Despite his personal reticence, he also continued to spread the imperial cult(s) in general by, for example, divinizing Livia, by publicly sacrificing to both his parents, and by treating "By Augustus!" as his most sacred oath.[445] He also hosted another round of Secular Games (claiming that Augustus was wrong in his calculation of the dates).[446] After his death, the cult of Claudius spread and, as a god, he is said to have had power not only over the people of the earth but also over natural forces, subjecting even the sea and making it calm so that it would carry his ships peacefully.[447]

NERO

Finally, with Nero, who reigned from 54–68 CE, we see a resurgence of large-scale hope focused upon the living emperor as a divine figure. As Suetonius notes, Nero started with a parade of virtue, giving Claudius a lavish funeral, personally delivering the oration, and deifying the deceased emperor.[448] Given that he had been adopted by Claudius, Nero was then referred to as the "Son of the greatest of gods" and was also referred to as the "good God."[449] Here, it was particularly important to the Roman ideo-theology that Nero came to power without shedding any blood (even if Nero's mother is said to have poisoned Claudius). He is compared to Augustus for his unique ability to be the means by which peace may be created after the turmoil caused by his predecessors. But for some (Seneca is one

442. For example, in a move that would have appalled Augustus, given his proclivity for family values, Claudius changed the legal code so that he was able to marry his niece (Tacitus, *Annals* 7.6).

443. See Tenney, *New Testament Times*, 115–16.

444. See Winter, *Divine Honours for the Caesars*, 89.

445. Suetonius, *Twelve Caesars*, 189.

446. Tacitus, *Annals* 11.11.

447. Seneca, *Octavia* 41–44.

448. Suetonius, *Twelve Caesars*, 215.

449. See Deissmann, *Light from the Ancient East*, 345, 347.

example), Nero is even greater than the divine Augustus because Augustus was still stained by the bloodshed of the civil wars.[450] Similarly, Lucan, in his account of the civil wars—surely the most traumatic event in recent Roman history—asserts that ultimately these wars were worthwhile since they became the reason for Nero's ascension to power. Lucan writes: "But if the Fates could find no other way for Nero's coming, if eternal kingdoms are purchased by the gods at great cost, if heaven could serve its Thunderer only after wars with the ferocious Giants, then we have no complaints, O gods; for this reward [i.e., Nero] we accept even these crimes and guilt."[451] Thus, Lucan is assured of Nero's divinity:

> You [Nero], when your duty is fulfilled and finally you seek the stars, will be received in your chosen palace of heaven, with the sky rejoicing. Whether you choose to wield the scepter or to mount the flaming chariot of Phoebus and to circle with moving fire the earth entirely unperturbed by the transference of the sun, every deity will yield to your decision, nature will leave which god you wish to be, where to set your kingdom of the universe. . . . Then may humankind lay down its weapons and care for itself and every waring nation love one another, may Peace be sent throughout the world and close the iron temple-gates of warring Janus. But already to me you are a deity.[452]

Although Nero initially began his reign by refusing divine honors for himself, he later came to accept all divine honors.[453] He reshaped the calendar in order to rename the month of April after himself.[454] He also furthered the spread of the imperial cult(s) by encouraging the building of temples to Claudius in the provinces, renaming other months after Claudius and Germanicus, reviving the law of treason in relation to the imperial cult(s) (which had fallen into disuse after Tiberius), and including his deceased daughter and deceased second wife, Poppaea, as divine members of the imperial cult (even though he had, in a fit of rage, kicked Poppaea to death while she was pregnant).[455]

---

450. Seneca, *Octavia* 468–77.

451. Lucan, *Civil War* 1.33–38 (text modified from poetry to prose).

452. Lucan, *Civil War* 1.46–52, 60–63.

453. Tacitus, *Annals* 13.10, 41; 15.74. Also note the divine honors given to Nero in the treatise on mercy that Seneca writes to the emperor (*De clementia* 1.1, 7–8, 19).

454. Tacitus, *Annals* 15.74.

455. Tacitus, *Annals* 14.31; 16.12; 14.48; 15.23; 16.6, 22, respectively.

Nero was also venerated as *the* chief among the gods in a manner similar to the veneration of Augustus. Thus, Seneca writes that "no man these days talks of the deified Augustus or of the early years of Tiberius Caesar, or looks for a model that he would have you copy other than yourself."[456] Additionally, in a story similar to that which emerged around the birth of Augustus, it is said that snakes were seen by his cradle when Nero was an infant.[457] Thus, it is not surprising to see that Nero also sought to follow the example set by Augustus and blur the lines that existed between the emperor and Jupiter.[458] Developing this idea in his play, *Octavia*, Seneca has Nero state the following: "I, who make gods, would be a fool to fear them."[459] The veneration of Nero was especially strong in Achaea, which Nero freed from taxation and which, in return, venerated him as lord of all the cosmos, as Zeus Liberator, the father of the fatherland and of the cosmos.[460] Corinth especially celebrated Nero as savior, liberator, and lord of all the world.[461]

Of course, even at Rome, this rose-tinted perspective of Nero's reign does not last long. Suetonius notes many ways in which Nero fell short of the standards set for emperors and for virtuous people. For example, while Augustus was noted for his triumphs, Suetonius observes the various defeats of Rome and her allies, not to mention internal revolts, that occurred during the reign of Nero.[462] Furthermore, while others like Augustus and Tiberius were known for their pious restoration of temples, Nero is reported to have plundered the temples of Rome in order to fund the rebuilding needed after the fire he was suspected of starting in order to refound the city.[463] Nero also becomes notable for breaching all the protocols related to family values. The elaborate plots he developed in order to murder his own mother (who played the central role in Nero's rise to power) are recounted in detail by several sources (and, as already mentioned, he kicked

---

456. Seneca, *De clementia* 1.1.

457. Tacitus, *Annals* 11.11.

458. Kahl, *Galatians Re-Imagined*, 142–44.

459. Seneca, *Octavia* 451.

460. Maier, *Picturing Paul in Empire*, 74.

461. Winter, *Divine Honours for the Caesars*, 73.

462. See Suetonius, *Twelve Caesars*, 232, 234–35. Suetonius also describes the nightmares that Nero had about being crushed by the statues of the vanquished nations contained in the theater of Pompey (237).

463. See Tacitus, *Annals* 15.45.

his pregnant wife to death).[464] Ultimately, all of these things, along with Nero's debaucheries and oppressive economic policies, led to a widespread revolt against him in 68 CE. This concluded with Nero being condemned by the senate and him committing suicide before he could be brought before the courts. However, some came to believe that Nero had not really died (or, if he had died, that he would come back from the dead). It is interesting to note that faith in *Nero Redivivus* was especially strong the East—if Nero was forced to flee Rome, some astrologers forecast that he would find another throne there, specifically in Jerusalem.[465]

Summary of the Central Themes of the Imperial Cult

Thus, we arrive at the primary cluster of themes associated with the Roman imperial cult: (a) predestination to universal rule; (b) the gospel of Roman peace, salvation, and liberty; (c) war, victory, and justice; (d) piety; (e) mercy; (f) the rule of law; (g) the cult of Roma; and (h) the reverence of the divine Caesars. Put more succinctly, one could summarize the ideo-theology of Rome in this way: the Romans has been predestined to rule the world forever due to their piety and their commitment to justice and the rule of law. Therefore, they were guaranteed victories in wars with those who were less pious, less just, and who, in actuality, were in need of liberation, which came through Roman rule and was graciously expressed in the practice of mercy. The result of this was the appropriate veneration of Rome herself, but also of the emperors who were the supreme examples of piety, the primary agents of peace and salvation, the best suited for the practice of mercy, and who were, for all intents and purposes, divine—the makers of gods, the greatest of gods.

---

464. Tacitus, *Annals* 14.1–10; Seneca, *Octavia* 312–73.

465. Suetonius, *Twelve Caesars*, 234. It is interesting to note that these rumors of "resurrections" began in relation to important Roman personages at least as early as the reign of Augustus. For example, Postumus Agrippa, a close friend of Augustus, was believed to have been saved by death by heaven, and his imminent return was anticipated by some (Tacitus, *Annals* 2.39–40). The rumor of *Caligula Redivivus* has already been noted above.

Conclusion

We have covered a great deal of ground in this chapter. Having first examined the four building blocks of Roman imperialism and of the Roman imperial cult—the household, cultural conceptions of honor and shame, the practice of patronage, and traditional Roman religiosity—we looked at critical (and often non-literary) sources for the study of the imperial cult and then explored the key themes of that cult. Therefore, at this point, we are well positioned to understand how Paul and his coworkers (engaging with communities of people who were suffering under Roman rule and as a consequence of the Roman ideo-theology as it was embodied in their contexts) engaged with and attempted to systematically dismantle, replace, subvert, or destroy everything Rome held dear in order to create and maintain a way of structuring life together that was life-giving to those left for dead.

4

CONCLUSION: ASSEMBLING THE LIVING IN THE EMPIRE OF DEATH

IN 2003, ACHILLE MBEMBE argued that Foucault's notion of biopower "is insufficient to account for contemporary forms of subjugation of life to the power of death."[1] Instead, Mbembe put forward the ideas of "necropolitics" and "necropower" in order to

> account for the various ways in which, in our contemporary world,
> weapons are deployed in the interest of maximum destruction of
> persons and the creation of *death-worlds*, new and unique forms
> of social existence in which vast populations are subjected to
> conditions of life conferring upon them the status of *living dead*.[2]

Particularly striking examples of those assigned to this status are the figure of the slave and of the colonized. Hence, Mbembe asserts, "Slave life . . . is a form of death-in-life" and "the sovereign's right to kill is not subject to any rule in the colonies."[3] Furthermore, in the commodified wars of "the globalization era," States interact (sometimes as allies, sometimes as accomplices, sometimes as opponents) with those whom Mbembe refers to as "war machines" (i.e., "segments of armed men that split up or merge with one another depending on the tasks to be carried out and the circumstances . . .

1. Mbembe, "Necropolitics," 39–40.
2. Mbembe, "Necropolitics," 40.
3. Mbembe, "Necropolitics," 21, 25, respectively.

[war machines are] characterized by their capacity for metamorphosis").[4] In this context, and over and against Foucault's out-dated (in Mbembe's opinion) examination of the technologies and *dipositifs* of biopower, Mbembe argues that "the new technologies of destruction are less concerned with inscribing bodies within disciplinary apparatuses as inscribing them, when the time comes, within the order of the maximal economy now represented by the 'massacre.'"[5]

Sayak Valencia develops Mbembe's thesis in her examination of the kind of political economy that can arise in border spaces among populations of people consigned to the status of the living dead.[6] In this context, and expressly against those who romanticize liminal spaces—as though they automatically confer upon all their inhabitants some sort of liberating, creative, anti-hierarchical, rhizomatic, community of resistance—Valencia speaks of "endriago subjects" who have become enamored by the vision of abundance held out by capitalism but prevented from participating in that abundance due to their race, nationality, or socioeconomic location.[7] Frustrated by this, Valencia argues that the endriago subject embraces an incredibly brutal form of "necroempowerment," wherein he (this subject is generally a male who is enamored with a form of machismo that has deep roots in patriarchal heteronormativity) seeks to transform the situation of vulnerability "into possibilities for action and self-empowerment, and that reconfigure this situation through dystopian practices and perverse self-affirmation achieved through violent means."[8] Here, rather than encouraging an ethics rooted in the commandment to "do no harm," we find an ethics that says, "*Receive no more harm*, or *Participate in harm as agents and no longer (only) as victims*."[9] In this context, death itself becomes "the most profitable business in existence."[10] Of course, Valencia emphasizes, by acting in this way, the active agents of gore capitalism are simply mirroring

---

4. Mbembe, "Necropolitics," 31–32.

5. Mbembe, "Necropolitics," 34.

6. See Valencia, *Gore Capitalism*.

7. See Valencia, *Gore Capitalism*, 184–86, 124–38. Valencia takes the term "endriago" from a medieval text (*Amadis of Gaul*), wherein the endriago is "a monster, a cross between a man, a hydra and a dragon. It is noted for its large stature, agility and beastliness . . . the island where it lives is described as uninhabited, a kind of earthly hell" (*Gore Capitalism*, 132).

8. Valencia, *Gore Capitalism*, 301; 74.

9. Valencia, *Gore Capitalism*, 114.

10. Valencia, *Gore Capitalism*, 21; see also 62–68.

the actions and ethics of mainstream economic actors (like pharmaceutical companies, for example, who steal Indigenous knowledge and then privatize manufactured medicines that could [but then do not] save millions of lives, because they desire the highest profits regardless of the human cost).[11] Following Mbembe, Valencia argues that this produces a necropolitics that supersedes biopolitics because it is centered upon negotiating with, producing, and profiting from death.[12] This then gives rise to a large scale "thanatophilia" (understood as "the predilection for the spectacularization of death in contemporary hyperconsumerist societies") in both popular and underground cultures.[13]

Both Mbembe and Valencia are highly attuned to the specific contexts that they examine and the ways in which the unique intra-actions and entanglements situated in those contexts require us to develop new critical lenses—in order to advance our analyses beyond what earlier theorists have postulated—and find new ways of speaking that not only do justice to the world of which they are a part but also in order to find new ways to transform that world.[14] I respect their efforts and priorities and do not mean to seriously question their methodology except to say that, for all that is new here, there is much that is very old as well. Twenty-first-century capitalism does not have a monopoly on prioritizing profits over people or on producing death on a massive (and massively profitable) scale, of falling into thanatophilia, or of engaging in blood-soaked necropolitics and necropower. And it is not only those oppressed by capitalism who have found ways to mimic or glory in the violent, life-denying ethics of the oppressors in order to advance their own personal status and wealth. In many ways, although they are embodied in a wide variety of permutations and overcoded with many different glosses, ideologies, or gods, these dynamics are representative of imperialism *qua* imperialism. Certainly, it is not difficult to find almost all of these elements within the ideo-theology of Roman imperialism and the practices of elite Romans. From the forced relocation, enslavement, rape, and torture of millions of vanquished peoples to the use

11. Valencia, *Gore Capitalism*, 78.

12. Valencia, *Gore Capitalism*, 209–11.

13. Valencia, *Gore Capitalism*, 219. See also her section on the trendiness of "decorative violence" (228–33) and on death in the realm of art and fashion (246–48).

14. I borrow the language of "intra-actions" and "entanglement" from Karen Barad's stunning defense of what she refers to as "agential realism" in *Meeting the Universe Halfway* (which is also a text that seeks to both describe "the world" and to transform our engagement therein).

of captives as torches at garden parties hosted by the rich (who learned to space women evenly among the men in order to cause the flame to burn at an equal height, rather than having it flare up higher in areas where women were clustered together), Rome was no stranger to necropower, extravagant consumption, the willingness to sacrifice the lives of others in order to accumulate massive fortunes, and thanatophilia. And the Pauline faction recognized this. In their analysis, the rulers, Powers, and other forces who persecuted the Pauline faction and those to whom they gospeled, were all subservient to one Lord—Death (which is why, as per 1 Cor 15:26, Death is the final enemy to be defeated). Empires are like a necrotizing fasciitis. Wherever they go, pain, rot, and, ultimately, annihilation quickly follow. The Caesars, far from being agents of liberation, universal saviors, pious peacemakers, and merciful victors divinely predestined to rule, are actually the sword hand of Death.

However, for the Pauline faction, empire does not have the last word, and this is why Paul and his coworkers do not pursue the forms of necro-empowerment that tempt other members of subaltern populations within the Roman Empire (as we saw in our earlier study of conflicts at Corinth, early Jesus loyalists were not immune to this temptation—and, of course, in the end, this temptation was too strong and overwhelmed the Jesus movement as it transitioned into what we now call Christianity). For the Pauline faction, the future was not closed, resistance was not futile, and the Spirit of *anastasis* Life was already moving and working among those left for dead. Furthermore, the Pauline faction believed that the gospel that was being assembled by Jesus loyalists throughout the eastern portion of the Roman Empire was the surest proof of the downfall of any system premised upon dealing death to others and hoarding the abundance of life to one's self and one's small, elite, peer group. For, as we will see in volume 3, abundance is definitive of the political economy of the Jesus loyalists who, far from being counted among the living dead, now experience a form of Life that is stronger than Death.

BIBLIOGRAPHY

Agosto, Efrain. "Patronage and Commendation, Imperial and Anti-Imperial." In *Paul and the Roman Imperial Order*, edited by Richard A. Horsley, 103–23. Harrisburg, PA: Trinity, 2004.

Alexander, Michelle. *The New Jim Crow: Mass Incarceration in the Age of Colorblindness*. Foreword by Cornel West. New York: New Press, 2012.

Althusser, Louis. "Ideology and Ideological State Apparatus." In *Lenin and Philosophy and Other Essays*, by Louis Althusser, 85–126. Translated by Ben Brewster. New York: Monthly Review, 2001.

Anderson, Carol. *White Rage: The Unspoken Truth of Our Racial Divide*. New York: Bloomsbury, 2017.

Ando, Clifford. *Imperial Ideology and the Provincial Loyalty in the Roman Empire*. Berkeley: University of California Press, 2000.

Augustus. *Res Gestae Divi Augusti: The Achievements of the Divine Augustus*. Edited by P. A. Brunt and J. M. Moore. Oxford: Oxford University Press, 1967.

Aune, David E. *Apocalypticism, Prophecy, and Magic in Early Christianity: Collected Essays*. Grand Rapids: Baker Academic, 2008.

————. *The Cultic Setting of Realized Eschatology in Early Christianity*. Supplements to Novum Testamentum 28. Leiden: Brill, 1972.

————. *Prophecy in Early Christianity and the Ancient Mediterranean World*. Grand Rapids: Eerdmans, 1983.

Badiou, Alain. *Being and Event*. Translated by Oliver Feltham. Bloomsbury Revelations Series. London: Bloomsbury Academic, 2005.

————. *St. Paul: The Foundations of Universalism*. Translated by Ray Brassier. Cultural Memory in the Present. Stanford: Stanford University Press, 2003.

Bakunin, Michael. "Letter to the Comrades of the Jura Federation." October 12, 1873. Online. https://www.marxists.org/reference/archive/bakunin/works/1873/letter-jura.htm.

Balthasar, Hans Urs von. *A Theology of History*. San Francisco: Ignatius, 1994.

Bammel, Ernst. "Romans 13." In *Jesus and the Politics of His Day*, edited by Ernst Bammel and C. F. D. Moule, 363–85. Cambridge: Cambridge University Press, 1984.

Bammel, Ernst, and C. F. D. Moule, eds. *Jesus and the Politics of His Day*. Cambridge: Cambridge University Press, 1984.

Barad, Karen. *Meeting the Universe Halfway: Quantum Physics and the Entanglement of Matter and Meaning*. Durham: Duke University Press, 2007.

Barclay, John M. G. "The Family as the Bearer of Religion in Judaism and Early Christianity." In *Constructing Early Christian Families: Family as Social Reality and Metaphor*, edited by Halvor Moxnes, 66–80. London: Routledge, 1997.

Barclay, William. *The Mind of Saint Paul*. New York: Harper & Row, 1975.

Bauckham, Richard, ed. *God Will Be All in All: The Eschatology of Jürgen Moltmann*. Edinburgh: T & T Clark, 1999.

———. "Time and Eternity." In *God Will Be All in All: The Eschatology of Jürgen Moltmann*, edited by Richard Bauckham, 155–226. Edinburgh: T & T Clark, 1999.

Beacham, Richard. "The Emperor as Impresario: Producing the Pageantry of Power." In *The Cambridge Companion to the Age of Augustus*, edited by Karl Galinsky, 151–74. Cambridge: Cambridge University Press, 2005.

Beker, J. Christiaan. *Paul the Apostle: The Triumph of God in Life and Thought*. Philadelphia: Fortress, 1984.

———. *Paul's Apocalyptic Gospel: The Coming Triumph of God*. Philadelphia: Fortress, 1982.

Bell, Daniel. *The End of Ideology: On the Exhaustion of Political Ideas in the Fifties*. New York: Free Press, 1960.

Blanton, Ward. *A Materialism for the Masses: Saint Paul and the Philosophy of Undying Life*. Insurrections: Critical Studies in Religion, Politics, and Culture. New York: Columbia University Press, 2014.

Brueggemann, Walter. *Mandate to Difference: An Invitation to the Contemporary Church*. Louisville: Westminster John Knox, 2007.

Brunner, Emil. *Eternal Hope*. Translated by Harold Knight. London: Lutterworth, 1954.

Brunt, P. A. "*Laus Imperii*." In *Paul and Empire: Religion and Power in Roman Imperial Society*, edited by Richard A. Horsley, 25–35. Harrisburg, PA: Trinity, 1997.

Carter, Warren. *John and Empire: Initial Explorations*. New York: T & T Clark, 2008.

———. "Matthew Negotiates the Roman Empire." In *In The Shadow of Empire: Reclaiming the Bible as a History of Faithful Resistance*, edited by Richard A. Horsley, 117–36. Louisville: Westminster John Knox, 2008.

———. "Paul and the Roman Empire: Recent Perspectives." In *Paul Unbound: Other Perspectives on the Apostle*, edited by Mark D. Given, 7–26. Peabody, MA: Hendrickson, 2010.

———. *The Roman Empire and the New Testament: An Essential Guide*. Nashville: Abingdon, 2006.

———. "Vulnerable Power: The Roman Empire Challenged by the Early Christians." In *Handbook of Early Christianity: Social-Science Approaches*, 453–88. New York: Altamira, 2002.

Chow, John K. "Patronage in Roman Corinth." In *Paul and Empire: Religion, Power, and the Life of the Spirit*, edited by Richard A. Horsley, 104–25. Harrisburg, PA: Trinity, 1997.

Cicero, Marcus Tulius. *Cicero: Political Speeches*. Translated by D. H. Berry. Oxford World's Classics. Oxford: Oxford University Press, 2006.

———. *The Orations of Marcus Tulius Cicero*. Translated by C. D. Yonge. London: George Bell and Sons, 1891. Online. http://www.perseus.tufts.edu/hopper/text?doc=Cic.%20Balb.

Collins, John J. *The Apocalyptic Imagination: An Introduction to Jewish Apocalyptic Literature*. Grand Rapids: Eerdmans, 1998.

Comack, Elizabeth. *Racialized Policing: Aboriginal People's Encounters with the Police.* Winnipeg: Fernwood, 2012.

Coulthard, Glen Sean. *Red Skins, White Masks: Rejecting the Colonial Politics of Recognition.* Minneapolis: University of Minnesota Press, 2014.

Countryman, Louis William. *The Rich Christians in the Church of the Early Empire: Contradictions and Accommodations.* New York: Edwin Mellen, 1980.

Cousar, Charles B. *An Introduction to the New Testament: Witnesses to God's New Work.* Louisville: Westminster John Knox, 2006.

Crary, Jonathan. *24/7: Late Capitalism and the Ends of Sleep.* London: Verso, 2014.

Crossan, John Dominic. *God and Empire: Jesus Against Rome, Then and Now.* San Francisco: HarperSanFrancisco, 2007.

———. "Roman Imperial Theology." In *In The Shadow of Empire: Reclaiming the Bible as a History of Faithful Resistance,* edited by Richard A. Horsley, 59–73. Louisville: Westminster John Knox, 2008.

Crossan, John Dominic, and Marcus J. Borg. *The First Paul: Reclaiming the Radical Vision Behind the Church's Conservative Icon.* New York: HarperOne, 2009.

Crossan, John Dominic, and Jonathan L. Reed. *In Search of Paul: How Jesus's Apostle Opposed Rome's Empire with God's Kingdom. A New Vision of Paul's Words and World.* San Francisco: HarperSanFrancisco, 2004.

Cullmann, Oscar. *Christ and Time: The Primitive Christian Conception of Time and History.* Translated by Floyd V. Filson. Philadelphia: Westminster, 1964.

Davies, William David. *Jewish and Pauline Studies.* Philadelphia: Fortress, 1984.

Deissmann, Adolf. *Light from the Ancient East: The New Testament Illustrated by Recently Discovered Texts of the Graeco-Roman World.* Translated by Lionel R. M. Strachan. Grand Rapids: Baker, 1978.

———. *Paul: A Study in Social and Religious History.* Translated by William E. Wilson. New York: George H. Doran, 1926.

Derrida, Jacques. *Specters of Marx: The State of Debt, the Work of Mourning, and the New International.* Translated by Peggy Kamuf. Routledge Classics. New York: Routledge, 1994.

deSilva, David A. *Honor, Patronage, Kinship, and Purity: Unlocking New Testament Culture.* Downers Grove, IL: InterVarsity, 2000.

Dewey, Arthur J. *Spirit and Letter in Paul.* Studies in the Bible and Early Christianity 33. Lewiston: Edwin Mellen, 1996.

Downs, David. "Is God Paul's Patron? The Economy of Patronage in Pauline Theology." In *Engaging Economics: New Testament Scenarios and Early Christian Reception,* edited by Bruce W. Longenecker and Kelly D. Liebengood, 129–56. Grand Rapids: Eerdmans, 2009.

Dunn, James D. G. *Beginning from Jerusalem.* Christianity in the Making 2. Grand Rapids: Eerdmans, 2009.

———. *The Theology of Paul the Apostle.* Grand Rapids: Eerdmans, 1998.

Eaton, George. "Francis Fukuyama Interview: 'Socialism Ought to Come Back.'" *The New Statesman,* October 17, 2018. Online. https://www.newstatesman.com/culture/observations/2018/10/francis-fukuyama-interview-socialism-ought-come-back.

Eder, Walter. "Augustus and the Power of Tradition." In *The Cambridge Companion to the Age of Augustus,* edited by Karl Galinsky, 13–32. Cambridge: Cambridge University Press, 2005.

Elias, Jacob W. *Remember the Future: The Pastoral Theology of Paul the Apostle*. Waterloo: Herald, 2006.

Elliott, Neil. "The Apostle Paul's Self-Presentation as Anti-Imperial Performance." In *Paul and the Roman Imperial Order*, edited by Richard A. Horsley, 67–88. Harrisburg, PA: Trinity, 2004.

———. *The Arrogance of Nations: Reading Romans in the Shadow of Empire*. Paul in Critical Contexts. Minneapolis: Fortress, 2008.

———. "Disciplining the Hope of the Poor in Ancient Rome." In *Christian Origins: A People's History of Christianity*, edited by Richard A. Horsley, 177–97. Minneapolis: Fortress, 2005.

———. "Ideological Closure in the Christ-Event: A Marxist Response to Alain Badiou's Paul." In *Paul, Philosophy, and the Theopolitical Vision: Critical Engagements with Agamben, Badiou, Žižek, and Others*, edited by Douglas Harink, 135–54. Eugene, OR: Cascade, 2010.

———. "Strategies of Resistance and Hidden Transcripts in the Pauline Communities." In *Hidden Transcripts and the Arts of Resistance: Applying the Works of James C. Scott to Jesus and Paul*, edited by Richard A. Horsley, 97–122. Atlanta: Society of Biblical Literature, 2004.

Esler, Philip F., ed. *The Early Christian World*. Vol. 1. London: Routledge, 2000.

———. "The Mediterranean Context of Early Christianity." In *The Early Christian World*, edited by Philip F. Esler, 3–25. London: Routledge, 2000.

———. *New Testament Theology: Communion and Community*. Minneapolis: Fortress, 2005.

Faulkner, William. *Requiem for a Nun*. New York: Vintage, 2011.

Federici, Silvia. *Caliban and the Witch: Women, the Body and Primitive Accumulation*. Brooklyn: Autonomedia, 2014.

———. *Re-Enchanting the World: Feminism and the Politics of the Commons*. Foreword by Peter Linebaugh. Kairos Series. Oakland: PM, 2019.

———. *Witches, Witch-Hunting, and Women*. Oakland: PM, 2018.

Fee, Gordon D. *Paul, the Spirit, and the People of God*. Peabody, MA: Hendrickson, 1996.

Feeney, Denis. *Caesar's Calendar: Ancient Time and the Beginnings of History*. Sathers Classical Lectures 65. Berkeley: University of California Press, 2007.

Finley, M. I. *The Ancient Economy*. Sather Classical Lectures 43. Berkeley: University of California Press, 1973.

Foucault, Michel. *The Archaeology of Knowledge and the Discourse on Language*. Translated by A. M. Sheridan Smith. New York: Pantheon, 1972.

———. *Discipline and Punish: The Birth of the Prison*. Translated by Alan Sheridan. New York: Vintage, 1995.

———. *Power/Knowledge: Selected Interviews and Other Writings 1972–1977*. Edited by Colin Gordon. Translated by Colin Gordon et al. New York: Pantheon, 1980.

Frankopan, Peter. *The Silk Roads: A New History of the World*. New York: Alfred A. Knopf, 2016.

Friedman, Milton. *Capitalism and Freedom*. Chicago: University of Chicago Press, 1962.

Friesen, Steven J. "Paul and Economics: The Jerusalem Collection as an Alternative to Patronage." In *Paul Unbound: Other Perspectives on the Apostle*, edited by Mark D. Given, 27–54. Peabody, MA: Hendrickson, 2010.

Fukuyama, Francis. *The End of History and the Last Man*. New York: Avon, 1992.

Furnish, Victor Paul. *Theology and Ethics in Paul*. Nashville: Abingdon, 1968.

Galinsky, Karl. *The Cambridge Companion to the Age of Augustus*. Cambridge: Cambridge University Press, 2005.

Garnsey, Peter, and Richard Saller. "Patronal Power Relations." In *Paul and Empire: Religion and Power in Roman Imperial Society*, edited by Richard A. Horsley, 96–103. Harrisburg, PA: Trinity, 1997.

———. *The Roman Empire: Economy, Society, and Culture*. Berkeley: University of California Press, 1987.

Georgi, Dieter. "God Turned Upside Down." In *Paul and Empire: Religion and Power in Roman Imperial Society*, edited by Richard A. Horsley, 148–57. Harrisburg, PA: Trinity, 1997.

———. *Theocracy in Paul's Praxis and Theology*. Translated by David E. Green. Minneapolis: Fortress, 1991.

Given, Mark D., ed. *Paul Unbound: Other Perspectives on the Apostle*. Peabody, MA: Hendrickson, 2010.

Gordon, Richard. "The Veil of Power." In *Paul and Empire: Religion and Power in Roman Imperial Society*, edited by Richard A. Horsley, 126–37. Harrisburg, PA: Trinity, 1997.

Gorman, Michael J. *Apostle of the Crucified Lord: A Theological Introduction to Paul and His Letters*. Grand Rapids: Eerdmans, 2004.

———. *Cruciformity: Paul's Narrative Spirituality of the Cross*. Grand Rapids: Eerdmans, 2001.

———. *Reading Paul*. Cascade Companions. Eugene, OR: Cascade, 2008.

Graeber, David. *Debt: The First 5,000 Years*. New York: Melville, 2011.

Green, Joel B. *The Gospel of Luke*. New International Commentary on the New Testament. Grand Rapids: Eerdmans, 1997.

Hansen, Ryan L. "Messianic or Apocalyptic? Engaging Agamben on Paul and Politics." In *Paul, Philosophy, and the Theopolitical Vision: Critical Engagements with Agamben, Badiou, Žižek, and Others*, edited by Douglas Harink, 198–223. Eugene, OR: Cascade, 2010.

Hardin, Justin K. *Galatians and the Imperial Cult: A Critical Analysis of the First-Century Social Context of Paul's Letter*. Wissenschaftliche Untersuchungen zum Neuen Testament 2. Reihe 237. Tubingen: Mohr Siebeck, 2008.

Harink, Douglas. "Introduction: From Apocalypse to Philosophy—And Back." In *Paul, Philosophy, and the Theopolitical Vision: Critical Engagements with Agamben, Badiou, Žižek, and Others*, edited by Douglas Harink, 1–10. Eugene, OR: Cascade, 2010.

———. *Paul Among the Postliberals: Pauline Theology Beyond Christendom and Modernity*. Grand Rapids: Brazos, 2003.

———, ed. *Paul, Philosophy, and the Theopolitical Vision: Critical Engagements with Agamben, Badiou, Žižek, and Others*. Theopolitical Visions Series. Eugene, OR: Cascade, 2010.

Harries, Jill. "Armies, Emperors and Bureaucrats." In *The Early Christian World*, edited by Philip F. Esler, 26–52. London: Routledge, 2000.

Harrill, J. Albert. "Paul and Slavery." In *Paul in the Greco-Roman World: A Handbook*, edited by J. Paul Sampley, 575–607. New York: Trinity, 2003.

Hart, Trevor. "Imagination For The Kingdom of God? Hope, Promise, and the Transformative Power of an Imagined Future." In *God Will Be All in All: The Eschatology of Jürgen Moltmann*, edited by Richard Bauckham, 49–76. Edinburgh: T & T Clark, 1999.

Hayek, Friedrich A. *The Road to Serfdom*. Introduction by Milton Friedman. Chicago: University of Chicago Press, 1994.

Hays, Richard B. *The Moral Vision of the New Testament: A Contemporary Introduction to New Testament Ethics*. San Francisco: HarperSanFrancisco, 1996.

Heen, Erik M. "The Role of Symbolic Inversion in Utopian Discourse: Apocalyptic Reversal in Paul and the Festival of the Saturnalia/Kronia." In *Hidden Transcripts and the Arts of Resistance: Applying the Works of James C. Scott to Jesus and Paul*, edited by Richard A. Horsley, 123–44. Atlanta: Society of Biblical Literature, 2004.

Holsclaw, Geoffrey. "Subjects between Death and Resurrection: Badiou, Žižek, and St. Paul." In *Paul, Philosophy, and the Theopolitical Vision: Critical Engagements with Agamben, Badiou, Žižek, and Others*, edited by Douglas Harink, 155–75. Eugene, OR: Cascade, 2010.

Hopkins, Dwight N. "The Religion of Globalization." *Other Journal* 5 (2005). Online. http://theotherjournal.com/print.php?id=53.

Horace. *The Complete Works of Horace*. London: J. M. Dent & Sons, 1936.

Horne, Gerald. *The Counter-Revolution of 1776: Slave Resistance and the Origins of the United States of America*. New York: New York University Press, 2014.

Horrell, David G. *An Introduction to the Study of Paul*. T & T Clark Approaches to Biblical Studies. London: T & T Clark, 2006.

———. *The Social Ethos of the Corinthian Correspondence: Interests and Ideology from 1 Corinthians to 1 Clement*. Studies of the New Testament and Its World. Edinburgh: T & T Clark, 1996.

Horsley, Richard A. *Covenant Economics: A Biblical Vision of Justice for All*. Louisville: Westminster John Knox, 2009.

———. "The Gospel of Imperial Salvation: Introduction." In *Paul and Empire: Religion and Power in Roman Imperial Society*, edited by Richard A. Horsley, 10–24. Harrisburg, PA: Trinity, 1997.

———, ed. *In the Shadow of Empire: Reclaiming the Bible as a History of Faithful Resistance*. Louisville: Westminster John Knox, 2008.

———. "Introduction." In *Paul and the Roman Imperial Order*, edited by Richard A. Horsley, 1–23. Harrisburg, PA: Trinity, 2004.

———. "Jesus and Empire." In *In the Shadow of Empire: Reclaiming the Bible as a History of Faithful Resistance*, edited by Richard A. Horsley, 75–96. Louisville: Westminster John Knox, 2008.

———. *Jesus and Empire: The Kingdom of God and the New World Disorder*. Minneapolis: Fortress, 2003.

———. *Jesus and the Powers: Conflict, Covenant, and the Hope of the Poor*. Minneapolis: Fortress, 2011.

———. *The Liberation of Christmas: The Infancy Narratives in Social Context*. Eugene, OR: Wipf & Stock, 1989.

———. "Patronage, Priesthoods, and Power: Introduction." In *Paul and Empire: Religion and Power in Roman Imperial Society*, edited by Richard A. Horsley, 88–95. Harrisburg, PA: Trinity, 1997.

———, ed. *Paul and Empire: Religion and Power in Roman Imperial Society*. Harrisburg, PA: Trinity, 1997.

———, ed. *Paul and the Roman Imperial Order*. Harrisburg, PA: Trinity, 2004.

———. *Religion and Empire: People, Power, and the Life of the Spirit*. Facets Series. Minneapolis: Fortress, 2003.

Horsley, Richard A., and Neil Asher Silberman. *The Message and the Kingdom: How Jesus and Paul Ignited a Revolution and Transformed the Ancient World.* Minneapolis: Fortress, 1997.

Howard-Brook, Wes, and Anthony Gwyther. *Unveiling Empire: Reading Revelation Then and Now.* Foreword by Elizabeth McAlister. The Bible and Liberation Series. Maryknoll, NY: Orbis, 1999.

Hurtado, Larry. *Destroyer of the Gods: Early Christian Distinctiveness in the Roman World.* Waco, TX: Baylor University Press, 2016.

Jeffers, James S. *The Greco-Roman World of the New Testament Era: Exploring the Background of Early Christianity.* Downers Grove, IL: InterVarsity, 1999.

Jennings, Theodore W., Jr. *Outlaw Justice: The Messianic Politics of Paul.* Stanford: Stanford University Press, 2013.

Jensen, L. Paul. *Subversive Spirituality: Transforming Mission Through the Collapse of Space and Time.* Princeton Theological Monograph Series 113. Eugene, OR: Wipf & Stock, 2009.

Jewett, Robert. "The Corruption and Redemption of Creation: Reading Rom 8:18–23 within the Imperial Context." In *Paul and the Roman Imperial Order*, edited by Richard A. Horsley, 25–46. Harrisburg, PA: Trinity, 2004.

———. "Paul, Shame, and Honor." In *Paul in the Greco-Roman World: A Handbook*, edited by J. Paul Sampley, 551–74. New York: Trinity, 2003.

———. *Romans: A Commentary.* Hermeneia Series. Minneapolis: Fortress, 2007.

Judge, Edwin A. "Did the Churches Compete with Cult Groups?" In *Early Christianity and Classical Culture: Comparative Studies in Honor of Abraham J. Malherbe*, edited by John T. Fitzgerald et al., 501–24. Leiden: Brill, 2003.

———. *Social Distinctives of the Christians in the First Century: Pivotal Essays by E. A. Judge.* Edited by David M. Sholer. Peabody, MA: Hendrickson, 2008.

Juvenal. "Satires." In *The Sixteen Satires*, by Juvenal, 65–297. Translated by Peter Green. Penguin Classics. London: Penguin, 1967.

Kahl, Brigitte. *Galatians Re-Imagined: Reading with the Eyes of the Vanquished.* Paul in Critical Contexts Series. Minneapolis: Fortress, 2010.

Käsemann, Ernst. *New Testament Questions of Today.* Translated by W. J. Montague. Philadelphia: Fortress, 1969.

Kautsky, Karl. *Foundations of Christianity.* Translated by Henry F. Mins. New York: S. A. Russell, 1953.

Kaye, Julie. *Responding to Human Trafficking: Dispossession, Colonial Violence, and Resistance among Indigenous and Racialized Women.* Toronto: University of Toronto Press, 2017.

Kee, Howard Clark. *The Beginnings of Christianity: An Introduction to the New Testament.* London: T & T Clark, 2005.

———. *Christian Origins in Sociological Perspective: Methods and Resources.* Philadelphia: Westminster, 1980.

———. *The Renewal of Hope.* New York: Association, 1959.

Keresztes, Paul. *From Herod the Great to about 200 AD.* Vol. 1 of *Imperial Rome and the Christians.* New York: University Press of America, 1989.

Koester, Helmut. *History, Culture, and Religion of the Hellenistic Age.* Vol. 1 of *Introduction to the New Testament.* Berlin: de Gruyter, 1995.

Lampe, Peter. "Paul, Patrons, and Clients." In *Paul in the Greco-Roman World: A Handbook*, edited by J. Paul Sampley, 488–523. New York: Trinity, 2003.

Lassen, Eva Marie. "The Roman Family: Ideal and Metaphor." In *Constructing Early Christian Families: Family as Social Reality and Metaphor*, edited by Halvor Moxnes, 103–20. London: Routledge, 1997.

Levine, Amy-Jill, with Marrianne Blickenstaff. *A Feminist Companion to Paul*. Cleveland: Pilgrim, 2004.

Lietzmann, Hans. *The Beginnings of the Christian Church*. Translated by Bertram Lee Woolf. London: Lutterworth, 1953.

Livy. *Ab Urbe Condite, Book VI*. Edited by Christina Shuttleworth Kraus. Cambridge Greek and Latin Classics. Cambridge: Cambridge University Press, 1998.

Lohse, Eduard. *The New Testament Environment*. Translated by John E. Steely. Nashville: Abingdon, 1976.

Longenecker, Bruce W., and Kelly D. Liebengood. *Engaging Economics: New Testament Scenarios and Early Christian Reception*. Grand Rapids: Eerdmans, 2005.

Lopez, Davina C. *Apostle to the Conquered: Reimagining Paul's Mission*. Paul in Critical Contexts. Minneapolis: Fortress, 2008.

Loy, David. "The Religion of the Market." *Journal of the American Academy of Religion* 65 (1997) 275–90.

Lucan. *Civil War*. Translated by Susan H. Braund. Oxford World's Classics. Oxford: Oxford University Press, 2008.

MacMullen, Ramsay. *Changes in the Roman Empire: Essays in the Ordinary*. Princeton: Princeton University Press, 1990.

———. *Paganism in the Roman Empire*. New Haven, CT: Yale University Press, 1981.

Maier, Harry O. *Picturing Paul in Empire: Imperial Image, Text and Persuasion in Colossians, Ephesians and the Pastoral Epistles*. London: Bloomsbury T & T Clark, 2013.

Malina, Bruce J. *The New Testament World: Insights from Cultural Anthropology*. Louisville: Westminster John Knox, 2001.

———. "Social Levels, Morals and Daily Life." In vol. 1 of *The Early Christian World*, edited by Philip F. Esler, 369–400. London: Routledge, 2000.

Malina, Bruce J., and Jerome H. Neyrey. *Portraits of Paul: An Archaeology of Ancient Personality*. Louisville: Westminster John Knox, 1996.

Malina, Bruce J., and John J. Pilch. *Social-Science Commentary on the Letters of Paul*. Minneapolis: Fortress, 2006.

Martyn, J. Louis. "The Gospel Invades Philosophy." In *Paul, Philosophy, and the Theopolitical Vision: Critical Engagements with Agamben, Badiou, Žižek, and Others*, edited by Douglas Harink, 13–33. Eugene, OR: Cascade, 2010.

———. *Theological Issues in the Letters of Paul*. Nashville: Abingdon, 1997.

Maynard, Robyn. *Policing Black Lives: State Violence in Canada from Slavery to the Present*. Winnipeg: Fernwood, 2017.

Mbembe, Achille. "Necropolitics." Translated by Libby Meintjes. *Public Culture* 15 (2003) 11–40.

Meeks, Wayne A. *The First Urban Christians: The Social World of the Apostle Paul*. New Haven, CT: Yale University Press, 1983.

———. *In Search of the Early Christians: Selected Essays*. Edited by Allen R. Hilston and H. Gregory Snyder. New Haven, CT: Yale University Press, 2002.

———. *The Moral World of the First Christians*. Library of Early Christianity. Philadelphia: Westminster, 1986.

————. *The Origins of Christian Morality: The First Two Centuries*. New Haven, CT: Yale University Press, 1993.

Merkley, Paul. *The Greek and Hebrew Origins of our Idea of History*. Toronto Studies in Theology 32. Lewiston, ID: Edwin Mellen, 1987.

Moltmann, Jürgen. *A Broad Place: An Autobiography*. Translated by Margaret Kohl. Minneapolis: Fortress, 2008.

————. *The Church in the Power of the Spirit: A Contribution to Messianic Ecclesiology*. Translated by Margaret Kohl. Minneapolis: Fortress, 1993.

————. *The Coming of God: Christian Eschatology*. Translated by Margaret Kohl. Minneapolis: Fortress, 1996.

————. *Experiences in Theology: Ways and Forms of Christian Theology*. Translated by Margaret Kohl. Minneapolis: Fortress, 2000.

————. *God in Creation: A New Theology of Creation and the Spirit of God*. Translated by Margaret Kohl. Minneapolis: Fortress, 1993.

————. "The Liberation of the Future and Its Anticipation in History." In *God Will be All in All: The Eschatology of Jürgen Moltmann*, edited by Richard Bauckham, 265–89. Edinburgh: T & T Clark, 1999.

————. *Theology of Hope: On the Ground and Implications of a Christian Eschatology*. Translated by James W. Leitch. New York: Harper & Row, 1967.

————. *The Way of Jesus Christ: Christology in Messianic Dimensions*. Translated by Margaret Kohl. Minneapolis: Fortress, 1993.

————. "What Has Happened to Our Utopias? 1968 and 1989. Response to Timothy Gorringe." In *God Will be All in All: The Eschatology of Jürgen Moltmann*, edited by Richard Bauckham, 115–21. Edinburgh: T & T Clark, 1999.

Mumford, Lewis. *Technics and Civilization*. London: Routledge & Kegan Paul, 1934.

Osiek, Carolyn. "Family Matters." In *Christian Origins: A People's History of Christianity*, edited by Richard A. Horsley, 201–20. Minneapolis: Fortress, 2005.

Oudshoorn, Daniel. "Hurtado Responds." *On Journeying with Those in Exile* (blog), November 3, 2016. Online. https://poserorprophet.wordpress.com/2016/11/03/hurtado-responds.

————. "Response to Larry Hurtado's *Destroyer of the Gods: Early Christian Distinctiveness in the Roman World*." *On Journeying with Those in Exile* (blog), October 27, 2016. Online. https://poserorprophet.wordpress.com/2016/10/27/response-to-larry-hurtados-destroyer-of-the-gods.

Oudshoorn, Judah. *Trauma-Informed Youth Justice in Canada: A New Framework toward a Kinder Future*. Foreword by Howard Zehr. Toronto: Canadian Scholars, 2015.

Ovidius Naso, Publius. *The Metamorphosis*. Translated by Mary M. Innes. Penguin Classics. London: Penguin, 1955.

Pagels, Elaine. *Why Religion? A Personal Story*. New York: HarperLuxe, 2018.

Pate, C. Marvin. *The End of the Age Has Come: The Theology of Paul*. Grand Rapids: Zondervan, 1995.

Peppard, Michael. *The Son of God in the Roman World: Divine Sonship in Its Social and Political Context*. Oxford: Oxford University Press, 2011.

Petronius, Arbiter. "The Satyricon." In *Petronius/The Satyricon. Seneca/The Apocolocyntosis*, 1–204. Translated by J. P. Sullivan. London: Penguin, 1977.

Pickett, Ray. "Conflicts at Corinth." In *Christian Origins: A People's History of Christianity*, edited by Richard A. Horsley, 113–37. Minneapolis: Fortress, 2005.

Plutarch. *The Lives of the Noble Grecians and Romans.* Translated by Thomas North. Selected by Judith Mossman. Wordsworth Classics of World Literature. Hertfordshire: Wordsworth, 1998.

Portier-Young, Anathea. *Apocalypse Against Empire: Theologies of Resistance in Early Judaism.* Foreword by John J. Collins. Grand Rapids: Eerdmans, 2011.

Price, Simon R. F. *Rituals and Power: The Roman Imperial Cult in Asia Minor.* Cambridge: Cambridge University Press, 1984.

Ramsaran, Rollin A. "Resisting Imperial Domination and Influence: Paul's Apocalyptic Rhetoric in 1 Corinthians." In *Paul and the Roman Imperial Order,* edited by Richard A. Horsley, 89–101. Harrisburg, PA: Trinity, 2004.

Razack, Sherene H. *Dying from Improvement: Inquests and Inquiries into Indigenous Deaths in Custody.* Toronto: University of Toronto Press, 2015.

———, ed. *Race, Space, and the Law: Unmapping a White Settler Society.* Toronto: Between the Lines, 2002.

Rehman, Luzia Sutter. "To Turn the Groaning into Labor: Romans 8:22–23." In *A Feminist Companion to Paul,* edited by Amy-Jill Levine with Marianne Blickenstaff, 74–84. Cleveland: Pilgrim, 2004.

Roetzel, Calvin J. *Paul—A Jew on the Margins.* Louisville: Westminster John Knox, 2003.

———. *The World That Shaped the New Testament.* Atlanta: John Knox, 1985.

Saller, Richard P. *Personal Patronage Under the Early Empire.* Cambridge: Cambridge University Press, 1982.

Sampley, J. Paul. *Walking Between the Times: Paul's Moral Reasoning.* Minneapolis: Fortress, 1991.

———, ed. *Paul in the Greco-Roman World: A Handbook.* New York: Trinity, 2003.

Sanders, E. P. *Paul: The Apostle's Life, Letters, and Thoughts.* Minneapolis: Fortress, 2015.

Sauter, Gerhard. *What Dare We Hope? Reconsidering Eschatology.* Theology for the Twenty-First Century. Harrisburg, PA: Trinity, 1999.

Scheid, John. "Augustus and Roman Religion: Continuity, Conservatism, and Innovation." In *The Cambridge Companion to the Age of Augustus,* edited by Karl Galinsky, 175–94. Cambridge: Cambridge University Press, 2005.

Schnackenburg, Rudolf. *The Moral Teaching of the New Testament.* Translated by J. Holland-Smith and W. J. O'Hara. London: Burns & Oates, 1967.

Schoeps, H. J. *Paul: The Theology of the Apostle in the Light of Jewish Religious History.* Translated by Harold Knight. Philadelphia: Westminster, 1961.

Schrage, Wolfgang. *The Ethics of the New Testament.* Translated by David E. Green. Philadelphia: Fortress, 1988.

Schüssler-Fiorenza, Elisabeth. *In Memory of Her: A Feminist Theological Reconstruction of Christian Origins.* New York: Crossroad, 1994.

Schweitzer, Albert. *The Mysticism of Paul the Apostle.* Translated by William Montgomery. London: Black, 1931.

Seneca, Lucius Annaeus. "The Apocolocyntosis." In *Petronius/The Satyricon. Seneca/The Apocolocyntosis,* 221–33. Translated by J. P. Sullivan. Penguin Classics. London: Penguin, 1966.

———. *Four Tragedies and Octavia.* Translated by E. F. Watling. Penguin Classics. London: Penguin, 1966.

———. *Seneca: Dialogues and Essays.* Translated by John Davie. Oxford World's Classics. Oxford: Oxford University Press, 2007.

Sherwin-White, A. N. *The Roman Citizenship.* Oxford: Clarendon, 1973.

Stauffer, Ethelbert. *New Testament Theology*. Translated by John Marsh. London: SCM, 1955.

Suetonius Trannquillus, C. *The Twelve Caesars*. Translated by Robert Graves. London: Folio Society, 2005.

Tacitus, Publius Cornelius. *The Complete Works of Tacitus*. Translated by Alfred John Church and William Jackson Brodribb. Edited by Moses Hadas. Modern Library. New York: Random House, 1942.

Taubes, Jacob. *Occidental Eschatology*. Translated by David Ratmoko. Cultural Memory in the Present. Stanford: Stanford University Press, 2009.

Taylor, Keeange-Yamahtta. *From #BlackLivesMatter to Black Liberation*. Chicago: Haymarket, 2016.

Tellbe, Mikael. *Paul between Synagogue and State: Christians, Jews, and Civic Authorities in 1 Thessalonians, Romans, and Philippians*. Coniectanea Biblica New Testament Series 34. Stockholm: Almqvist & Wiksell, 2001.

Tenney, Merrill C. *New Testament Times*. London: Lowe & Brydone, 1965.

Terkel, Studs. *Hope Dies Last: Keeping the Faith in Troubled Times*. New York: New Press, 2003.

Valencia, Sayak. *Gore Capitalism*. Translated by John Pluecker. Semiotext(e) Intervention Series 24. Pasadena, CA: Semiotext(e), 2018.

Vergilius Maro, Publius. *The Aeneid*. Translated by Robert Fitzgerald. Vintage Classics. New York: Vintage, 1990.

———. *The Eclogues. The Georgics*. Translated by C. Day Lewis. Oxford World Classics. Oxford: Oxford University Press, 1983.

Vos, Geerhardus. *The Pauline Eschatology*. Grand Rapids: Eerdmans, 1972.

Walsh, Brian J., and Sylvia C. Keesmaat. *Colossians Remixed: Subverting the Empire*. Downers Grove, IL: InterVarsity, 2004.

Welborn, L. L. *Paul, the Fool of Christ: A Study of 1 Corinthians 1–4 in the Comic-Philosophic Tradition*. Early Christianity in Context Series. London: T & T Clark International, 2005.

———. *Paul's Summons to Messianic Life*. Insurrections: Critical Studies in Religion, Politics, and Culture. New York: Columbia University Press, 2015.

Wengst, Klaus. *Humility: Solidarity of the Humiliated. The Transformation of an Attitude and Its Social Relevance in Graeco-Roman, Old Testament-Jewish and Early Christian Tradition*. Philadelphia: Fortress, 1988.

———. *Pax Romana and the Peace of Jesus Christ*. Translated by John Bowden. Minneapolis: Fortress, 1987.

Winter, Bruce W. *Divine Honours for the Caesars: The First Christians' Responses*. Grand Rapids: Eerdmans, 2015.

———. *Seek the Welfare of the City: Christians as Benefactors and Citizens*. First Century Christians in the Graeco-Roman World. Carlisle: Paternoster, 1994.

Witherington, Ben, III. *Jesus, Paul, and the End of the World: A Comparative Study in New Testament Eschatology*. Downers Grove, IL: InterVarsity, 1992.

———. *The Paul Quest: The Renewed Search For the Jew of Tarsus*. Downers Grove, IL: InterVarsity, 1998.

Wright, N. T. *New Tasks for a Renewed Church*. London: Hodder & Stoughton, 1992.

———. *The New Testament and the People of God*. Christian Origins and the Question of God 1. Minneapolis: Fortress, 1992.

———. *Paul: In Fresh Perspective*. Minneapolis: Fortress, 2005.

———. *Surprised by Hope: Rethinking Heaven, the Resurrection, and the Mission of the Church*. New York: HarperOne, 2008.

Yarbrough, O. Larry. *Not Like the Gentiles: Marriage Rules in the Letters of Paul*. SBL Dissertation Series 80. Atlanta: Scholars, 1985.

Yeo, Khiok-Khng. *Chairman Mao Meets the Apostle Paul: Christianity, Communism, and the Hope of China*. Grand Rapids: Brazos, 2002.

Zanker, Paul. *The Power of Images in the Age of Augustus*. Jerome Lectures 16th Series. Translated by Alan Shapiro. Ann Arbor: University of Michigan Press, 1990.

Zimmerman, Jens. "Hermeneutics of Unbelief: Philosophical Readings of Paul." In *Paul, Philosophy, and the Theopolitical Vision: Critical Engagements with Agamben, Badiou, Žižek, and Others*, edited by Douglas Harink, 227–53. Eugene, OR: Cascade, 2010.